MASKING EVIL

WHEN GOOD MEN AND WOMEN TURN CRIMINAL

CAROL ANNE DAVIS

D1291163

...ersdale

MASKING EVIL

Summersdale Publishers Ltd
46 West Street
Chichester
West Sussex
PO19 1RP
UK

www.summersdale.com

Printed and bound by CPI Group (UK) Ltd, Croydon, CR0 4YY

ISBN: 978-1-84953-883-1

Substantial discounts on bulk quantities of Summersdale books are available to corporations, professional associations and other organisations. For details contact Nicky Douglas by telephone: +44 (0) 1243 756902, fax: +44 (0) 1243 786300 or email: nicky@summersdale.com.

For Ian
1957–2009

ABOUT THE AUTHOR

Carol Anne Davis was born in Dundee, moved to Edinburgh in her twenties and now lives in south-west England. She left school at 15 and was everything from an artist's model to an editorial assistant before going to university. Her Master of Arts degree included criminology and was followed by a postgraduate diploma in Adult and Community Education.

Since graduating from Edinburgh University in 1987, she has been a full-time writer. Her crime novels *Near Death Experience*, *Extinction*, *Sob Story*, *Kiss It Away*, *Noise Abatement*, *Safe as Houses* and *Shrouded* have been described as chillingly realistic for their portrayals of sex and death.

She is also the author of the true crime books *Parents Who Kill*, *Doctors Who Kill*, *Youthful Prey*, *Sadistic Killers*, *Couples Who Kill*, *Children Who Kill* and *Women Who Kill*.

www.carolannedavis.co.uk

CONTENTS

INTRODUCTION

What makes a mild-mannered bank clerk kidnap little girls? What drives a deacon to use and murder prostitutes? Why would a respected airline pilot bludgeon his wife to death? All of the men and women profiled in the following pages were in good professions – some were doctors, clergymen, criminologists, policemen and educationalists – but all of them fell spectacularly from grace. Most committed murder, though two stopped short of this, perpetrating repeated acts of extreme child abuse. The younger killers were model pupils, the type voted most likely to succeed.

Criminologists used to see violence as an act of frustration often borne out by an inability to articulate strong emotion, hence the unemployed young man lashing out at his girlfriend or the drunken layabout slapping his energetic kids. These professionals also believed that men and women who had no control at work would take out their rage on weaker victims during their leisure time.

And, at first, this seems borne out by a quick look back at recent history's most heinous crimes. Raymond Morris, profiled in one of my previous books, felt demeaned by his factory job and would go to work in a suit and lie to his relatives and neighbours about his work life. His rage spilled over and he became a murderous paedophile. Similarly, Peter Sutcliffe, the serial-killing Yorkshire Ripper, felt that he was too bright to be a lorry driver and had a sign in his cab saying that genius lurked within. Moors murderer Ian Brady saw himself as an intellectual and abhorred being an office clerk, whilst labourer Fred West told anyone who would listen that he was a skilled abortionist.

There was nothing wrong with the work that these men did, but they viewed themselves as superior to it and carried some of their frustration into their increasingly pathological sex lives. They also found that stalking their prey brought them an excitement that the nine-to-five simply lacked.

The culprits featured in this book broadly fall into several categories. First, the predatory personalities who knew from an early age that they wanted to molest women or children and joined the clergy in the hope that it would provide them with a lifelong moral framework. It didn't. Similarly, some of these emotionally fractured men entered the police force in the hope of becoming extra good. But other police officers, such as the sadistic Gerard Schaefer and the misogynistic Craig Peyer, deliberately entered the force to lure young women into their lethal traps.

Some of the other professionals featured here fit into the intelligent-but-hugely-damaged-in-childhood category. Though they became everything from a church organiser to an Ivy League lawyer, they were at heart angry and neglected children with numerous unmet needs.

Greed is one of the motives which rears its ugly head, particularly in the case of the foster mother from hell, Eunice Spry, who was willing to keep one of her foster daughters in a wheelchair, despite the fact that she could walk, in order to claim additional benefits. Her other motive was sadism. Greed also motivated policewoman Antoinette Frank, who turned a thriving family restaurant into a bloodbath in the hope of stealing the day's takings.

Fear also plays its part, as evidenced in the case of FBI Agent Mark Putnam, a basically good man who murderously overreacted when his lover threatened to tell his wife and employer about their relationship. Fear equally influenced Steven Rios, who was terrified that his gay lover would tell Rios' wife about his true sexual desires, and terror was the main motivator for Donny Tison, a criminal justice student who helped his father, a known killer, to escape from jail as he feared his father would be killed by another prisoner if he remained behind bars.

Extreme jealousy was behind a few of the crimes, notably those committed by John Tanner and Jean Harris, both bookish and sensitive individuals – at opposite ends of the age scale – who murdered their lovers. Meanwhile, madness motivated the doctor who became part of a cult and turned into a half-starved survivalist, and there was also increasing mental illness in Cokeville town marshal David Young, who plotted to kill an entire classroom of kids in Wyoming.

Though some of the most sadistic adult murderers deserve to die behind bars (and several of the serial killers already have), this is not a book without hope: two of the youngest killers – and a middle-aged FBI officer – have been released and gone on to lead useful lives in their new communities. Others will become eligible for parole in due course, though only time will tell if they deserve a second chance.

1

THE DEPUTY SHERIFF
GERARD SCHAEFER

Though he applied to train for the priesthood and, when rejected, went on to become a law enforcement officer, Gerard Schaefer was one of America's most sadistic serial killers.

Early life

Gerard John Schaefer was born on 25 March 1946 to Doris and Gerard Schaefer. He was their firstborn and they went on to have a girl, then a second boy. The family initially lived in Wisconsin but relocated to Georgia when the children were small.

The Schaefers were staunch Roman Catholics and sent their children to a religious school. It's not known if Gerard was unhappy there – but he *was* unhappy at home and felt strongly that his father, a salesman, favoured his sister Sara. By the time that he was 12, he had started wearing her underwear – boys who feel unloved often start to wear their mother's lingerie as a way of feeling close to her, so perhaps wearing his sister's panties was a variation on this. The young boy somehow found out about the act of autoerotic asphyxiation and would take a rope into the local woods and half hang himself whilst masturbating. This is unusually precocious for a 12-year-old, so it's highly likely that an adult told him about this masochistic act.

When he was 16, the family moved to Fort Lauderdale in Florida and he was again enrolled in a Catholic school. But he didn't fit in and was regarded as different, especially when he dared to question religious doctrine. He had an IQ of 130, which put him in the top five per cent of the population, and had an enquiring mind. He became a reluctant loner (as opposed to a happy loner who actively prefers his own company) and retreated to the Everglades at weekends, killing animals for sport. At 18 he briefly had a girlfriend – he was handsome, with a friendly and honest-looking face – and told her that he enjoyed spying on his neighbour, Leigh Hainline, when she sunbathed in the nude. He said that Leigh Hainline was just asking to be raped. He continued to indulge in Peeping Tom activities, peering through her bedroom window whilst she undressed. He also spied on one of her female friends.

After leaving school, Schaefer decided to train as a priest but he was turned down and rejected the church thereafter. He turned to creative writing but his teacher was alarmed that so many of his stories involved the murder of young female victims. Referred to the student counsellor, he admitted that he had fantasies about butchering animals and defiling their carcasses, and that he longed to enter the army so that he could kill men. But he hadn't committed a crime and wasn't referred for more intensive psychotherapy. In truth, his fantasies were so ingrained by this stage that it's unlikely that any talking therapy could have helped.

He went on to graduate with an Associate's degree in business studies, after which he applied for a teacher training course, a chilling occupation for a young man who was already obsessed with thoughts of hanging teenage girls and raping their corpses. But he failed his preliminary exams so was sent a draft notice for the Vietnam war. At his evaluation he was wearing women's underwear, perhaps because he knew it would be discovered during the physical exam, and a psychiatric assessment found that he was unstable, so he was deemed unfit to serve. He would later state that he deliberately dodged the draft by telling the psychiatrist that he was contemplating suicide.

A first failed marriage

That same year, 1968, his parents divorced and that summer he starting dating a girl called Martha. They married in December (unstable men will often push for a swift marriage, knowing that they cannot maintain a normal facade for a lengthy dating period) and he returned to teacher training but behaved inappropriately with his female teenage pupils when doing his student teaching at various high schools in 1969. He was asked to leave.

He continued to feel rage towards flighty women, and told his acquaintances that his neighbour Leigh Hainline was a slut and didn't behave like a good Catholic girl. On 8 September 1969, he paid her a visit and she was never seen alive again. There was confusion as to whether she had run away, as she had told her husband that she was leaving him for a family friend. Her locket was later found in the house that Gerard Schaefer was now living in with his mother and wife Martha. It was found with his trophies from other victims: he had kept everything from passports to diaries. (Leigh's skull was found nine years later but not identified until 2004.)

Later in 1969, nine-year-old Peggy Rahn and eight-year-old Wendy Stevenson were seen with a young man resembling Gerard Schaefer, after which they disappeared and were never seen again. He would subsequently tell a girlfriend that he had murdered and cannibalised both children, frying parts of their flesh with peppers and onions, and he wrote short stories about how easy it was to permanently hide bodies in the woods or on construction sites. (Much later, in prison, perhaps to avoid being labelled as a paedophile, he would claim that he hadn't sexually assaulted either child, saying that he just wanted to experience what it was like to eat human flesh as he had been reading about the exploits of cannibalistic serial killer Albert Fish.)

The following year, Martha filed for divorce and Gerard went abroad, to Europe and North Africa, for a change of scene. He would later tell investigators that he killed teenage girls throughout this extended trip. At the time, hitchhiking was common and girls often travelled extensively with a friend so weren't reported missing for some months, by which time the trail had gone cold.

A second marriage

On his return to the States, he began working as a security guard and soon married a woman called Teresa who was several years his junior. He was accepted into the police force at Wilton Manors but had an argument with the police chief in 1972 and tried to transfer to Broward County. They conducted psychological tests, which he failed, so he was promptly rejected. But he merely forged a letter of recommendation, took it along to Martin County and was hired as a deputy sheriff. He loved the power that this new position gave him.

On 21 July 1972, a month after securing the post, he was driving along in his patrol car when he saw two girls, 18-year-old Nancy Trotter and her 19-year-old friend Pamela Wells, hitchhiking at the roadside. He gave them a lift to the beach and said that he would take them back there the following day. He lectured them gently about the dangers of accepting lifts from strangers and they were delighted to know that they were now in safe hands.

The following day, a Saturday, he picked up the girls at their holiday accommodation and said that he would show them a historical monument which necessitated a drive to a remote part of Martin County. When they reached the woods, he ordered them out of the car, handcuffed both women and looped a rope around Nancy's neck before fastening it to a tree. He balanced her on a large root and pointed out that, if she lost her footing, she would be hanged to death. He tied Pamela to another tree then left the scene when his police radio alerted him to the fact that he was needed at work. He warned the girls not to move, that he would return.

Fortunately, Nancy managed to struggle free of the noose and she ran to the roadside in a distressed state and flagged down a car. The police were called and freed an equally distressed Pamela. When Schaefer returned to the scene he found both victims gone and knew that they would have reported this attempted murder to the police. He drove back to headquarters and told his superiors that he had pretended to hang the girls in order to frighten them as they had laughed when he warned them about the dangers of hitchhiking. He admitted that he had gone too far.

He was sacked and charged with false imprisonment and aggravated assault but after two months was released on his own recognisance, awaiting trial. It's thought that he was given preferential treatment because he had been in the police force. The former deputy sheriff must have suspected that he would be going to prison for a long time so he had nothing to lose by continuing to act out his fantasies.

A murder spree

On 27 September 1972, he befriended 17-year-old Susan Place and 16-year-old Georgia Jessup, telling them that his name was Jerry. Susan told her mother that she'd met him at the beach and that he was taking them back there on that same day. Mrs Place didn't like the man and wrote down his number plate, but the teenagers insisted on going off with him and were never seen alive again. (Six months later, their bodies, cut in half, were found partially buried in Blind Creek. Schaefer's fantasies included dismemberment and he was known to own extremely sharp knives.)

On 23 October 1972, two 14-year-old girls disappeared whilst hitchhiking to the shops. Elsie Farmer's remains were found on a construction site near a school campus the following year and her jewellery was located at Gerard Schaefer's home. Her friend Mary Briscolina's body was discovered at the construction site the following month. The bodies were too decomposed to ascertain the cause of death and they were only identified through dental records. Schaefer later confessed to both homicides.

In December, the disgraced deputy sheriff was tried for the false imprisonment of Nancy Trotter and Pamela Wells and was given a mere six-month suspended sentence, the judge believing his account that he had merely intended to persuade the girls not to hitchhike. He was told by the court that he had behaved like a fool – surely the understatement of the year. His wife and mother stood by him and the judge regarded him as a basically good family man who had made one mistake. Schaefer was free to continue his killing spree...

On 8 January 1973, two 19-year-olds disappeared as they hitchhiked from Iowa to Florida. The driving licences of both Colette Goodenough and Barbara Wilcox were later found in Gerard Schaefer's home along with several of Colette's teeth. (Their skeletal remains were discovered in a forest in Port St Lucie, Florida in 1977.)

Alarmed at the number of hitchhikers who were going missing, investigators turned their attention to Schaefer and a search of his mother's home found a trunk filled with photographs of his dead victims, including one photograph of a dead nude male. Many of the bodies had been mutilated and the former policeman had kept some of the bones. They also found his stories, which drew on actual murderous events, and the sketches which he had made of hanged women. He'd also cut photos of women out of newspapers and magazines and drawn nooses around their necks.

Schaefer was arrested and tried for the murders of Susan Place and Georgia Jessup. Mrs Lucille Place, Susan's mother, had identified Schaefer as the man that had driven the two teenagers away, and Georgia's handbag had been found at Schaefer's house – he was using it to store a gun and ammunition. The authorities decided to concentrate on this case as the evidence was so strong.

The former cop was also damned by his own words as he had written an essay about how to get away with murder, suggesting how to torture the victim, tie the noose, hang her and dispose of the body. He wrote that kidnapping two women at a time was a good idea as their guard would be down if they were travelling as a pair. He wrote that he also enjoyed making one girl hurt or kill the other to stave off her own imminent torture and death.

Following the conclusion of his trial in Florida in October 1973, the jury returned with a guilty verdict and he was sentenced to life in prison, whereupon his second wife served him with divorce papers, got a quickie divorce and soon married his attorney. Schaefer began communicating with a Filipino woman who started off as his pen pal and he married her whilst in prison but, after she got her green card, she too filed for divorce. The years passed slowly and he was very, very bored.

In 1983, he offered to take investigators to 34 murder sites in Florida so that they could solve their missing persons cases, but his offer was not taken up. He continued to be a thorn in the authorities' side, filing frivolous lawsuits against the prison and against various true-crime writers for describing him as a serial killer. But, though he protested his innocence to the outside world, he boasted to other prisoners about his many crimes.

Living by numbers

Whilst incarcerated in Starke, Florida, Schaefer became friends with serial killer Ted Bundy, a notorious necrophiliac. The latter had killed 33 women, whereas Schaefer was suspected to have murdered 34. Schaefer's victims were believed to have included a girl aged eight and one aged nine while Bundy had murdered a 12-year-old, so they were well matched in their depravity. Schaefer was upset when Bundy was put to death by electrocution, but, that same year, he started a new romance with a former girlfriend after she wrote to him and he replied avidly.

Determined to remain in the public consciousness, he managed to get two books of his short stories published and got in touch with a missing persons agency, offering to point out which of the missing females on their books he was responsible for murdering. He added that he had been linked to 170 victims but that only six corpses had been found.

Arrogant and unfriendly, he was disliked by many of his fellow prisoners: they regarded him as a snitch who would pass on information to the guards for extra favours, and he was further hated for being a former police officer and deputy sheriff. As a result of his poor reputation, the other prisoners often threw waste matter at him. But, on 3 December 1995, one of his enemies went further, entering his cell and stabbing him over 40 times with a crudely fashioned knife. The killer, Vincent Rivera, already serving a sentence for double murder, also gouged out Schaefer's eyes.

Unfortunately, Schaefer's death means that the families of many missing women in Florida have lost the opportunity to find out if the depraved cop was responsible for the demise of their loved ones, and most are still searching for answers to this day.

2

THE DEACON
SAM SMITHERS

Firefighters and the clergy are among the professions profiled in this book, and sex killer Sam Smithers was both.

The perfect husband

Everyone said that Deacon Samuel Smithers was a really nice guy, a family man who was custodian at the First Baptist Church in Plant City, Florida. Everyone, that is, except the young women who were forced to spend time alone with him. He embarrassed and frightened several attractive female parishioners by making explicit comments about their bodies and suggesting that they have sex with him. On one occasion he lifted up a woman's blouse and, in another instance, he talked about one of his ex-lovers whilst he rubbed his penis through his clothes. Some of the women reported his conduct to the church's custodian and, by 1994, the church realised that he was an ongoing problem and asked him to have psychological counselling. He refused and they asked him to resign, which he duly did.

It would later transpire that Smithers had had counselling in 1986 when he lived in Tennessee. Whilst acting as a volunteer fireman and as a church deacon, he'd started several fires and attempted to help put them out, hoping to be hailed as a hero. But police became suspicious about the number of accidental blazes starting in and around the church and a full enquiry showed that these were arson attacks and that Sam Smithers was responsible. He resigned from the church but they forgave him and accepted him as a parishioner, holding a prayer meeting in his honour in the hope that he would be mentally healed. The state also showed leniency, giving him a three-to-five-year sentence which was suspended on account of his good behaviour and upon his promise to have psychological counselling. Smithers turned up to a few sessions but soon quit.

The former deacon retrained and became a welder, but his mother kept phoning him to be critical of his lifestyle. The couple moved to Florida to be nearer his wife Sharon's parents and he got a job as an electrician's apprentice and was respected as a good, steady worker. He was also an ideal husband who always came home for his evening meal and was loving and attentive. But he led a secret life in which he would sneak out to see prostitutes when his wife went to bed.

By the late eighties, he was working as a handyman and also as a church custodian, whilst Sharon was a teacher's aide and their adopted teenage son was at college. (Smithers had a low sperm count so had not been able to father a child, a source of humiliation for him and sadness for them both as they had wanted a large family.) He had loving, dutiful sex with his supportive wife, but what he really wanted was to have rough intercourse which hurt women. He also enjoyed slapping them around.

Childhood

Sam himself had endured many beatings at the hands of his devoutly religious mother, Linnie, as had his three brothers. She was still taking off her belt to him in their home town of East Ridge, Tennessee, when he was 17. He was not allowed to play baseball, despite showing real prowess at the game, because she thought that the other baseball players would use bad language. And he was not allowed to stay over with school friends as evenings were devoted to family prayer.

Her husband, Alvin, couldn't stand the repressed atmosphere and spent his evenings drinking and smoking, occasionally picking up women. He also beat Linnie. She was so afraid of her sons seeing her naked that she would sleep in her clothing and only bathed every three or four days, when she would insist that the menfolk leave the house. She told the boys that premarital sex was sinful and that prostitutes deserved to be killed.

Murder

By 1996, the former deacon was sometimes visiting a brothel in Tampa, Florida and also picking up prostitutes on the street and going to a hotel room with them. He asked several of these working girls to come to his home instead, offering more money, but they declined.

Streetwalker Denise Roach, however, accepted his offer in mid May 1996 and he drove her to a remote house where he was caretaker. They went into the bedroom, where the 24-year-old divorcee fellated him. Afterwards they walked out into the yard, where he grabbed an axe from the garage, beat her repeatedly about the head and put his hands around her throat, strangling her to a point of near unconsciousness. He then grabbed an awl – a sharp metal instrument which he used to punch holes in leather – and stabbed her in the face and head, several of the wounds cutting so deeply that they penetrated her brain. The man of God dragged the still-warm corpse to a nearby pond and threw her in, before going home to mow the lawn for his wife.

Within a fortnight, he was ready to kill again. This time the unfortunate victim was 31-year-old Christy Cowan, a crack-addicted prostitute whom he had had sex with in the past. After leaving work on 28 May, he picked her up and drove her to the same house where he'd taken Denise Roach. This time the couple had full sex then walked downstairs and through the garage, where Smithers grabbed the same axe that he'd used previously and brought it down on the divorced mother-of-two's head. She was still alive, so he strangled her before dragging her body to the pond and throwing her in.

At that very moment he heard a car drive up and went to meet the driver, the resident of the property. She complimented him on how well he had tidied and swept the yard and mowed the grass, then stopped and stared at the pool of blood on the garage floor. Smithers stammered that someone must have killed a squirrel then froze as he heard moaning sounds coming from the direction of the pond. Christy Cowan was still alive…

Alarmed, the woman left the property and contacted the sheriff, who found the recently deceased body of Christy Cowan as well as Denise Roach's decomposing remains in the stagnant pond. Smithers had returned to the moaning woman and finished her off by battering her with a garden hoe.

A police officer went to the former deacon's home and told him about the bodies before asking him to come down to the station. He said calmly that he would but that he wanted his wife to accompany him. At police headquarters they were separated and an officer explained to Sharon that they believed her husband had murdered someone and that the death had been particularly gruesome. She said that this wasn't possible, that he wouldn't commit such an atrocity.

Meanwhile, Smithers was refusing to talk unless Sharon could sit with him. The police acquiesced and she told her husband to tell the truth, but he again said that he hadn't caused the pool of blood, surmising that a small animal had been killed and had bled out. When told that two corpses had been found on the property, both bludgeoned, he merely said that he was sorry to hear that but it was nothing to do with him. The police let him go home for the night but arranged to collect him and resume questioning the following day. They also persuaded Sharon to go and stay with relatives, but she remained loyal to her husband of 23 years and phoned him several times that night.

At the mortuary, Christy Cowan was quickly identified by her fingerprints, but Denise Roach's body was so decomposed (her entire face was missing and the skin had slipped from her fingers) that she was originally registered as a Jane Doe.

The next day, detectives resumed questioning Sam Smithers. He failed a polygraph test then admitted that he hadn't been completely truthful, that he'd picked up a woman whose car had broken down and was traumatised when she said that she'd accuse him of rape if he didn't give her $50. He added that he had driven her to the house where he was caretaker and had thrown her in the pond. As the interrogation continued he admitted to killing a second woman, though he denied having sex with either of them. Because he had moved around the country when he was younger, police forces in other areas began to consider him as a suspect in the unsolved murders of prostitutes.

Sam Smithers' trial began on 15 December 1998. The prosecution told the jury that Smithers had confessed to both murders, whilst the defence alleged that he had been coerced into making this confession by overzealous police.

The court heard about the blood on the garage floor and about Smithers' strange behaviour when he was confronted about it. The jury were shown the graphic autopsy photographs and the murder weapons. They also saw a security tape from a convenience store where Smithers and one of the victims, Christy Cowan, had gone to buy a soda before their sex session. And they heard from a forensic expert that semen found on a rug in the bedroom of the house where Smithers was caretaker (he was only supposed to look after the grounds of the property) belonged to Smithers and that another stain on the bedroom rug was probably from the mouth of Denise Roach.

One of Christy Cowan's friends testified that she had given Christy a condom just hours before she was murdered – and the condom's wrapper was found in the house that Smithers was looking after. Everyone was surprised when Smithers elected to testify in his own defence.

He took the stand and said that he'd had adulterous sex with a woman at his church who was called Mimi and that a mysterious man had seen them with their arms around each other, had taken photographs and threatened to tell Sharon about the liaison if he didn't give him access to the house which he was tending. This man, he added, had killed both women and made him dispose of their bodies in the nearby pond.

The prosecution had a field day, asking Smithers what Mimi's surname was. He didn't know, despite being the record keeper at the church. What about the name of the mysterious man, then? He didn't know that either, he said. Why hadn't he gone to the police after being forced to drag the bloody bodies to the pond? He'd feared that the mysterious man would kill his wife and teenage son. Sam Smithers had gotten by in life by being superficially charming but, under questioning, his flimsy story soon fell apart. That same day, the jury went out and returned in less than 2 hours with a verdict – guilty of first-degree murder on both counts.

At the penalty phase, the prosecution said that both murders had been premeditated: after all, he could have had sex in his car or at various quiet road-stops but had instead chosen to take both women to a more remote location where he could butcher them and dispose of the bodies. He'd phoned his wife to say that he was stuck in a traffic jam so would be late home. The defence argued that the killer had been so traumatised by his abusive childhood that he hadn't really known what he was doing. He had also apparently been dropped on his head as a baby, and the defence suggested this might have left him with permanent brain damage.

His wife took the stand and said that he had been a wonderful husband and an excellent adoptive father, that the family had done everything together. He had told her that it had felt as if someone else had committed the murders, not him. The defence's psychiatrist said that this meant he might have been having dissociative episodes, breaks with reality. But the jury were unconvinced and took only 90 minutes to recommend that he be put to death.

The former Baptist deacon appealed the death sentences, but the Florida Supreme Court refused to overturn the convictions. At the time of writing, Samuel Smithers resides on death row, awaiting his date with the electric chair.

3

THE OBSTETRICS NURSE
NORMA JEAN ARMISTEAD

Though she was trained to help women through their pregnancies, this nurse stole one baby and cut another out of its mother's womb in a desperate bid to keep her lover by her side.

A cruel plan

In 1974, Norma Jean Armistead was living with her lover Charles Armistead and had taken his surname but he was losing interest and she feared he'd return to his wife. He'd said that he'd like a son as his marriage had only produced daughters, so Norma Jean, who was in her early forties, kept quiet about the fact that she'd had a hysterectomy 13 years before. She had a grown-up son and daughter from a previous relationship so he had no reason to question her fertility. It's likely that she also failed to tell him that she'd spent time in a Texas mental hospital before becoming a nurse.

That autumn Norma Jean told him that she was pregnant and that she was sure that it was going to be a boy. As the months passed, she used more and more padding to fake an expanding stomach and wore voluminous garments to bed. The other nurses at her workplace, Kaiser Permanente Hospital in Los Angeles, believed that she was having a late baby with her new beau.

Norma Jean needed a black or mixed-race baby as her lover was black, so when 26-year-old Mary Childs was admitted in the early stages of labour on 20 September 1974, she seized her chance. She befriended the younger woman and injected her with strong sedatives in the early hours of the morning so that she was lapsing in and out of consciousness. She also gave her labour-inducing drugs. At one stage Mary woke up to find that she was paralysed but she soon drifted back into unconsciousness, gave birth to the child and slept for many hours afterwards. Meanwhile, Norma Jean took a three-pound stillborn foetus from the mortuary, put it between Mary's legs and walked out of the hospital with her healthy baby girl.

She took the baby, whom she called Carrie, to another hospital in the area and said she'd had a home birth and had had a medical examination at the hospital where she was employed as a nurse. She added that, in her opinion, the hospital she was in now offered better postnatal care and that's why she'd come here to register the birth. Medics were surprised at Norma Jean's decision but she was entirely plausible and they completed the necessary paperwork.

When Mary Childs eventually regained consciousness, doctors told her that her drug use had killed the baby in her womb the week before. Distraught, Mary protested that she didn't take drugs and that she had felt the baby kicking en route to the delivery room. Doctors said that the dead foetus must have shifted inside her but she countered that it was her third child so she knew how a baby's kick felt. They added that she'd had a massive amount of sedative in her system: they had no idea that their very own obstetrics nurse had injected her with this. Mary, a hard-working grocery store assistant, protested that she'd had a blood test when she was admitted which showed that she was drug-free and that the doctor had estimated that her baby would be about eight pounds, not the three-pound foetus which they now claimed that she'd delivered. Moreover, a doctor had registered a foetal heartbeat which she had seen on the screen. Despite these numerous inconsistencies the hospital claimed that she was in denial about the stillbirth and sent her home.

A savage murder

Meanwhile, Norma Jean presented Charles with his new daughter but he was disappointed that it wasn't a son and again the relationship faltered. Norma Jean, by now 44 years old, began looking around for another pregnant victim and soon befriended Kathryn Viramontes, a 26-year-old who was having her boyfriend's child.

Norma Jean attacked the younger woman on 16 May 1975 as they sat in Kathryn's apartment, injecting her with a medication which would paralyse her muscles. She taped Kathryn's mouth shut, cut her throat and also cut her from the navel to the pubic bone, effectively carrying out a home caesarean. The unfortunate mother died quickly of blood loss.

Norma Jean took the baby boy to a nearby hospital where she again refused a medical exam, explaining she was fine and only wanted to register the birth but the baby had a slight fever and a nurse took him away for treatment. Meanwhile, the bloody body of Kathryn Viramontes was found and it was obvious that someone had cut her child from her womb. Detectives contacted the nearest hospitals and found that Norma Jean was at one of them and acting suspiciously. A doctor who insisted on examining her discovered that she didn't have a uterus or a cervix so couldn't possibly have given birth to this child or the one that she claimed to have delivered the previous year.

Detectives went to her house and discovered that Mary Childs' daughter, now eight months old, was being cared for by one of Norma Jean's adult relatives. They belatedly united the real mother with her child and an anguished Mary Childs sued the hospital for originally preventing an investigation into what really happened. She received $275,000 and her baby daughter received $100,000.

A film, *Empty Cradle* (1993), was loosely based on the case. In the movie, the killer nurse is played by an ultra slim and glamorous Kate Jackson, whilst the real Norma Jean Armistead was overweight and matronly. The mother of the stolen baby in the film is white whereas the real mother was black. Norma Jean's lover, Charles, is also portrayed as being white rather than black and still lives with his unsuspecting wife and kids. Nevertheless, Kate Jackson accurately depicts the sudden mood swings and hysterics which borderline personalities like Norma Jean Armistead display in real life.

The motive

Romantics often believe that a woman who steals a baby is overwhelmed by her maternal instincts, but Norma Jean had given birth twice and had difficult relationships with her adult children. She'd had a hysterectomy many years before so her biological clock simply wasn't ticking and, after she stole Mary Childs' baby, she did not spend a great deal of time with it. Rather, she wanted a son for the bond that she hoped this would create with her increasingly indifferent lover, Charles, and the item to hold their union together could just as well have been a puppy or a kitten if that's what he desired. With her borderline personality she saw her victims as collateral damage and has never shown full awareness of the terror that she wrought.

Still protesting

At the time of writing, Norma Jean Jackson (she has reverted to her real surname) is in a female correction centre in Chowchilla, California. Now in her eighties, she is suffering from heart disease, the after-effects of a stroke and arthritis, and believes that she should be released or at least moved into a halfway house. Her few supporters note that she's on ten prescription medications a day and say that she's paid for her crimes, but her detractors remember the full horror of Kathryn's murder and the fact that she robbed the young mother of potentially more than 50 years of life, as well as causing Mary Childs untold pain.

A psychologist explains

This was such an unusual case that I sought the input of Dr David Holmes, a senior lecturer at Manchester Metropolitan University, director of their Forensic Research Group and author of the landmark text *Abnormal Clinical and Forensic Psychology*. I said that Norma Jean Armistead appeared to have a borderline personality disorder, evidenced by her mood swings and volatile relationships, and asked if he agreed with this and could identify any other personality disorders which she personified.

He replied as follows: 'Personality-disordered individuals are almost always diagnosed with two or more personality disorders – it is very rare to have a single diagnosis. Ms Armistead shows borderline personality features such as mood swings and rapid reaction to others but also in her desperate measures to avoid abandonment and gain attention. This attention-seeking and her pathologically overconfident levels of lying would tick boxes for narcissism, but, with her lack of concern for others or consequences, more clearly indicates psychopathy. There are elements of Munchausen syndrome by proxy in her acts as she fabricates her pregnancy at the ultimate expense of the suffering and death of others. Her professional manipulation of medical skills and overconfident ambition to fool other medical professionals also fits this syndrome.'

I commented that most of us couldn't cut a foetus from the womb even if we badly wanted a baby and asked if he believed this lack of empathy is only found in psychopaths.

'Lack of empathy can be found on the schizoid spectrum but such individuals lack the motivation to harm and do not appreciate that others may be suffering or in pain, whereas psychopaths such as Armistead know full well they are inflicting harm but feel nothing and care even less.' He added thought-provokingly that 'some individuals share the lack of revulsion at the grotesque visceral acts characteristic of psychopaths but train to put this layer of insensitivity to good use as surgeons, nurses or emergency personnel'. He also noted that 'there is an area of the frontal brain behind the eyes that prevents us acting out our darkest violent fantasies. This does not function properly in psychopaths.'

We know virtually nothing about Norma Jean Armistead's childhood, so it's impossible to find her place on the nature-versus-nurture scale, but Dr Holmes believes that 'most callous killers such as Armistead have had their dangerous traits all their lives but only display them when the opportunity arises. Some show incidences in childhood and in some cases their extreme traits can dominate the family home and destroy its emotional fabric, thus causing a broken home rather than vice versa.' He continued: 'Most individuals who suffer abandonment or loss in childhood compensate by being overdutiful and caring as adults. However, some professionals believe that dependent personalities can develop from this.

Although Armistead shows dependent traits, she fits the picture of borderline psychopath better.'

I asked him if this type of killer typically loses herself in a particularly rich fantasy life. After all, she must have known that the police would soon be looking for a baby taken via a home caesarean so it seems incredible that she believed that she could pass the baby off as her own, particularly when a medical examination would show that she'd had a hysterectomy.

Dr Holmes explained: 'One clear trait of psychopaths is a lack of concern for the future. They live for the satisfaction of the moment and are overconfident, even arrogant, about their abilities to maintain lies. Although manipulative and cunning, they make mistakes and become careless when reality does not fall in line with their selfish and often unpleasant fantasies. Oddly, in Munchausen by proxy, perpetrators enjoy the challenge of fooling professionals into thinking they, the perpetrators, are superior. If they have any plan at all, psychopaths think they will simply use force or manipulation if found out by someone.'

I confided that a lawyer involved in the case recently referred to Armistead as an elderly Charles Manson and asked Dr Holmes if, in his opinion, someone who committed such brutal crimes could ever become normal and present no further danger to society.

'Dangerous personalities are lifelong propensities,' he replied, 'not temporary or curable diseases. When psychopaths agree to treatment they are most likely to manipulate the therapist into giving them a good report by faking good behaviour. Those that genuinely want to change can have their traits moderated though not removed. Personality traits often moderate as individuals pass through middle age but they do not change to anything like normal, thus they will always present a risk to others.'

4

THE BISHOP
MARVIN PENTZ GAY

Though ostensibly a man of God, this bishop didn't follow the edict that not one hair on a child's head should be harmed. Instead, he beat every one of his family members mercilessly and murdered his firstborn son.

Unmitigated cruelty

Though Bishop Marvin Gay was a leader of the House of God church, he was a ruthless father who beat his little boy, Marvin junior, whenever the boy failed to accurately cite biblical chapter and verse. He went on to have another son and two daughters, whom he also beat on a regular basis, but he reserved the worst of his hatred for his oldest child.

As the years passed, the beatings became increasingly sadistic and the father would send Marvin junior up to his bedroom then spend up to an hour jangling his belt on the stairway to increase the child's trepidation. Little Marvin began to have night terrors and wet the bed and his father beat him for this. There was little respite at school, as he was bullied because of the homosexual connotations his surname had. He often saw his father beating up his mother, Alberta, and he was confused by his father's insistence on dressing in his mother's clothes, something which his father did for sexual kicks.

A musical career

Though Marvin junior was emotionally crippled by the years of abuse, he had one talent which gave him a level of self-belief: a remarkable singing voice. At first, he only used this to sing hymns in church. When the other parishioners praised him, his father became enraged, so he began to sing in the local clubs instead.

By the time that Marvin turned 15, he was tall enough to challenge his father when he tried to beat him. He left school, much to the bishop's disgust, and embarked on a professional singing career, changing his surname from Gay to Gaye, which further enraged his father. The bishop began to drink more and more alcohol and went to work less and less. The long-suffering Alberta, who had worked as a cleaner for years to help support the family, had to take on a second menial job to make ends meet.

As the young man's musical career flourished with hits like 'I Heard It Through the Grapevine', 'What's Going On?' and 'Sexual Healing', Bishop Gay became increasingly irate, claiming that the human voice was only designed to praise God. When his son came home after suffering a nervous breakdown, the religious leader barely spoke to him. The younger man remained holed up for days in his childhood bedroom, listening to records and snorting cocaine.

The bishop's background

So what kind of upbringing leaves a man so full of hate and so lacking in pity that he brutalises his own children? Marvin Pentz Gay senior was born on 1 October 1914 to impoverished farm workers. He was the third of their 13 children and had to work long hours with his family in the tobacco fields. He often went hungry and was also traumatised by watching his father beat up his mother, a pattern he would repeat later with his own wife.

When he was four, his parents joined the House of God, a church which combined Pentecostal Christianity with Judaism. The little boy took on his parents' religious views, even when it meant that he couldn't play football at school or sing popular songs, as any form of entertainment was disallowed.

At 20, he became a minister and, that same year, he married Alberta. She already had a daughter by another man, but Marvin insisted on sending this child away. Two years later they had a daughter together but he also rejected her as he wanted a son. Another two years elapsed before Alberta gave birth to Marvin junior, but her husband was inexplicably jealous of the boy and hated it when Alberta lavished affection on him. He even suggested that the child wasn't his.

Bishop Gay had often gone hungry throughout his childhood and now he made his children – he eventually had two boys and two girls – submit to fasting, explaining that this would bring them closer to God. He repeatedly warned them that, if they did not please their deity, they would go to hell.

A change of heart

The years passed in a religious fervour until Marvin senior had a midlife crisis: he decided that he had to go public about his love of dressing in women's clothes, and this clashed with the beliefs of his church peers and his parishioners. He opted to resign from his ministry and began to spend his days drinking alcohol on the porch whilst wearing a dress and ladies shoes. His children often saw him in women's undergarments – he enjoyed parading around the house in drag – and were deeply ashamed.

When Marvin Gaye became famous and rich, he bought his parents an expensive house in LA and begged his mother to divorce his father but she, too, was religious and believed that marriage was for life.

Marvin's own marriage failed and his career began to flag. Increasingly dependent on drugs, he moved back in with his parents in August 1983. He started to tell his fellow musicians and his siblings that he was going to die, and that he might be poisoned or shot dead. Such drug-induced paranoia is common, but the singer would prove to be chillingly correct…

Murder

On 1 April 1984, the former bishop, now 69, couldn't find an insurance policy which he had taken out the previous week. He accused his son of stealing it, and a row developed in which the younger man shoved his father out of the way. The patriarch's response was to walk into his bedroom, retrieve his pistol and return to the room where Marvin was by now resting with his mother. He shot his firstborn son at point-blank range and the 44-year-old (who was a day short of his forty-fifth birthday) fell to the floor. Standing over him, Bishop Gay aimed at his heart and fired again. His mother screamed and begged him not to kill her, too, but he reassured her that she had nothing to fear from him, then walked out and sat on the porch, waiting for the police.

Arrested, he claimed that he had killed his son in self-defence. He was refused bail and put on suicide watch, his defence lawyer claiming that he was mentally unfit to stand trial. Gay later claimed that he thought the gun had been empty or that it only fired blanks.

That summer, doctors discovered and removed a small tumour from the killer's brain. The charge against him was reduced from murder to voluntary manslaughter and he was given five years' probation. He returned to the death house and continued to drink heavily, spending hours alone in his bedroom. His wife, still mourning the loss of her beloved son, divorced him after he showed no contrition for the crime.

When his health failed, Marvin Gay senior moved into a retirement home in Long Beach, California and lived a quiet life. In October 1998, 14 years after killing his son, he died of pneumonia.

5

THE PUBLIC SAFETY OFFICER
ROBERT FRATTA

Despite it being his sworn duty to safeguard the community, Bob Fratta was increasingly violent towards his estranged wife.

Murder in suburbia

Wednesday 9 November 1994 was a typically quiet night in Timber Trails, a residential area of Humble, Texas, so residents were alarmed when shots rang out. They raced to their windows to see that their neighbour Farah Fratta was lying beside her car and that the man they presumed to be her shooter was trying to hide behind a tree. Moments later a car screeched to a halt, the murderer jumped in and the small, silver vehicle, which had only one working headlight, sped away. Farah's neighbours called the emergency services but the attractive 33-year-old was dead by the time that she reached the hospital.

Shortly after the murder, Robert Alan Fratta, her estranged husband (known as Bob), arrived at the house with their three children. A religious man who worked as a public safety officer – that is, a policeman who also doubles as a firefighter, a dual role that is common in small-town America – he was well known for his hatred of Farah. He admitted to police that he was involved in a bitter custody dispute which was due to be heard in less than three weeks, but professed shock at her sudden death. Farah's parents took the three youngsters – sons aged seven and five and a four-year-old daughter – home with them and broke the news of their mother's demise the following day.

An autopsy showed that Farah had been shot twice in the head at almost point-blank range. She had screamed and fallen to the floor after the first shot, after which the shooter had stood over her and fired a second time. This shot had proved fatal and her body had already been convulsing and was close to death when paramedics arrived.

The investigation

Police soon established that Bob Fratta had asked several friends and people who he worked out with at the local gym if they would kill his wife. He had wanted an open marriage and she had refused to accommodate him.

But Fratta's demands hadn't ended there, for, during the nine-year marriage, he had asked her repeatedly to urinate on him, to punch him in the testicles and to defecate in his mouth. The popular airline clerk was understandably disgusted by these extreme requests and they had separated for a time, but Fratta, who was handsome and charismatic, had persuaded her to give him a second chance, saying that he would be happy with a monogamous marriage if only she had a breast enhancement.

Farah had agreed to this and had the surgery in August 1992, but, within weeks, her husband was demanding that they have sex with lesbians or with transsexuals: he'd started to meet the latter in gay bars. The couple split up again that autumn and she filed for divorce. She had reluctantly told her lawyer about Bob Fratta's behaviour and said that she feared he would behave inappropriately with their little girl.

Farah had also told the judge at the custody suite that her husband had no parenting skills, that he often brought the children home hungry and dirty and that his pet snake, a python, had bitten their eldest son on the back. He had also allowed the children to play with his gun and, on other occasions, to play with live ammunition. She had listed all of her estranged husband's faults during the custody battle and, when he found out, he had been enraged.

Questioned further by the police, Fratta admitted asking various acquaintances to kill Farah, but claimed that he just wanted word of this to get back to her so that she would fear for her life and give him custody of the children. He said that he didn't want to pay child support and that he didn't want another man to enjoy the breast enhancement that he had paid for. He also claimed that he would not benefit financially in any way from her death.

But, three days after the shooting, he phoned Farah's insurance company and asked when he would be getting the $100,000 payout from her life assurance policy. He was amazed and incensed to hear that she had recently changed the policy so that he was no longer a beneficiary. As a widower, he'd expected to be a very rich man, but now his children would inherit the money instead. He'd also hoped to get full custody of the children so that he could access the $135,000 that Farah had put into a savings account for their education. (A judge would soon award custody to Farah's parents, stating that Bob Fratta's bizarre sexual practices, and the cloud that he was under regarding his wife's murder, rendered him unfit.)

Police also suspected very strongly that Bob Fratta was behind the murder, but he'd been with his offspring in catechism class in church around the time of the shooting. People at the church remembered that he'd been very tense that night and had made several calls, out of earshot, on his mobile phone. Could he have been talking to the would-be assassin and arranging the last details of the hit?

The authorities also suspected Bob Fratta of being the mastermind behind the torture of the unfortunate Farah on 28 June 1994. She'd woken at 4 a.m. to find a man, dressed all in black and wearing a ski mask, in her bedroom. He'd said, 'I've come to talk about Bob,' and had pressed a Taser gun – widely used by police in the area – into her flesh, burning her. Her children, alerted by her screams, had started pounding on her locked bedroom door, but her assailant had ignored them and pressed the Taser against her throat, torn the phone from the wall and fled the house. Farah had used a second telephone to call police and explain that the torturer was too large to be her husband and that it wasn't his voice. Everyone who knew the couple was convinced that Bob Fratta was indirectly responsible, but no one had ever been charged.

The frightened mother-of-three, who was badly burnt in the attack, had her father come to the house and increase her security measures, and she took to wearing a panic-alert pendant so that she could notify the police if she was assaulted. Her new boyfriend, David, was also protective, though the couple were keeping their relationship discreet as Farah wasn't yet divorced. Farah told David that the man who had tortured her had sounded like her husband's friend from the gym, a man she'd said hello to a few times, though she couldn't remember his name. She was referring to Joe Prystash, a man whom the police would later become very interested in.

A breakthrough

For the next few months, detectives continued to build a case against Bob Fratta. They investigated his gym buddy, Joe Prystash, and found that the man had a criminal record. He had been involved in various burglaries in Dade County in 1977, for which he had been placed on probation. He had also assaulted his brother-in-law and had initially been charged with the man's attempted murder, though the charge had later been dropped. He had two failed marriages and was unemployed but living with a girlfriend.

In turn, Joe had a friend called Howard Guidry, a young black man who lived in the same apartment complex, was similarly unemployed and always looking for easy money. On 6 March 1995, Guidry and three associates robbed a bank but were caught as they fled from the premises. Guidry's gun was found to be the same gun that had shot Farah Fratta: it had belonged to Bob Fratta and was identified by her father. And bullet fragments found at the murder scene matched the bullets used by the gun.

Questioned at length, Howard Guidry admitted killing the mother-of-three at the request of Joe Prystash, who had promised him $1,000, blood money that he would get from Bob Fratta. The older and more streetwise Prystash had driven the getaway vehicle but neither man had received payment as the money was in the glove compartment of Fratta's car when he was taken in for questioning by police and Fratta had avoided both men since. Joe Prystash had fixed the broken headlight on the getaway car (later scrapping the vehicle entirely) and had asked the teenage killer to dispose of the gun, but Howard had kept it as a pay-off for committing the crime.

Howard Guidry, police found, had been in minor trouble with the law as a boy, and had gravitated to breaking into cars by the age of 16. Now, at 18, he was facing a murder charge.

When arrested, Joe Prystash, aged 38, admitted that Bob Fratta had asked him to kill his wife, stating that he'd pay $1,000 to the killer upfront, then make additional payments at later dates until he'd paid a total of $5,000. Prystash had asked Guidry to carry out the murder and the teenager had agreed as he wanted enough money to get his own place rather than continue residing with his sister. He also wanted to buy cocaine and sell it to make additional cash.

On 21 April 1995, detectives arrested Bob Fratta at his mother's house. He told journalists outside jail that he was innocent and praying for justice. The prosecution decided to try Bob Fratta first as they reasoned that he was the ringleader, the man who had masterminded the murder: if he hadn't hated Farah, she would still be alive.

Bob Fratta's trial

On 9 April 1996, Fratta's trial began in Harris County. He pleaded not guilty. The prosecution spoke of the many motives which had led him to hiring a killer: rage that his wife wouldn't agree to his sexual demands; jealousy that another man was enjoying the breast enhancement that he had paid for; and anger that he'd have to pay child support for well over a decade if she succeeded in getting custody. He had also believed that he would benefit financially from her life insurance policy if she died.

Joe Prystash's girlfriend, Mary Gipp, took the stand and admitted that she had heard him on the phone to Bob Fratta on several occasions, planning Farah Fratta's murder. She had not informed anyone of this at the time and had been given immunity from prosecution in return for her testimony.

She said that Bob had given his gun to Joe five months before the murder, as payment for work which Joe had done on Bob's car. Joe, in turn, had given it to Howard Guidry when he needed a murder weapon.

Several churchgoers testified that Bob Fratta had received several phone calls in the hour leading up to the murder and the telephone records showed that these calls were made between himself and Joe Prystash, no doubt as they discussed Farah's movements and as Prystash prepared to drop Guidry off outside her house.

A psychologist testified that Bob Fratta was a narcissist, a man who was shallow and had an inflated sense of his own importance. He was also sexually masochistic and had scored highly on the psychopathic and paranoid scales. Several of his colleagues testified that his love of coprophagy (ingesting bodily wastes, in this case excrement) was common knowledge, that he was open about his desires. He had said that he loved his wife when they first started dating as she would do whatever he wanted but that she now refused many of his requests.

The trial unearthed relatively little about his childhood, apart from the fact that he was a Catholic of Italian heritage but had grown up in New York with his mother and sister. His father had died when he was young. Fratta had been an overly polite and somewhat repressed teenager who didn't lose his virginity until he had graduated from college at age 22, after which he had seemed desperate to make up for lost time. Attractive and with a perfect physique (he worked out for hours every week at the gym and also took steroids), he began to do well with women and kept a notebook detailing his sexual conquests, a book which was misogynistic and which objectified women or saw them as little girls to be dominated and used solely for his own sexual needs. He had told Farah that he regretted waiting so long to lose his virginity and that he wanted his children to start having sex when they were 12.

The defence said that Farah had not mentioned her husband's sexual deviance to her doctor when she was being treated for depression, that she had only disclosed this information when trying to get custody of the children. They said that Joe Prystash and Howard Guidry could have been coerced into making their statements and that the $1,000 found in Bob Fratta's glove compartment on the night of the murder was for buying carpet underlay, not to pay for his wife's assassination. They produced two ex-girlfriends who had dated Fratta and who said that he had never made any unusual sexual demands.

The jury deliberated for under an hour before finding the public safety officer guilty of capital murder. He was subsequently sentenced to death by lethal injection.

Joe Prystash's trial

Whilst Robert Alan Fratta languished on death row in Texas, Joseph Prystash's trial began. It started on 1 July 1996 and mainly involved the same witnesses as those in the Fratta trial. Another gym member explained that, at almost 10 p.m. on the night of Farah's murder, Prystash had left the gym to go looking for Bob Fratta. The prosecution said that Prystash wanted the $1,000 which the public safety officer had promised him for arranging the murder, but Fratta was being questioned by detectives, so Prystash didn't get the cash.

The trial lasted eight days, after which the jury found him guilty of capital murder. At the punishment sentencing phase, his ex-girlfriend Mary Gipp said that Prystash was also the man who had broken into Farah's apartment and tortured her with the Taser. Gipp added that he was doing so at Bob Fratta's request. Both of Prystash's ex-wives said that he was a man who showed little conscience and was subject to mood swings and always on the lookout for money. On 10 July he was sentenced to death.

Howard Guidry's trial

The teenage killer, Howard Guidry, was in court for a mere two days – from 19 to 21 March 1997 – before the jury went out. He had given lengthy statements to the police admitting his guilt, and this was corroborated by a polygraph test. Bank tellers spoke of the terror that they had felt when the 18-year-old and his friends robbed them at gunpoint: this showed the jury his propensity for violence. The gun which he pointed at the bank staff was the same revolver which had previously been used to kill Farah. The jury quickly returned with a guilty verdict and, five days later at the penalty phase, he was sentenced to death.

Retrials

In 2006, Howard Guidry was granted a retrial on the grounds that the police hadn't allowed him access to a lawyer before his confession, even when he requested this. He was convicted for a second time.

Subsequently, Robert Alan Fratta was also granted a retrial when his lawyers alleged that Howard Guidry had been tricked into making a confession. The trial lasted for six weeks, and Guidry and Prystash refused to testify. Several witnesses again told of how Bob Fratta had asked them to kill his wife. In May 2009, after 7 hours of deliberation by a jury in Houston, he was again found guilty and was subsequently re-sentenced to death. He lost an appeal in October 2011 and remains on death row, as do Guidry and Prystash.

6

THE FBI AGENT
MARK PUTNAM

Ambitious, hard-working and devoted to his wife, no one could have predicted that this FBI Agent would kill to save his reputation...

A lethal rage

He had to silence her – he just had to. As the woman screamed that she would tell his wife about their affair, the man grabbed her around the throat and held tight. She struggled in the limited space of the front seat of the car, scratching his jaw and arms and biting his hand but he held her more tightly and she eventually went limp. When he regained his composure, he realised to his horror that she was dead. The murder victim was Susan Smith, an attractive divorcee and an FBI informant, the murderer FBI Agent Mark Putnam, a married father of two.

Their relationship had started as one of mutual convenience when Putnam was sent to his first posting in Pikeville, a small town in Eastern Kentucky, to get intelligence on the local criminals. The Bureau was especially keen to catch bank robber Carl Lockhart in the act. The criminal was on probation and was living with a man called Kenneth Smith, Kenneth's girlfriend and his ex-wife Susan. The Smiths' two children also lived at the house.

Mark Putnam befriended Susan and asked her to keep him updated about Lockhart's plans. In turn, he gave her money from the FBI coffers for becoming one of their informants. Susan liked to take recreational pills, and was struggling to support her two-year-old son and five-year-old daughter on welfare, so was grateful for the extra cash. Soon they were meeting at least twice weekly and before long the 27-year-old had fallen for the tall, dark and handsome federal agent.

Initially, he just felt sorry for Susan as her relationship with her ex-husband was volatile and she was poorly educated and had no future plans. In contrast, he had a promising career with the Bureau and a beautiful, intelligent wife, Kathy. The Putnams had a daughter and Kathy was pregnant with their second child.

In early September 1987, Susan reported to Mark Putnam that her bank-robber friend had brought home sawn-off shotguns and ski masks. He told his colleagues and they put local banks on red alert. On 10 September, Lockhart entered the First National Bank, 15 miles from Pikeville, and left with the takings, unaware that the teller had dropped a dye pack into the pillowcase with the cash. It exploded, rendering most of the money useless, so he laid low for a week before going to another bank and attempting to exchange some of the notes which were only stained red around the edges. The suspicious teller alerted police but Lockhart fled to his mother's house. Susan Smith told the FBI where he was and he was promptly arrested. Mark promised Susan that she'd be paid $4,000 if she testified at his trial.

The unhappy young woman needed the money but she also wanted to please Mark Putnam, with whom she had fallen in love. He was easy to talk to, sophisticated and treated her like a lady. When she found out that he liked to go out running every night, she started going running too. She frequently phoned his house and spoke to Kathy, asking about which meals and TV programmes her husband liked and disliked. Kathy felt sorry for the unemployed housewife, an impoverished coalminer's daughter who wanted to be someone but had no idea how to escape from small-town life.

An alleged affair

Susan took her role as an informant very seriously and told anyone who would listen that she was working for the government. Naturally, this made her enemies and people began to spread rumours that she was sleeping with Putnam. The Putnams laughed off the rumours and went back to Connecticut for Kathy to give birth to their second child, a boy.

They soon returned to Pikeville with their latest addition and Mark threw himself back into his job, determined to impress his superiors and be sent to a more upmarket location. Kathy loathed small-town life and was becoming increasingly depressed, but Mark's spirits were raised when Susan testified at Carl Lockhart's trial and he was found guilty and sent back to the penitentiary. He needed Susan less now, so asked her to start reporting to another FBI Agent who had relocated to the area. Devastated, she began to call the Putnams at all hours of the day and night, talking to Kathy when Mark refused to answer the phone.

She wanted to sleep with Mark but, so far, he had resisted her advances. Now she increasingly retreated into a fantasy world, often fuelled by pills, where she believed that he had fallen in love with her and that they'd had sex in his house when Kathy was away. She told this story to her relatives, adding that he was going to divorce his wife and marry her.

In mid December 1988, Mark and Susan were talking in his car, parked in a clearing, when she began to massage his tense shoulders. Her hands travelled down his body to his inner thighs and he became aroused and had sex with her in the car. Putnam would later tell colleagues that he only ever had sex with Susan in his vehicle, but she would tell friends that they slept at his place whenever Kathy was visiting her parents. He would tell his biographer that after four sex sessions he felt sufficiently guilty to break off the relationship, but Susan gave her peers the impression that it was a lengthier affair. Whatever the time span, Susan felt both used and enraged when he ended the liaison, but was determined to get him back. She was desolate when he and his family moved to Miami, where he was taking up a new FBI post.

A few weeks later, in early June 1989, he returned to Pikeville to tie up some loose ends at work. Susan tracked him down to his motel and told him that she was expecting their baby. She said that she would fly down to Florida and tell his wife and the FBI. He said that he and his wife would raise the baby but this understandably hurt her further and she began to shriek at him that she was a good mother, that she wanted to keep the child and would call it Mark. He offered to drive her home, knowing that it would be easier to talk if they parked somewhere quiet.

A fatal argument

He drove them into the rugged hills, halfway to her house, and parked before asking her wearily what she expected of him. She said that he had to divorce his wife and marry her. He would later say that the verbal argument descended into a physical fight and they punched and scratched at each other. Enraged, he strangled her to death.

Afterwards, probably still in shock, he put her corpse in his rental car, drove back to his motel and lay awake all night with the light on. He attended a meeting the next day with the body still in the trunk. That evening, he drove until he came to a ravine with a creek at the bottom, took out the corpse and rolled it a little way down the slope, about 15 feet from the road. Susan's body was now hidden by bushes but close to a dirt bike track used by children, and near to a popular dog walkers' route.

Three days later, Mark Putnam reported to the FBI that his informant, Susan Smith, was missing, but they weren't particularly alarmed as local intelligence showed that she sometimes went AWOL for a few days, perhaps staying with friends in a nearby town. Her sister then phoned the state police and reported her missing, stressing that she was a good mother who had never before deserted her children like this. A local detective did some background checks and was interested to hear that she had had a positive pregnancy test at the Health Centre a fortnight earlier and had named the father as Mark Putnam, a married agent with the FBI. As a result of this lead, two detectives visited Mark and spoke to him informally for an hour.

The detectives were suspicious of him as he seemed nervous and was almost too co-operative, but they had no proof that he had anything to do with the young woman's disappearance and couldn't be sure that she hadn't disappeared for her own good reasons. After all, her relationship with her ex-husband had been combative and she had made enemies amongst the local criminal fraternity because she'd become an informant for the FBI. The Bureau had given her a total of $9,000 in payment for her intelligence work, enough for her to relocate and start a new life in another town.

Plagued by guilt

For now, Mark Putnam was off the hook, but his conscience was troubling him. He slept badly, his appetite diminished and he lost a stone in weight. He developed a patch of dermatitis on his chest and scratched it repeatedly. He bought and read several newspapers every day, always looking for news that Susan's body had been found.

A year passed, and the local police decided to take another look at Susan Smith's disappearance. They re-interviewed Mark Putnam and this time he let slip that he had broken the windshield of his rental car by kicking it in an act of frustration after accidentally hurting his hand. Until now, detectives hadn't even realised that Putnam had rented a vehicle – and they immediately realised that Putnam and Susan Smith must have fought within its confines and that it was probably the murder site.

That same week, Putnam took and failed a polygraph test. He flew home and admitted to his wife that he had had sex with Susan, believed she was carrying his baby, and had choked her to death. The couple engaged a lawyer who told him that the authorities didn't have a case: after all, they had no body and, as long as he remained silent, no proof that he'd done Susan Smith any harm.

But by now Putnam had lost another stone in weight and his conscience continued to trouble him. He entered into talks with the authorities whereby it was agreed that he would plead guilty to the charge of first-degree manslaughter and be imprisoned for 16 years in a New York prison rather than a Kentucky penitentiary (American prisons offer a more relaxed regime than penitentiaries). Putnam told them where to find the body and they recovered Susan's skeletal remains and her crucifix on a chain. Some of her fingernails and toenails, both painted red, were also recovered at the scene.

Putnam started his sentence at Otisville in New York but was later transferred to a federal prison in Rochester, Minnesota and then to a Massachusetts prison. Kathy visited him whenever she could but the loneliness took its toll and she began to drink heavily. She died in 1998 of a heart attack. Putnam's sentence was reduced to ten years because of good behaviour and he was released in September 2000 and relocated to Florida where he remarried and started a new life. Unlike many of the men profiled in these pages, he appears to be a good man who made one terrible, life-altering mistake.

7

THE CHARITY WORKER
ROBERT SPANGLER

Though he was very well liked by friends and neighbours, Robert
Spangler murdered at least four family members when he tired
of their company.

Unwanted

Though nothing is known of his birth family, Robert Spangler was
born on 10 January 1933 and spent time in an orphanage before
being adopted by Merlin and Ione Spangler, who lived in Iowa. He
would later speculate that he had inherited bad genes which made
him capable of killing without guilt.

Merlin was an engineering professor at the local university, an
erudite but affable man who married his childhood sweetheart. The
couple also adopted another son.

Bob (he preferred this to the more formal Robert) was
intelligent, but he got into lots of fights at junior school, and
especially hated another 11-year-old. When the boy died by
drowning in a sewage treatment plant, police suspected that Bob
had played a part in his death and he was questioned at the police
station. Classmates spoke out about his propensity for violence,
but, without sufficient proof of foul play, the case was eventually
written up as a tragic accident.

But by secondary school he had found his niche as features editor on the school newspaper and began to date a sweet-natured teenager, Nancy. He went on to study technical journalism at university and married Nancy in 1955 shortly after their graduation. He started a career in television and their son David was born in 1961, with daughter Susan following in 1963.

Later, he got work as a publicist with a large charity and moved the family to Denver, Colorado. Once again, he excelled at his job and raised a great deal of money to provide clean water to impoverished overseas communities. He kept fit by helping coach a children's football team and was always happy to listen to the youngsters' problems. He also formed lifelong friendships with some of the people he met whilst out hiking, sending them long, articulate letters about his life and future hiking plans.

But by the mid seventies, he was bored with his stay-at-home wife, although Nancy still doted on him. He still enjoyed his work and liked riding his motorbike and going hiking, but he increasingly disliked going home. He didn't approve of his daughter's boyfriends and, though he was closer to his son, wasn't pleased that the youngster was experimenting with marijuana. He wanted a peaceful household but often came home to find the teenagers' music blaring from their rooms.

So, when he had to recruit a new assistant for himself, he hired attractive and outdoor-loving Sharon Cooper, 11 years his junior. Though she was highly strung, she initially hid this with flirtatious behaviour. Soon the duo embarked on a passionate affair.

Bob left Nancy and the children and set up home with Sharon, but she wasn't as easy-going as Nancy and the pair were soon having regular arguments. Meanwhile, Nancy took temping work and found that she really enjoyed it. She also completed a university course and was planning a new public relations career. The Spanglers decided to reconcile and Bob moved back into the family home in the autumn of 1978 and they all celebrated Christmas together. But he missed his more exciting life with Sharon and decided to return to her immediately after that Christmas. A normal man would perhaps have asked for a divorce and started over, but divorces are costly and he would have had to pay maintenance for his children, whereas if all three died...

Familicide

On 30 December of that same year, he typed an ostensible suicide note from Nancy which said that she had found a gun, was tired of life and had decided to end it all and take the kids with her. He then persuaded her down into the basement office and sat her down, telling her to close her eyes as he had a surprise for her. He did indeed, but it wasn't the gift she was doubtless expecting. Instead, he fatally shot her through the head.

He next made his way to his daughter's bedroom and shot the sleeping teenager through the heart. She died instantly. Moving on to his son's bedroom, he shot the boy through the chest. But David was only wounded, sat up in bed and grappled with his father. Panicking, Bob Spangler suffocated him with a pillow after a fierce struggle which saw blood spatter over the bed and floor.

The dead teenagers were found hours later by Susan's horrified boyfriend, who alerted the authorities and waited outside for the paramedics. Meanwhile, Bob Spangler went to a burger bar and to the cinema, expecting to come home eventually and pretend to discover the bodies. Medics took the children's bodies away and detectives searched the residence. They were further shocked to find Nancy dead in her typist's chair in the basement. The suicide note gave the impression that she had killed her children in a fit of depression before turning the gun on herself.

As the recently estranged husband, Bob Spangler was an obvious suspect and was asked to take a polygraph test. He hyperventilated throughout, making the test results worthless. He did the same thing when asked to retake the test. An examination of the typed suicide note showed that it had been signed merely with a capital N and it was determined that Nancy often signed letters in this way.

Understandably, Nancy's siblings had their suspicions. She'd been building herself a more interesting life and making plans for the future, and hadn't seemed to be depressed or despairing. Moreover, she dearly loved her children and would never have harmed them. She also adored Bob and wanted to make their marriage work. She was a small, slender woman with an arthritic right hand so it was doubtful whether she could have fired the gun, far less overpowered her 17-year-old son with a pillow whilst he fought for his life.

Bob also changed his story after it was determined that the gun was too far away from Nancy's hand for it to have dropped naturally to the floor. Now he told detectives that he'd in fact found his wife dead, picked up the gun and dropped it again, then panicked and fled the house, going to the burger bar and the cinema. In the circumstances, it seems incredible that he wasn't arrested and sent to trial.

Curiouser and curiouser

Spangler's behaviour continued to raise red flags as, days after the murders, he moved Sharon into the death house. Strangers often baulk at living in such Amityville Horror properties and they are usually either knocked down or sold at a substantial discount. How could Spangler bear to live in the rooms where his wife, son and daughter had bled to death? It's equally surprising that Sharon, who considered herself to be in tune with the elements and who wrote eloquently about nature, could live in such an unhappy residence.

Bob and Sharon married on 14 July 1979 and spent part of their honeymoon at the Grand Canyon, but their relationship remained volatile. The community, who had really liked Nancy, were naturally shocked that she had been replaced with indecent haste so they were wary of befriending Sharon. They also found her New Age beliefs risible. Feeling increasingly adrift, she alternated between bouts of hypermania and excessive sleeping, symptoms which today would point towards bipolar disorder – in those days known as manic depression. Though she had been 37 when she married, she often acted like a much younger woman.

By now Bob wanted to devote more of his time to his hobbies but couldn't afford to give up work. His mother had died ten days after he murdered Nancy and the two children, but his 92-year-old father was still going strong so he couldn't claim his inheritance.

In 1986 he visited the old man and shortly afterwards Merlin had a terrible fall from which he never recovered. Within a fortnight he was dead. Bob now inherited a substantial sum of money and was able to take early retirement. That same year, Sharon's book, *On Foot in the Grand Canyon*, was published to great acclaim.

But by the following December the couple's fights had reached fever pitch and Sharon fled to a nearby market claiming that Bob had refused to give her the car keys. She hid in a storeroom and, when the police arrived to investigate, starting kicking out at them. She was taken to hospital for an evaluation where she stated that her husband was trying to 'get' her. By the end of the month the pair had agreed to divorce.

In the summer of 1988, the lawyers finished allocating their assets and Bob was unhappy that Sharon got the car, stocks and bonds and $400 a month in maintenance. But they both wanted to maintain their contact with Sharon's three dogs so agreed to keep in touch. Bob would take the animals, which he loved, whenever Sharon was out of town. In 1989 her book about the canyon went into its second printing so, for a while, her life was on the up.

Another murder

Never able to remain alone for long, Spangler was soon dating several women, but before long he focused on a 56-year-old accountant called Donna Sundling, whom he had met in April 1989. They were the same age and both liked to keep fit, and Donna taught aerobics. She agreed to go hiking with him in the Grand Canyon but secretly hated it. She wanted to please him, however, so gave the impression that she enjoyed the outdoor life.

Donna had raised five children and maintained good relationships with them all. She had no reason to disbelieve Bob's version of events, in which he said that Nancy had killed the children and herself. Doubtless he explained the failure of the second marriage by alluding to Sharon's mental health problems. A more streetwise woman would have insisted on a long courtship until she really got to know him, but Donna fell in love and they were married in August 1990.

Unfortunately, those who marry in haste often repent at leisure and the couple soon found that they didn't have much in common. Donna suffered from vertigo to the extent that she wouldn't even stand on a ladder to hang a painting, whereas Bob adored the dizzying heights of the Grand Canyon and returned there with friends at every opportunity. He was angry that Donna didn't want to return there with him. Her relatives noticed that he was very controlling, though he showed no propensity for violence. He found part-time work at a local radio station as a DJ and began to flirt openly with other women. Desperate to win back her husband's attention, Donna asked him to go skiing with her, but he was understandably afraid that he would break a leg, so he demurred.

As Easter 1993 approached, Bob Spangler knew that he wanted out of the marriage but that, by walking away, he would lose all of his wife's assets, including their palatial home. But if she died he would inherit everything.

He pleaded with her to go hiking with him in the Canyon, giving the impression that it would strengthen their flagging relationship, and she eventually agreed. Perhaps sensing subconsciously that she was about to die, she phoned her adult children and told them that she loved them. They would never hear her voice again.

At first the couple walked alongside other hikers who were taking the same trail but, as 11 April 1993 wore on, he suggested that they leave the main path and camp illegally overnight near a disused mineshaft. He had planned his strategy carefully as, from this point on, they wouldn't be overlooked. He waited until Donna was distracted then ran at her and pushed her over the edge so that she fell down a 140-foot drop. He scrambled down by a safe route to ascertain that she was dead. If she hadn't been, he planned to suffocate her.

He then calmly walked back to the park ranger's office, stood casually in line and, on reaching the desk, reported that his wife had lost her footing and fallen to her death.

Suicide

As usual, Spangler's grief was short-lived and he was soon scouting around for another relationship. In the interim period, his ex-wife Sharon had endured another failed relationship and was feeling lost and alone. Absence makes the heart grow fonder and she must have forgotten the more difficult periods of their marriage in the eighties, concentrating instead on the many good times that they'd had. Whatever her hopes, in the April of 1994, she moved in with him as a lodger and by June had written her last will and testament.

Though Sharon had suffered from depression all her life, at that particular period she had good reason to feel down. Her attempts at self-employment had failed, one of her beloved dogs had died and her mother was seriously ill. She even gave up her beloved walking jaunts and became increasingly agoraphobic. She had lost her way.

On 1 October, she wrote several farewell notes to her friends and relatives, including one to Bob which said 'your nurturing love gave me so much'. She then took a bottle of prescription medication and washed it down with alcohol.

Spangler found her barely conscious and rushed her to the nearest medical centre, where she was admitted to the Intensive Care Unit and managed to tell a doctor that she had taken an overdose. Twelve hours later she died.

Spangler had now had three wives and two children die on him, so the authorities were understandably suspicious. Ironically, he probably had no hand in Sharon's death, though he benefited financially as he no longer had to pay her monthly alimony.

The net closes

Donna's children were shocked to hear that Sharon had now died in Bob's home, especially as they also knew about the death of Nancy and the children. They contacted the authorities, telling them that all three of Bob Spangler's wives and both of his children had died very young.

Detectives went back and re-examined the photographs taken of Nancy after she died. They sent them to ballistics experts who said that the shot to her head appeared to have been fired at intermediate range rather than up close as is usual in a suicide. There had been a man's sock over the handle of the pistol making it impossible to dust for fingerprints. There was no powder from the gun on Nancy's blouse and none of her prints on the note or pen. Records of the tyre tracks outside the house on the morning after the murders suggested that Bob Spangler lied about the number of trips that he had made to and from the death house.

When questioned now, he remained cool under pressure. Indeed, he was so confident that the police would never pin anything on him that he began yet another relationship, this time via the internet, and relocated to Pennsylvania to pursue the woman. But she lost interest and he moved to Grand Junction, Colorado and began scouting for dates.

He soon got involved with a woman called Judy Hilty and they went into the house-renovating business together. He also asked her to go hiking with him in the Grand Canyon. By now, alarmed detectives were keeping a close tab on him as they feared that he might kill again.

Always keen for new experiences, he joined an amateur dramatics company but in the summer of 2000 realised he was having difficulty in memorising his lines. He also started to have eyesight problems and Judy persuaded him to have medical tests. To everyone's surprise, he was found to have lung cancer which had already spread to his brain, creating the loss of concentration. The disease was already terminal.

A fourth marriage

On 1 September of that same year, Bob and Judy married and he signed over his house to her. By now, police had increased their surveillance, worried that yet another spouse would meet an untimely end. When they heard that Spangler probably had six months to a year left, they decided to bring him in for questioning. If they waited much longer he would take his secrets to the grave.

They asked him to come down to the sheriff's office for questioning and he agreed but asked them to collect him by car as his brain cancer was affecting his ability to drive. They did so. Knowing that he loved to feel important, they had mocked up a room peopled by the Spangler Task Force and he was interviewed by, amongst others, an FBI officer. He stuck by his story that Nancy had killed herself and the children, but admitted that his marriages to Sharon and Donna had been mistakes. As the day wore on he seemed close to confessing, saying, 'This information will be hard on Judy.' They brought his fourth wife down to the station and the couple talked then went home, with Bob promising to return the next day.

When he returned, he said that he wanted to talk to the FBI Agent, that he wanted to understand himself. He had already said that he compartmentalised his life and that he didn't dwell on the past. Now he admitted luring Nancy down to the basement, adding, 'I shot her. It was easier than divorce.' Later in the interview he said, 'The next step was to shoot David and Susan. And this was simply a matter of me being enamoured with Sharon.' After describing the struggle to kill his teenage son he asked rhetorically, 'Why was I capable of such a thing?' Investigators already knew the answer, as they had determined that he was a fully fledged psychopath who would always put his own self-interest first and who was incapable of remorse.

He also talked about murdering Donna, saying that she had become jealous and that they lacked a connection. He had lost interest in their sex life. He had pushed her over the edge then leaned over to see the body and had almost fallen over. The profiler noticed that he became more animated when talking about this near brush with death. Yet he remained fearless now that he was terminally ill. At that stage, though, he still had enough energy to go on short hikes and visit friends.

He spoke about being adopted and said he had no idea who his parents were, that perhaps this had made him different. The profiler explained that most of us feel like killing someone at times but that we're able to fight the urge. Bob Spangler simply lacked that mechanism. It was agreed that he would be given a month to put his affairs in order before his arrest.

But within three days he was having second thoughts and wrote to the authorities saying that he wanted a news blackout. He argued that his friends and remaining family thought highly of him and that there was no need for them to know of his darker side. He said, incredibly, that he had only been bad on two days (when he killed his first family and when he killed his third wife) out of 67 exemplary years. He truly was incapable of understanding the lifelong pain that Nancy's siblings and Donna's children felt at their early deaths. Articulate to the last, he described himself as 'an eminently admirable human being, a good friend, able mentor, solid role model' and added later that he was 'worthy of respect'.

The police had suggested strongly that Judy, his fourth wife, stay with friends, but she said she loved Bob and that he would never harm her. Nevertheless, the authorities feared that he might stage a murder–suicide so they arrested him earlier than planned. On 3 October 2000 he was handcuffed at his home and taken into custody.

As he'd surmised, his friends and neighbours were stunned and spoke out about how kind he had been to them, how he'd made them laugh with his dry sense of humour. He'd helped coach numerous children on the football field and his years as a local radio host had brought him additional fans.

Though crime writers now wondered if he had also had a hand in Sharon's death, it seems unlikely. She had a lifelong history of depression and had clearly been contemplating suicide by the time she moved in with her former husband. And, though she and Spangler had many rocky moments, they were never totally free of each other, always keeping in touch. In her Grand Canyon book, which is written in the first person, her admiration for him shines through and she writes briefly about everything from how he helped her climbing style to his determination to complete the hike even when in agony from an injured knee. In turn, it's likely that an egotist like Spangler loved being credited as the photographer in a well-respected tome about his favourite place on earth.

But Bob Spangler would never go hiking again, except in his imagination. In November 2000 he was convicted of Donna's murder and sentenced to life imprisonment, to be served at a federal prison in Missouri. It would be a short life sentence as by the following February his health was failing and that summer he was transferred to a prison hospital. He died there on 5 August 2001, aged 68, but didn't get his final wish for his remains to be scattered over the Grand Canyon, the scene of his final murder.

8

THE FOSTER MOTHER
EUNICE SPRY

Though she stopped short of murder, this woman's catalogue of abuses against her adopted and foster children was described by a judge as the most shocking that he had ever seen.

Adoption and fostering

Eunice was born on 28 April 1944 to a married couple from Gloucestershire who were devout Jehovah's Witnesses. Her father, an army man, was considered to be a disciplinarian and had been one of the first Jehovah's Witnesses in Cinderford. He insisted that the family, which included Eunice's brother, make the 15-mile journey to the nearest Kingdom Hall by bicycle three times a week. Holidays were seen as sinful, as was celebrating your birthday as there are only two birthday parties mentioned in the Bible and someone dies at both. Television and radio were not allowed and Eunice was encouraged to mainly mix with other Jehovah's Witnesses.

Eunice and her first husband Frank had two daughters and the older one, Judith, would later admit that she was regularly horsewhipped throughout her childhood. Her sister must have been the favourite as she only recalls being horsewhipped once. Judith sometimes lived with her mother in adulthood and was desperate to please her, becoming increasingly involved with her religion. When Eunice's marriage broke up she remarried, this time to a man called Jack Spry.

Eunice Spry applied to the local social services to become a childminder in 1979 but was turned down as she was seen as an unsuitable candidate. Yet shortly afterwards the decision was reversed and she began to take care of other people's children in her own home. When she first applied to foster a child she was again turned down but she persevered and she and her husband were allowed to adopt a newborn baby girl in Gloucestershire in 1983. By then they had bought their council house in Tewkesbury and Eunice was still a registered childminder who was good with very young babies.

In 1986 she fostered a two-year-old girl, Alloma Gilbert, for a month when her parents were having problems with substance abuse. (Children in child-abuse cases normally have their identities protected but Alloma opted to waive this right and has written a book, *Deliver Me from Evil*, about her experiences at her foster mother's hands. One of Eunice's foster sons, Christopher Spry, also went public and his book is called *Child C*.) Six months later she contacted Alloma's parents for a reference so that she could foster another little girl, a child she went on to adopt.

By the time that Alloma was six her mother was suffering increasing health problems and Alloma's grandmother was taking on most of her childcare. When she heard that Eunice was still fostering, she asked if she'd babysit Alloma on a regular basis. At first, it seemed like an ideal place for a child as the adoptive mother had a dog, five cats, an aviary in the garden and lots of toys.

In 1992, Alloma went to live with Eunice permanently. By then, Eunice's second marriage had broken down and there was no longer a man on the premises, though her first husband, Frank, often visited to spend time with his dog and brought the children cakes, crisps and sweets.

By now Gloucestershire Social Services had deregistered Eunice Spry as an official foster carer as they could see that she was already taking care of enough children, but Eunice made a private fostering arrangement with Alloma's mum and dad. The following year she privately fostered the Christopher who would later write the book and his younger brother, an arrangement made with the help of social services. She later applied for a residency order for them and this was granted, making her their legal guardian. She would use some of the children as child labour but resented spending money on them, so they were regularly underfed. The others, her clear favourites, were given an excessive number of toys and were never beaten.

At first, when Alloma was still visiting her parents occasionally, Eunice was nice to her but eventually she told Alloma that her parents didn't want to see her any more and that she was the Devil's child. She told Christopher the same thing, that he was evil and had to have the demon beaten out of him. A devout Jehovah's Witness like her parents, she began to take them to church meetings three or four times a week, telling them that this was the only hope of saving their evil souls. She also took them to bring-and-buy sales at the local community centre, where they were told to mainly mix with other Witnesses to avoid becoming too worldly.

A teacher at Alloma's school complained to social services that she and her fostered siblings were unnaturally timid, dressed in exceptionally shabby clothes and often hungry. A doctor at the local hospital then questioned Christopher about injuries he had received, but Christopher said nothing – the injuries had been inflicted when

Eunice battered him about the head. In spite of all this, Eunice Spry somehow persuaded social services that all was well.

To limit their access to the outside world, she began to home-school them all and they were force-fed her disturbing take on life. She said that they were wicked and that they would be put to the sword when the end of the world came. She also made the youngsters watch horror films aimed at adults and said the awful cruelties enacted in these movies would happen to them.

With none of the children's parents around and no teachers to report signs of abuse, Eunice Spry was free to do what she liked with her increasingly traumatised charges. She began to give each of them an enema every morning and would do this to Alloma until she left home aged 17. She also washed out their mouths with soapy water if they used words which displeased her and, if they vomited, she made them eat the vomit and keep it down.

She moved the children to an isolated farmhouse, owned by an ailing bachelor farmer whom she'd befriended, and kept in his good books in the hope that he would leave the farm to her after his death.

The youngsters were robbed of all normal childhood fun as playing at being Ninja Turtles, the craze of the period, was considered 'worldly' and they were beaten for it. When they couldn't sleep, she would make them stand all night and would hit them every time they attempted to lie down.

She often threw things at them and even knocked out one of the children's front teeth, claiming to the dentist that it was an accident. She also began to beat their feet. Alloma ran away and hid in a barn, becoming mildly hypothermic, but the police brought her back. For a few days Eunice was nicer, fearing further police and social worker involvement, but the abuse soon escalated again and Christopher was battered in the knee with a cricket back, leading to a permanent injury.

The torture continued and Spry would force a stick down the children's throats whilst Judith stood on them to keep them from escaping. Eunice regularly starved them, and several of the children became so weak from lack of food that they only survived by sneaking into the pigsty and eating pigswill. She also locked them, naked, in a room for many days, and beat them when they emptied their bowels.

Her relatives visited and she once had a party at her house, so there was some awareness in the community that all wasn't well in the household. The local vicar called but she wouldn't let him in: however, he wrote to social services that he was worried about the state of the children and someone else phoned the department to complain that the youngsters were having washing-up liquid squirted into their mouths. In total there were 12 separate complaints to social services about her parenting methods – the house was also littered with animal faeces and there were geese living in the kitchen – but they were still left in her care.

Social services would later say that Spry was regarded as eccentric and controlling but that the children always claimed that they were well treated, which is hardly surprising when their tormentor remained in the room with them. The social workers were never allowed to speak to the children alone and Eunice Spry always knew in advance when they were arriving so would feed the children better, stop hitting them for a few days and make sure that the house was tidy and clean.

Additional benefits

Spry was already getting fostering allowances for the foster children and home-tutoring allowances for each child and was also making money by forcing the children to do all of the farmyard work. But she realised that she could get more money if the children were registered as disabled...

She managed to get one of the girls diagnosed as autistic and two of the boys diagnosed as hyperactive; the latter were put on Ritalin, a very powerful medication. When Alloma was 12, Eunice coached her on the symptoms of Asperger's syndrome (high-functioning autism) and took her to a specialist, but the psychologist wasn't convinced that she was genuinely suffering from this. Eunice now began to give Alloma some of the boys' Ritalin and she got hooked, taking so many that she went on psychedelic trips. Her foster mother's cruel acts continued and she sometimes filled the bath with cold water and held the teenager's face under it. Just as horrifying, she cut Christopher in the side with a kitchen knife, hit him with a piece of lead piping and even tied him to a rope and towed him behind her Transit van. Yet she showed occasional acts of kindness, taking her parents and the children to Florida for several weeks, including a trip to Disneyworld. Whilst there, they spent lots of time visiting American Jehovah's Witnesses.

A fatal car crash

In September 2000, the family (including Eunice's older biological daughter, Judith, and two of Judith's Jehovah's Witness friends) went to Brean Down, near Weston-super-Mare, for a four-day holiday. When it was over, the plan was for Judith to take three of the children swimming, then they would drive home. Meanwhile, Alloma (who had cut her head so couldn't go to the pool) would accompany Eunice in her car to the cattery to pick up their pets.

But Judith's car was involved in a pile-up on the A5 on the way home when a lorry crashed into them. Judith was killed, as was Eunice Spry's favourite adopted daughter, Charlotte, and two of the other children were seriously injured. One of them needed a blood transfusion but Spry refused to approve this and invited other Jehovah's Witnesses over to the house to plan some kind of intervention. Many Witnesses believe that it is better to let an injured child die as he or she will be resurrected in an afterlife and there have even been instances of Witnesses abandoning a child after they have been given blood. Fortunately, doctors in some countries, including the UK, can legally overrule a parent's decision and give a transfusion to save a young life.

At the hospital Eunice told the oldest child, Victoria (she has also waived her right to anonymity and would like to set up a residential home for young people escaping from religious cults), that it was appalling that she had survived as she was the scum of the earth. She was much kinder to her favourite young foster son and spent a month at his bedside, weeping with relief when he regained consciousness.

After six weeks, Eunice Spry signed 15-year-old Victoria and her eight-year-old foster brother out of hospital. Victoria was still in a wheelchair but when her ability to walk returned, Spry forbade it. She knew that having a wheelchair-bound daughter would allow her to claim a higher disability allowance and would also ensure a bigger financial settlement as Judith had not been at fault in the fatal crash. She continued to kick and beat the teenager as well as terrorising the other children in the house.

When Alloma turned 17, she kept saying that she wanted to leave home. A normal parent would have paved the way, helping the teenager to find a bedsit that she liked and making sure that she had a job and some kind of support system, but Eunice suddenly said, 'You're leaving tomorrow. I'm taking you to Bristol.' She drove the girl to a hostel where she had paid her first month's rent. At the door she said goodbye and handed her £3 in change before driving away. The youngster survived on plates of noodles until managing to find herself a catering job and a room to let.

Trial

The abuse continued. Christopher fought back once when he turned 15 and pushed his cruel foster mother to the ground. Fearing that she was losing control, Eunice sent him to live with her parents, who desperately needed a carer. By now Eunice's mother had cancer and was having chemotherapy, and her father, who had been confined to a wheelchair for years due to chronic arthritis and now weighed more than 20 stone, had become incontinent and had advanced Parkinson's.

Determined always to have a scapegoat, she continued to abuse Victoria. By now the teenager was spending more time with a couple of Jehovah's Witnesses and, when they asked about the various marks on her body, including strangulation marks on her neck, she confided that her foster mother had been hurting her all her life.

One day, Eunice used a punishment that she had previously used on several of the children, grabbing Victoria and rubbing her hands and face with sandpaper.

When her Witness friends saw the livid marks all over her cheeks, they offered to help her to escape. By now aged 18, she left the house with them whilst Eunice was out horse riding. Her legs were very weak as Eunice had stopped her doing her physiotherapy exercises, but she could walk.

On Boxing Day 2004, Victoria phoned the police and reported that she had been abused from the time that she was tiny and she had the marks to prove it. A police officer went to Alloma's house and asked her to talk about her childhood and her report tallied perfectly with Victoria's account. Police officers went to Eunice's rundown farmhouse and found that she had also been mistreating her pets and farmyard animals – the RSPCA became involved. The case shed light on the fact that home-schooled children are vulnerable if their home schooler is sadistic or mentally ill, and that there should be some kind of external organisation which sees such children on a regular basis, otherwise an abuser has free reign.

Christopher initially refused to tell the truth about his years of torture at Eunice's hands as he thought of her as his mother and fondly remembered the few times that she had hugged him when they were on holiday. But his foster siblings reassured him that they had made full disclosure and that Eunice would never be able to hurt him again. Taken to live with kinder foster parents, he gradually opened up about the abuse and agreed to testify against his tormentor in court.

Victoria and Christopher now had to catch up on their schooling as Spry had been such a poor home educator, refusing to buy them the required books. They also had to learn how to socialise with people other than Jehovah's Witnesses.

Spry was arrested in February 2005 (she remained emotionless), but it took two years for her case to go to trial. In the interim, the children were examined by doctors and talked with increasing candour to psychologists. Two of the children had scar tissue at the back of their throats through being repeatedly poked by a stick in that area and all of them had multiple scars through being hit and kicked.

Though she had been forbidden from making contact with her surviving victims, Eunice Spry kept sending Victoria letters saying that she loved her and wanted a chance to mother her. She also tracked Christopher down at work but was spotted by one of his co-workers, who would later testify to the fact at Eunice's trial. Unabashed, she cornered Christopher again, this time with a large male friend in tow, and offered him her boat (which was her pride and joy, having been bought with some of her savings) if he withdrew the charges. He refused and the case went to court.

At her trial, which began on 19 February 2007, the prosecution produced one of the sticks which had been forced into the children's mouths. It had a child's tooth marks and two inches of dried blood on the end of it. Victoria described her earliest memory at Spry's hands at the age of two, when she had been made to eat solids and a spoon had been forced violently between her lips until her mouth filled with blood. Whenever she had vomited she was made to eat up the vomit. The children had also been made to eat their own faeces and had been forced to ingest everything from bleach to lard.

Christopher said that Spry had held his hand close to the hotplate on the stove until it was badly burned. Alloma had also had her hand held close to the plate.

Spry denied all of the torture charges and said she had only occasionally smacked them on the bottom. She said she had put her life into caring for and educating them. But the children's scars told their own tale and she was found guilty on 20 March of 26 counts of child abuse. She was found not guilty of charges of indecency.

A month later she was sentenced to 14 years in prison, with the judge commenting that it was the worst cruelty case that he had seen during his 40 years in the criminal justice system. Eunice Spry smiled broadly at the verdict then resumed her usual emotionless look as she was led away. On appeal, her sentence was reduced to 12 years, leaving the public incensed. In prison she remained without remorse and refused to take part in any rehabilitative programme, so her mindset remained unchanged.

No return

As the first date loomed on which Spry would be eligible for parole, her victims panicked. It was likely that she would return to one of her previous haunts and the three children who had testified couldn't bear the thought of bumping into her whilst out at the local shops. In May of 2014 the organisation Children Have Rights launched a petition asking the authorities to ban Spry from Gloucestershire and Worcestershire, a petition which over 12,000 people (including this author) signed.

Her foster child Victoria told the press: 'We weren't just horrifically abused, we were controlled, deprived education, locked away from the world and subjected to some of the most horrendous torture imaginable.' She added that it was unfair that her abuser had more rights than she had.

A disordered mind

Victoria has described Eunice Spry as a psychopath, a label which few psychologists would argue with. Spry's entire life was about self-interest, apart from the care that she lavished on her two favourite foster children, Charlotte (who died in the car crash) and a little boy. But even here there was a selfish element as she kept these particular children in a juvenile role for as long as possible, perhaps because she loved babies and the early mothering years.

Spry was also deeply sadistic and read books about torture and mind control, books which police found at her farmhouse. She used many of the techniques in these books on the children and deliberately kept them in a state of perpetual fear.

All of the children and every professional who came into contact with her spoke of her immense need for total control, yet her house was completely out of control, with dirty laundry piled up in the corners and her possessions strewn about the rooms and outhouses. She hoarded junk and didn't house-train her many animals. She is an enigma and almost impossible to explain.

Eunice Spry, who remains convinced of her own righteousness, was released to an unknown location in July 2014, though she will be on licence until 2018.

9

THE CHIEF OF POLICE
DAVID BRAME

Shots rang out in the shopping centre car park and 34-year-old Crystal Brame collapsed, bleeding on the ground. Inside the car, her estranged husband David shot himself in the head and lapsed into unconsciousness...

A privileged start

David Brame was born in East Tacoma, Washington in 1960 to Beverly and Gene Brame, the youngest of four children. His father was a detective and his mother a housewife. He was the star athlete of the family and also performed well academically. The family was deeply religious and he wasn't allowed to date until he was 16.

When he left school he applied to join the police, but psychological reports showed that he was introverted almost to the point of being antisocial. However, the Blue Code – whereby the sons and daughters of detectives are given preference over strangers who apply to join the force – prevailed and he was taken on.

At 19 he married but kept his wife very short of money and insisted she provide receipts for every grocery and petrol bill. His spouse became depressed and took a boyfriend and the marriage collapsed after eight years. Brame didn't believe in premarital sex, which perhaps explained his desire to marry again as soon as possible, but he found it difficult to chat up women as he was so prudish and restrained.

When he was 28, a colleague alleged that he had driven her to his place after they'd been out to eat, had picked her up, carried her to his bedroom and violently raped her. But she didn't report the sexual assault for 15 months, by which time there was obviously no physical evidence.

Police believed her but could not corroborate her story, so Brame was never charged. He admitted to a fellow officer that he was guilty of the crime but said that he was a good Christian who was getting counselling from his pastor and that it wouldn't happen again. The young police officer had a previously unblemished record and the report was not lodged in his personnel file.

A difficult second marriage

Despite his good looks and six-foot frame, Brame found it hard to find a girlfriend. But when he was 29, he met Crystal Judson, a graduate in criminal justice who was working as an intern at the Tacoma Police Department. The beautiful 20-year-old was doing undercover work, in which she posed as a prostitute, when he offered her a lift home. There was an immediate physical attraction and she also appreciated the fact that he was the strong, silent type. Her family had misgivings as he was so controlling, to the extent that, when she looked for a new job, he insisted that she work in a women-only office. He thought that he could control her as she was younger and very much in love.

On 3 August 1991, the couple married. Crystal worked as a paralegal until 1994, when she gave birth to their daughter. She remained a stay-at-home mum until after the arrival of their son in 1997. They doted on their children but David controlled the purse strings and Crystal often had to admit to friends and relatives that she had no cash to spend. He demanded receipts for every grocery and petrol bill and also asked her to account for how she spent her time. He insisted that she step on the bathroom scales every morning as he was adamant that no wife of his would ever put on weight.

Other friends and relatives would later state that Crystal was abusive towards David, screaming at him and demanding his constant attention. He believed that she had developed a hormone imbalance after their daughter's birth.

As the years passed, the Brames' neighbours overheard their increasingly loud arguments and wondered what to do. Usually when there's verbal domestic violence, one calls the police – but David Brame was a police officer. Could they really report him to his force? Unbeknown to them, Brame had spoken to his fellow officers on two occasions saying that Crystal had punched and hit him and that he had left the house with his three service revolvers as he feared what she might do. He also showed various cuts and bruises to his friends and said that his wife had inflicted them when he refused to buy expensive furniture. She had previously spent hundreds of dollars on Christmas decorations. Her parents would later state that he caused the bruising to his own body so that he could counter her claims of violence if she ever filed for divorce.

The couple also had a complicated sex life. She told a friend that her husband would virtually rape her and that he handcuffed her to the bed, but photos were later found in the house where she happily posed semi-nude for him and they vacationed at a nudist colony together on three occasions. Brame had a high sex drive but felt that this contrasted with his Christian upbringing: as a result, he would later seek treatment for sex addiction, explaining that the subject dominated his thoughts.

Meanwhile, his dedication to his career paid off and, in January 2002, he was made Tacoma's police chief. But men in positions of power often produce more testosterone and therefore want more sex. Brame increasingly looked outside of his marriage for this. He propositioned two of his secretaries but was rebuffed. He also suggested to Crystal that they have a threesome or foursome but she wasn't interested. She had had enough.

On 24 February 2003, she packed up and left the marital home, whilst he was at work, and moved back in with her parents, taking both of the children. That same day, she filed for divorce, asking for half of her husband's salary and for him to pay her lawyer's fees.

Emotional collapse

To everyone's surprise, David Brame immediately went to pieces. For the next few weeks he skipped meetings and appointments at work, spending most of his time on the phone to lawyers or in tears, talking with colleagues about his failed marriage. He lost weight and often called Crystal, pleading with her to return to him. When she refused, he said that he would see her dead before giving her a penny. The threat was made in front of her parents and she later recorded it in her diary.

Her husband soon acquiesced to her financial demands, but she remained afraid that he would hurt or kill her and filed for a restraining order. She also consulted with a man who ran a karate school and he advised her to go to a secret location as Brame sounded so dangerous. She refused, wanting to remain close to her parents and keep the children in the same school.

Meanwhile, David Brame alternated between hunting for a new girlfriend and breaking down in tears before other cops. He continued to lose weight and his hair started to grey.

On 24 April, her thirty-fifth birthday, Crystal returned to the marital home, which her husband had now vacated, to clean the place up as she and the children were going to move back there. She was chilled to find that he had left the obituary page of the newspaper on the kitchen table for her. Crystal now had two days left to live…

The following day, the local paper headline was TACOMA POLICE CHIEF'S WIFE SAYS THAT HE POINTED A GUN AT HER. Both of the Brames were horrified by the leak and David was also irate. Crystal told her therapist that she now feared for her life.

Meanwhile, her estranged husband went into meltdown. He knew that, with the media firmly focused on him, someone would go public about his visits to the nudist colony. He'd also behaved inappropriately with various women and knew that they might tell their stories to the press.

On the morning of Saturday 26 April, Crystal attended a 4-hour seminar on divorce and how it affects children. She took over the class, talking nervously and incessantly about her fear of David and about how controlling he was. She added that she wanted to go to law school and reinvent herself. Eventually the social worker interrupted and explained that the other nine class members also needed time to tell their stories. She said that she'd be happy to talk to Crystal alone in the afternoon.

A murder-suicide

After lunch, Crystal Brame was driving to a tanning salon when she saw David's car. No one knows why she turned her own vehicle around and followed him into a shopping centre car park, though journalists would later surmise that she wanted to check he had picked up the children as agreed earlier.

David parked, spotted Crystal parking nearby and told the children to stay in the car, that he was going to talk to their mother. He got into her car and, a moment later, she got out. She leaned into the vehicle to say something, then a passer-by heard her shout: 'Don't!' Two gunshots rang out and the 34-year-old collapsed on the ground. As the couple's children rushed to their mother's aid, their father shot himself in the head.

Both of the Brames had lost brain tissue and copious amounts of blood but were still alive. Passers-by sent for help and did their best to staunch the bleeding. David Brame died of his injuries in hospital within a couple of hours.

On Saturday 3 May he was buried, his sister referring to him as an angel. That same day, his victim lost her fight for life. Their children, having witnessed the murder–suicide, are now being raised by Crystal's sister and brother-in-law.

David Brame falls into the If-I-can't-have-you-then-nobody-will category of killers, men who bully their female partner but fall apart when she leaves. They can only feel strong and in charge when dominating others, and the macho exterior often hides a frightened, repressed inner child. Some of these men also murder their own children and the family pets before committing suicide, seeing everyone and every animal in the household as mere possessions that they can dispose of at will.

10

THE DEVOUT CATHOLIC
DANILO RESTIVO

Though he never missed Mass and constantly stressed to his acquaintances the importance of being a good person, Danilo Restivo killed for the first time on his mother's saint's day and went on to kill again.

Early life

Danilo Restivo was born on 3 April 1972 to Maria Rose Fontana and Maurizio Restivo in Erice, Sicily. Maurizio was a powerful figure from a prominent Sicilian family and later moved his family to the mainland when he became the director of the Potenza branch of the National Library. He was an intellectual and enjoyed stimulating and thought-provoking company.

His son, however, fared badly in school and fared equally badly when it came to making friends. He would act the clown in order to get other children's attention but, when that failed, would become aggressive. He seemed steeped in self-pity and was widely disliked. He cut another child with scissors and was to become obsessed with the idea of cutting people, often carrying scissors around.

Criminologists would later speculate that his family's interest in Saint Agatha had had a devastating effect on the fantasies of this already disturbed boy. Saint Agatha had her breasts cut off by her torturers for refusing to renounce her Christian faith though she was allegedly healed afterwards by another saint. She is often depicted in paintings with multiple knife wounds and holding her severed breasts on a platter or above her head.

Just after Danilo's fourteenth birthday, in May 1986, he blindfolded a 12-year-old boy and a 14-year-old girl and tied their hands behind their back. He lured them to his outdoor den by promising them that he was going to give them a surprise – but the surprise came when he cut them with a knife and locked them in. The terrified youngsters eventually escaped and their parents reported the incident to the police, but the family accepted a substantial out-of-court settlement and the matter was dropped.

He continued to behave oddly, taking public transport and sitting behind girls with long hair. He would cut off an inch or more of their locks and take it away as a trophy. Many women saw him but no one knew his name. Years later they would identify him as Danilo Restivo.

The first victim

By the age of 15, he was approaching girls at Mass and trying to interest them in a date, but he was gently rebuffed on countless occasions. In 1992, he promised a girl a small gift if she would accompany him to the church's loft. She did so, but when he tried to persuade her to enter the tiny annexe she backed away and returned to the populated part of the church. His next target would be more trusting…

He was very attracted to Elisa Claps, a 16-year-old schoolgirl who attended the same church in Potenza. He had been asking her out for the last two years but she had always refused him. Though unsettled by his persistence, she felt sorry for the lonely boy and had tried to remain his friend. Elisa wanted to train as a medic and join Doctors Without Borders so that she could help the poor in the Third World. To this end, she was delighted to have passed her resit exams.

Danilo said that he had a present for her, a reward for doing so well in her studies, and persuaded her to meet him at the church on 12 September 1993. She would never be seen alive again.

Within hours of her disappearance, he returned home perspiring heavily and with dark stains on his trousers. He changed and showed his sister a small cut on his hand and insisted he be taken to hospital. He said that he had gone to look at some new escalators and had fallen, rolling over and over, all the way down but he had no other injuries and doctors put one small stitch in his hand. As it was his mother's saint's day (some Catholics choose a patron saint who they believe will bolster the power of their prayers), it seemed an especially odd time to go walkabout. He had a long talk with his father and later, when the police investigating Elisa's disappearance came round and asked if they could take away his clothing, his father said they would need a search warrant.

When Elisa Claps didn't return home for lunch, her family asked her friends what had happened and they said she'd gone with Danilo Restivo. The Claps then talked to Danilo, who admitted the meeting but said they'd only spoken for 15 minutes behind the altar and then Elisa had left, whilst he had stayed to pray. When Elisa's brother phoned later for more details, Danilo's father hung up on him. That night, Danilo left home and travelled to Naples to sit a pre-entrance exam for dental school. (He would fail in his bid to become a dentist, something he would later describe in court as 'his dream'.)

Criminal charges

Almost a year elapsed, as justice in Italy grinds exceedingly slow, before Danilo Restivo was arrested on a charge of making false statements about his movements on the day of Elisa Clap's disappearance. Whilst that case was ongoing, he was also charged with sending his neighbours – three young girls – pornographic drawings and obscene messages and making numerous late-night phone calls to their flat, during which he played the theme tunes from horror films over the line. He was fined for these offences on 23 February 1995. A fortnight later he was found guilty of the perjury charge and was sentenced to 20 months, the sentence being suspended pending an appeal. After the appeal it was increased by another year. But, as short sentences in Italy are automatically suspended, he didn't spend any time in custody.

In 1997, Danilo Restivo developed Graves' disease, an autoimmune disorder which affects the thyroid. This meant that sometimes he ran a very high temperature, had sleep disturbances and felt weak. The disease can also cause agitation, something which he seems to have suffered for most of his life. He became obsessed with his health and would discuss his symptoms at length.

The years passed and chaos followed in his wake. He applied to become a firefighter but failed the exams, so he started a fire near his house with the intention of putting it out and becoming a hero. But the flames took hold too quickly and he froze. He began to collect photos of and clippings about missing women. He continued to cut women's hair, sitting behind them on buses and touching their tresses whilst touching himself. He moved around Italy but never found acceptance and almost everyone who met him would marvel at his inability to connect.

In 2001, he had his thyroid removed but struggled to find the right dose of synthetic thyroid, which led to him having bulging eyes.

A new paramour

At the start of 2002, he began talking to Fiamma Marsango, 15 years his senior, in an internet chatroom. Though Fiamma was also Italian she had moved to Britain in 1977 and was now living in Bournemouth. She was divorced with two children and was suffering from rheumatoid arthritis. That March, he flew to England and moved into her house. Shortly afterwards, women on buses in that area were perturbed when a man with a swarthy complexion and bulging eyes cut their hair...

A hair-related murder

That summer, on 12 July, a 26-year-old South Korean girl, Jong-Ok Shin, known as Oki, was murdered three streets away from Danilo Restivo's Bournemouth home. A large clump of freshly cut brown human hair was found in the street nearby. The South Korean languages student had only arrived in Bournemouth eight months before and was on her way home from a nightclub when she was stabbed three times in the back. Taken to hospital, she told medics that she had been attacked by a man wearing a mask. But her English was poor and crime writers would later speculate that she meant a balaclava, something which Restivo had been seen wearing late at night on his walks. Shortly after giving this statement, she had a heart attack and died.

Police first focused on a boy she had dated for a month, also South Korean, as she had recently ended their relationship. He was arrested but not charged and soon returned to South Korea. Six weeks after the homicide, they arrested a heroin-addicted prostitute, Beverley

Brown, for shoplifting and she said she could help them solve Oki's murder. She claimed that she and three other men, whose names she gave, had been in a car in the early hours of 12 July, en route to a crack house in Boscombe to buy drugs, when they'd driven past the 26-year-old student. She claimed that two of the men had left the vehicle to talk to the girl and that when they returned, one man said that the other, Omar Benguit, had hurt her. Afterwards, she added, she herself had been raped and tortured by the men and they had inserted various tools into her.

Taken into custody, 30-year-old Omar Benguit, also a heavy heroin user and well known to the police because of his drug use, had no idea of his whereabouts six weeks before – but one of the other named men was able to show that he wasn't in the car with them but was in fact driving his own vehicle that night. And locals testified that the shouts and screams hadn't taken place in the area that Beverley Brown indicated, throwing further doubt on her testimony. She was also found to have made previous claims that various neighbours were paedophiles, but investigations had disproved this.

Despite there being no forensic evidence, Omar Benguit was tried three times for the student's murder. His girlfriend of two years claimed to be so intimidated by police that she refused to testify as a character witness and left the area. On the first two occasions juries failed to reach a verdict but after the third trial at Winchester Crown Court they found him guilty and he was sentenced to life imprisonment with the proviso that he serve at least 20 years.

Omar Benguit's legal team appealed, stating that Restivo, a known hair fetishist and knife carrier, lived three streets from the murder scene and was the true culprit. A man matching Restivo's description was seen on CCTV nearby minutes after the murder and a balaclava, like the kind he often wore, was found nearby. Furthermore, Oki's mobile phone and bag remained by her body; these were sources of income which would surely have been taken by a drug addict. But Benguit's appeal was rejected and he remains incarcerated in what many believe to be a miscarriage of justice.

Closer to home

Meanwhile, Danilo Restivo had become increasingly interested in 48-year-old seamstress Heather Barnett, who lived in the flat across the road from him. He could see into her bedroom and also see the frosted glass of her bathroom. Heather, a divorcee, shared her flat with her two children and a cat, and she took commissions from customers to make garments and upholstery.

She found Danilo Restivo frightening and felt uneasy when he paid her a visit in early November 2002, claiming that he wanted her to make curtains as a surprise present for Fiamma. After he left, she found that the key to her front door was missing and, believing that he had taken it, she had the locks changed.

The following week, on 12 November, she took the children to school as usual and returned home to start work. Within minutes there was a knock at the door...

Heather's 14-year-old son and 11-year-old daughter returned home late that afternoon and were perturbed when their mother didn't greet them as usual. They were even more concerned when they found her sewing machine had been knocked over and the radio had been left on. A search of the small flat uncovered her lying on the bathroom floor, covered in blood. Her breasts had been cut off and had been placed at her head.

Heather's devastated son phoned the police then the children ran out into the street, where Fiamma Marsango was parking her vehicle. Her large bulk prevented her from exiting the car quickly but Danilo Restivo got out and hugged the youngsters, asking them what was wrong and shepherding them into his house.

Forensic experts found that Heather had been bludgeoned about the head from behind with a blunt instrument such as a hammer, possibly as she sat at her sewing machine. She had a few defensive marks on her hands but had died within minutes. She was dragged into the bathroom, where her breasts had been hacked from her body and further post-mortem cuts had been made to her abdomen. Her jeans had been unfastened but there had been no attempt to mutilate her genitals. However, stains on her briefs suggested that a bloodstained glove had been in contact with them. Some of her own hair had been placed in her left hand and hair from an unknown donor in her right hand.

The bloodstained footsteps on the carpet suddenly ended and forensic scientists surmised that the killer had changed his shoes at this point in what had been a premeditated attack. The shoes which had left the prints were made by Nike and size 9–11.

Unfortunately, the police centred their suspicions on Heather's ex-husband. Even when they visited her neighbour Danilo Restivo and found his size-nine Nike trainers smelling of bleach in the bathroom, they didn't regard him as a suspect (even though they did take the trainers away with them). In fairness, he had an alibi in the form of a bus ticket stamped with the time of 8.44 a.m. He said he'd taken the bus to NACRO (National Association for the Care and Resettlement of Offenders) as he was a student there. He said he'd stayed there until 3.45 p.m.

A girl disappears

In the north of Italy on Easter Sunday, 20 April 2003, a South Korean girl who had been adopted by an Italian family mysteriously disappeared, never to be seen again. The 27-year-old Erika Ansermin had no reason to drop out of sight and is believed dead. When her photograph, downloaded from an Italian news channel, was later found by British police on Danilo Restivo's computer in Bournemouth during their investigations into the murder of Heather Barnett, the Italian authorities began looking in to him as a possible suspect for the Erika Ansermin murder, believing he might have returned home briefly to visit relatives.

Belatedly a suspect

Six months after Heather Barnett's murder, the police started to read her emails and found the one where she mentioned to a friend that she suspected Restivo of taking her key and that she'd had to have the locks changed, a significant expense for an impoverished single parent. They also found that she'd told one of her boyfriends that Restivo gave her the creeps. They also received a teletype from Italian police warning them Danilo Restivo was considered to be a serious danger to women. Investigating further, they found that he'd been a suspect in the murder of his teenage friend Elisa Claps and that the body had never been found.

Officers now visited NACRO and found that Restivo had signed in on the day of Heather Barnett's murder at 10.28 a.m. They realised he could have got on the bus at 8.44 and got off at the next stop, arriving back at her house within minutes. They decided to put him under surveillance and followed him to a local park where he lurked in the long grass watching women. Despite the warm May weather he wore his hood up and wore waterproof trousers. He was seen to change into identical clothing as if rehearsing what he might do after a bloody crime.

Detectives were so alarmed that they identified themselves and searched his car, finding a large knife, two pairs of scissors, a pair of gloves, a balaclava and a hooded jacket. He said that he had found the knife but it was later found to have come from the knife block in his own kitchen. They talked to Fiamma, and to the foreign students that she took in to make ends meet, and warned them that Danilo was extremely dangerous but Fiamma opted to remain in the relationship.

A month later they arrested Restivo and questioned him for three days but he admitted nothing and, fearing they didn't have enough evidence for a conviction, they reluctantly let him go. Shortly afterwards he married Fiamma, who seemed to be an almost maternal influence in his life. Now, as his wife, she couldn't be forced to testify against him…

Everyone knew that the hair left in Heather Barnett's hand was significant, perhaps even the killer's signature. Police also knew that, since 2002, women had had their hair cut by a swarthy overweight stranger on trains and buses. They appealed for victims to come forward and 13 women got in touch, identifying Danilo Restivo. Italian police made enquiries and a similar number of women came forward there. Searching Restivo's house in Bournemouth, detectives found a lock of hair tied with thread but were unable to establish who it had belonged to.

The net closes

Sixteen and a half years had elapsed since Elisa Claps had gone missing after meeting Danilo Restivo, but now the mystery was solved when a workman fixing the leaking roof of the church in Potenza found a mummified body in the attic space. On 17 March 2010 it was identified as the missing teenager.

Tests showed that she had been stabbed from behind and that her throat had been cut, possibly by a pair of scissors. Her bra had been cut open and her jeans had been undone and there were defence marks on her palms. A piece of her own hair, matted with blood, had been left in her hands and DNA, believed to be from the cut on Restivo's hand, was found on her jumper.

Two months later, Dorset police arrested Restivo for Heather Barnett's murder and, shortly afterwards, Italian police issued an arrest warrant for him in relation to Elisa Claps' murder.

On trial

Restivo's pre-trial hearing for the murder of Heather Barnett took place at Winchester Crown Court on 7 November 2010. He pleaded not guilty and was remanded in custody. The actual trial began in May the following year.

The prosecutor quickly demolished Restivo's alibi, showing that he could have left the bus at the first stop and been at Heather's flat within 8 minutes. He was found to have altered the time that he clocked in at NACRO.

An inspector talked of finding Nike trainers, wet and smelling strongly of bleach, in Restivo's bathroom the day after the murder. They had been taken away as footsteps in blood from a Nike trainer had been found on Heather Barnett's floor. Heather Barnett's own hair and that of an unknown person had been found in her hands and Danilo Restivo had admitted to having a hair fetish. Several women attended his trial and took the witness box, explaining how he'd pulled their hair over the back of the seat as he sat behind them on buses or at the cinema. Witnesses to the hair cutting said that Restivo had had both the ends of the hair and his own hands under his jacket and appeared to be masturbating.

Detectives spoke of putting the Italian under surveillance and watching him staring at women and changing into identical clothing. When they'd seen him do this on the eleventh of the month they'd arrested him, aware that Elisa Claps and Heather Barnett had died on the twelfth of a month, as, indeed, had Oki Shin. He was found to be armed with everything from scissors to a knife.

Various witnesses who had travelled from Italy took the stand to describe how Restivo had pestered girls when he was a teenager, how he was the last person to see Elisa Claps alive, and a professor showed the court a photograph of her mummified body. He said that her bra had been cut and her trousers unfastened. This, of course, had also been done to Heather Barnett shortly after her death. Clumps of her own hair, glued together with dried blood, had been found in her hands. Many of the tears on her jeans and jumper had been made with scissors and these happened to be one of Restivo's favourite tools. His DNA, believed to be blood from the cut he'd suffered to his hand, was found on her jumper.

To everyone's surprise, Danilo Restivo took the stand and admitted to his hair fetish. He said he'd originally done it as a bet then found that he enjoyed it. But he'd also found it frustrating as he wanted to smell the hair but had no sense of smell. He later had an operation to correct the problem. He also talked of various operations he'd had for everything from tendonitis to a hernia and for complications following his thyroidectomy.

When asked why he had a balaclava on his person in a park on a warm day he said it was to keep his sinuses warm as he suffered from sinusitis. Several people in court laughed. Asked why he was also carrying a bag with a knife in it, he said it was to kill insects and bring them home for his pet lizards. He further said that the hair found in his cupboard was to be used to make a fake moustache for a fancy dress party.

The jury were out for only a few hours before returning with a guilty verdict. The following day the judge said that he would never be released from prison. Two days later, Elisa Claps' mummified corpse was buried in her native Potenza.

A second trial

In November 2011 Restivo was tried in Salerno for the murder of Elisa Claps. He opted not to attend the trial or contest the evidence and was sentenced to 30 years.

But the legal process wasn't finished with the fetish-driven murderer and, in November 2012, his lawyers argued that the whole-life term he had been given for the Bournemouth murder was unlawful. They won and the sentence was replaced with a minimum 40-year term.

In 2013 he travelled to Italy to contest his conviction there but the appeal was dismissed and he was returned to Full Sutton Prison near York.

When he heard that the Home Secretary wanted him deported to Italy to serve out the rest of his sentence he immediately marshalled his legal team again and, in April 2014, attended an appeal hearing at Bradford Crown Court in which he claimed that he was able to enjoy visits from his wife whilst he was here in England and that returning him to Italy would be a breach of his human rights. He also said that, at the moment, he received a daily phone call from Fiamma but that this would be difficult if he was imprisoned in a different country. She, in turn, said that she had lived here for decades and had no ongoing links to Italy so didn't want to return. Restivo also complained that Italian jails were dirty and overcrowded. (Indeed, they are so overcrowded that some dangerous prisoners are being released early, something which understandably terrifies the relatives of his victims.) At the time of writing, a decision is still pending.

11
THE MODEL PUPIL
BRIAN BLACKWELL

To become a healthy autonomous adult, a teenager has to distance himself from his parents, but some overprotective parents simply won't allow this and insist on keeping the teenager at home in the evenings rather than letting them make friends. Most survive these difficult years but a few, often suffering from personality disorders, go on to kill the adults they see as standing between themselves and happiness.

Early years

Brian Blackwell was born in 1986 to 43-year-old Jacqueline and 54-year-old Brian in a small village near Liverpool. He was an exceptionally bright child (his parents nicknamed him 'Brains') and he was a model pupil. But he was increasingly unhappy as his parents didn't think that most of his friends were good enough for him. Neighbours noted that his elderly parents didn't appear to want to let him grow up and that he had an old-fashioned appearance and was always alone. (The children of elderly parents often become staid and are more likely to be overweight than the offspring of younger, fitter men and women. They are also more likely to have health problems.) Sad and solitary, he built himself a grandiose fantasy life in which he was all-powerful.

By the sixth form, Blackwell was telling his schoolmates that he was a professional tennis player and incredibly wealthy. To support these lies, he began to apply for credit cards in his father's name. His spending accelerated when he began to date a beautiful teenage girl and he used the credit cards to buy her gifts and take her on lavish nights out. He told her that he needed a secretary to keep track of his tennis career and, when she accepted the post, he paid her handsomely, though the cheque inevitably bounced. He also took a Mercedes for a test drive and used money from his trust fund to buy his girlfriend a £9,000 car. His mother, who doted on him, was understandably furious when she found out. On other occasions, he bought his girlfriend cheap jewellery and pretended that it was highly priced. Psychologists would later deduce that he was suffering from narcissistic personality disorder, leaving him with an extreme sense of entitlement coupled with a distinct lack of empathy.

Brian's parents didn't like his girlfriend and tried to stop him seeing her, but he was besotted with the teenager and at an age where he had the right to make his own choices. He started to stay over at her parents' house, where he felt valued and there was a happy family atmosphere.

But he still had a desperate need to impress others and fraudulently obtained 13 credit cards. Concerned at the number of designer goods he was buying, Jacqueline and Brian senior confronted him. They also found out that he had lied on a bank application form, telling the bank that he was a professional tennis player who needed a loan to play in the French Open. His embarrassed parents had to tell the bank manager that their son was still a schoolboy who only played tennis with his father. Blackwell now resolved to get his parents out of the way...

A double murder

On 25 July 2004, he booked two tickets to New York then spent the morning with his dad at the tennis club where they were regular attendees. The 71-year-old told staff how proud he was of the work which Brian had put in for his A-Levels. By now, the elderly man had only hours left to live. Sometime after their return home, Blackwell attacked his father from behind as the older man sat in a chair, battering him repeatedly about the head with a claw hammer. His mother rushed into the lounge to investigate and he hammered her with similar zeal. He also stabbed them both.

After the murders, he asked some local teenagers to burn down his house but they didn't take him seriously. The next day, he took his girlfriend to the USA on holiday, staying first at the Plaza Hotel in New York for three nights at a cost of over £2,000. He spent a phenomenal £30,000 during their two-week trip, which encompassed Florida, Barbados and San Francisco before they returned to New York and flew home. The killer returned expecting to find his childhood home reduced to a blackened ruin. Instead, the house was untouched and the corpses of his parents were still inside.

He immediately left the charnel house and went to stay with his girlfriend's parents in another part of Liverpool, explaining that he had lost his key and that his own family was away. A week later, he found out that he'd passed all of his A-Levels at A Grade and would be able to start medical school in Nottingham in October. Ironically, he would at last have what he craved most – freedom and recognition, the chance to be his own man. But, meanwhile, his parents' bungalow was filling with increasingly putrid odours and, when a neighbour tried to post a letter through their door on 5 September, he realised that the building was infested with thousands of flies.

He called the police, who discovered Mr Blackwell's badly decomposed corpse sitting in an armchair and Mrs Blackwell's corpse lying in a pool of blood in the bathroom. He had been stabbed 30 times in the chest and hit over the head with a hammer, whilst she had been similarly hit with a hammer and stabbed 20 times. Taken in for questioning, Brian Blackwell proclaimed his innocence to the authorities, stating that he had been on holiday then staying with his girlfriend and had believed that his parents must be on an extended vacation. He said that he was expecting them back on 7 September.

For seven interviews, he maintained his innocence, insisting that he must have been abroad when his parents were murdered and telling police that they shouldn't be treating him as a suspect. Then he spoke to a psychiatrist and admitted that he had killed them both. He gave an unconvincing portrayal of events, saying that his father had shaken him and that he'd retaliated by using the hammer he was holding, a hammer he'd been using to put up pictures. He'd gone on to kill his mother and said that, in both cases, they had died easily. (In reality, the couple were so horrifically bludgeoned that police initially thought they'd been shot to death.) He added that he had cried and told them that he loved them immediately after the double murder.

Later, he wrote a letter of apology, which was read out in court, in which he said that he regretted the murders and longed for the halcyon days when he was a child and felt loved by his family. He said that he missed them and was haunted by guilt 24 hours a day.

But psychologists were unconvinced as narcissists tend to share a trait with psychopaths, namely a lack of empathy. They know what they are doing is wrong but they simply don't care. Most narcissists merely cause havoc in their career and personal lives, because their overwhelming need for admiration and fantasies of unlimited success make them difficult to deal with, but a small number become delusional and turn violent. Because they see themselves as special, they invariably expect to get away with their crimes and are shocked when arrested and tried.

On 29 June 2005, Brian Blackwell, by now aged 19, was jailed at Liverpool Crown Court for the manslaughter of his 60-year-old mother and 71-year-old father. He pleaded guilty on the grounds of diminished responsibility because of his narcissistic personality disorder, the first time that this defence was used in a British court, and was jailed for life with a minimum tariff of 12 years.

Though teenagers in general are more narcissistic than adults, full-blown narcissistic personality disorder is only found in around one per cent of the population. Writing in his book *Abnormal, Clinical and Forensic Psychology*, Dr David Holmes notes that Brian Blackwell's plea reduced his sentence but also that he is likely to have his risk to others assessed before he is considered for parole.

Understanding youth crime

Keen to understand even more about such marginalised killers, I interviewed true crime writer R. Barri Flowers, whose books include *The Dynamics of Murder*, *The Adolescent Criminal*, *Street Kids* and *Kids Who Commit Adult Crimes*. His work has been praised by fellow true crime writer Harold Schechter as being of interest to everyone from law enforcement professionals to armchair criminologists.

I started by asking Barri whether he thought Blackwell was typical of the homicidal children he studies? He said that he was, adding 'Most teen murderers are narcissistic in their violent rage. Many are also often detached from reality in their homicidal impulses, as well as having a lack of value for human life (other than their own) and the ability to carry on with their lives normally as though they had never killed anyone. Such teens typically are so self-absorbed that they convince themselves that they will be able to get away with their crimes of violence, either by being able to outwit the authorities or by committing the perfect crimes – in effect, so that their crimes never lead directly back to them.'

He continued that most juvenile murderers he has studied tend to have other typical characteristics beside narcissistic personality disorder, including 'an early introduction to violence, aggressive behaviour, risk taking, hyperactivity, family dysfunction, school troubles and other antisocial behaviour'.

Barri has also found that 'violent juvenile offenders often acquire homicidal tendencies through learned behaviour such as child maltreatment and domestic violence or peer group violence. These young killers tend to see violence as an acceptable response to or reaction to problems encountered.'

He continued, 'Stress theory postulates that youth violence occurs as a means to cope with intolerable stress, which can occur when juveniles experience pressure from either a single traumatic incident or the gradual accumulation of a number of sources of trauma. The ensuing violent acts are often unplanned or unintended but may be directed towards family members or persons within the peer group, when the offender seeks to continue the intense emotional physical contact with the victim, even if the victim is responsible for their stress.' He added that 'studies have supported the correlation between stress theory and juvenile violence, finding that violent delinquents tend to be characterised by weak impulse control, low self-esteem, lack of empathy towards others, rage and little toleration for frustration'.

I asked Barri if he saw any particular traits in those teens who kill family members rather than strangers or their peers? 'Familicide youth offenders are further characterised as suffering from depression and are often under the influence of alcohol, drugs or both during their killing rage. Such killers not only tend to come from a disintegrating family core but typically experience a loss of control over many aspects of life, resulting in a deadly breaking point.'

It's certainly true that Brian Blackwell felt that he was losing control of his income and his hedonistic lifestyle, and that his parents were trying to limit the amount of time he spent with his girlfriend, but he was within months of legitimately escaping the family home by going to an out-of-town university. He bludgeoned his parents to death rather than wait a few more weeks. I asked Barri if he saw this level of impulsivity in many young killers?

'I do, often exacerbated by substance abuse, lack of parental discipline and peer group pressure. That notwithstanding, it's important to point out that many parents are overprotective or smothering yet most teenagers don't process this in a way that causes them to lash out violently at their parents or others.' He explained that 'youths who exhibit homicidal tendencies tend to act out of impulse, and often with little consideration for the rest of their actions, and tend to suffer from some form of mental disorder to one degree or another. Studies of homicidally violent children have correlated their deviant behaviour to psychomotor seizures, neurological impairment, suicidal tendencies, parental violence and a history of severe child abuse or witnessing such violence.'

There's no suggestion that Brian Blackwell had any neurological impairment or witnessed any violence between his parents. But it's clear that he saw himself as special and regarded the ordinary man in the street with disdain. I asked Barri if prison was liable to be a reality check.

'Yes, in fact Blackwell will find that there are more narcissistic murderers like him incarcerated than not. Further, he will be forced to confront to some degree the terrible crimes that landed him behind bars, with plenty of time to contemplate the ill-advised moves he chose to make in life and their consequences.'

As a teenager, Blackwell had many years to expand his consciousness as psychologists believe that the personality isn't fully formed until age 25. So, in Barri's experience, do teenage killers tend to change, personality-wise, in prison?

'Sadly, no. If there is a change it would likely be for the worse, perhaps reinforcing in the killer the dynamics that brought him or her to this point. The prison setting is inadequately set up to rehabilitate the majority of incarcerated youths and adults, but is rather a breeding ground for establishing criminal ties, solidifying mental illnesses and simply doing one's time. In an ideal world all violent inmates would come to positive terms with their crimes and learn to deal with them constructively whilst becoming better persons. The truth, however, is that more often than not incarcerated killers rarely take full responsibility for their actions and, if ever released, remain very likely to reoffend.'

12

THE PREACHER'S DAUGHTER
ERIN CAFFEY

Originally a model daughter, Erin Caffey couldn't bear to be parted from her teenage boyfriend. When her family intervened she decided they had to die...

A sheltered upbringing

Erin Caffey lived with her parents and two younger brothers in the small town of Emory, Texas, where her life revolved around religion. Her father, Terry, preached sermons at the Miracle Faith Baptist Church and was about to become a Baptist minister. Her mother, Penny, was the church organist and also part of a gospel singing group. Her two brothers played instruments at the church and Erin sang in the church choir. The children were also home-schooled for a year, further limiting their access to the wider world.

But when Erin reached ninth grade she was allowed to attend the local school and enjoy a more normal upbringing. At the age of 16, she got a part-time job in a restaurant and started dating another worker there, 18-year-old Charlie Wilkinson. He wanted to join the army and had already completed a pre-military course. Charlie fell in love with Erin and the pair would hold hands at church, but her family thought that he was disrespectful and arrogant and, as a result, they grounded her. When she continued to call her lover, they took away her mobile phone. By now, Erin was actively talking to friends about her desire to kill her parents, talk which went on for at least a month.

Towards the end of February 2008, her parents demanded that she finish with Charlie as they had found out through social networking sites that he and Erin had become sexually active and liked a drink, which didn't dovetail with their determination to be a Christian family. She didn't argue with them, but inside she decided that she had had enough. She asked Charlie to kill the entire Caffey clan so that they could be free to celebrate their love. He demurred, telling her that he'd help her to run away, but she was convinced that the Caffeys would find her. She told him that she also wanted her brothers, aged 13 and eight, murdered so that there wouldn't be any witnesses. The lovelorn girl added that, if Charlie then set fire to the house, no one would know what had happened and they would be free to live their own lives.

On Saturday 1 March 2008, when the household was asleep, she phoned her boyfriend and said that it was time to act. He roped in his friend, 20-year-old Charles Waid, and Waid's 18-year-old girlfriend, Bobbi Johnson. The latter did the driving and parked near the Caffeys' house. She and Erin sat chatting in the vehicle whilst the boys entered the house toting guns and a samurai sword.

Terry and Penny were shot first and Penny was then virtually decapitated, after which the killers made their way upstairs and herded 13-year-old Matthew and eight-year-old Tyler out of Erin's room and back to their own bedrooms. Matthew tried to defend himself and Charles Waid shot him. Both youths then stabbed eight-year-old Tyler with the samurai sword. It would later be established that most of the family had survived the initial brutal attack but died in the subsequent flames.

After the shootings and stabbings, the two youths used cigarette lighters to set fires throughout the house before fleeing the scene in Bobbi's car. At this point, Terry – though shot in the chest, back, shoulder and head – regained consciousness and was able to drag himself out of the burning building and alert the neighbours. He had heard his sons pleading with Charlie not to hurt them so knew who the perpetrator was. Meanwhile, as the house was engulfed in flames and the remaining Caffeys died of smoke inhalation, Charlie and Erin went to Charlie's trailer and made love.

At first, everyone assumed that Erin had also been stabbed or shot and had been cremated in the fire, but it was soon apparent that she wasn't among the horribly charred corpses. Detectives tracked down her boyfriend and his friends and all three said that Erin had put them up to it. Found hiding in Waid's trailer, she was arrested and charged, as were her three accomplices.

Charges

In January 2009, Erin Caffey, by now aged 17, pleaded guilty to capital murder and was given two life sentences plus an additional 25 years. Her boyfriend and his friend Charles Waid were facing the death penalty but Terry Caffey, still recovering from his horrific injuries, spoke up for them and they were both sentenced to life in prison without parole. Bobbi Johnson pleaded guilty to being an accomplice and was given a 40-year prison term though she will be eligible for parole in 20 years.

Though both witnesses and detectives dispute his version of events, Terry Caffey has chosen to believe that his daughter was bullied and manipulated by her boyfriend into not telling anyone about the murder plot. Seven months after the murders he started dating and has since remarried, becoming a stepfather. A regular on the church speaker circuit, he drives 200 miles every two months to visit his daughter in Gatesville Prison, Texas, where she will be eligible for parole at age 59.

13

THE ALTAR BOY
COLTON PITONYAK

Like many youngsters from upper-class backgrounds, Colton Pitonyak played at being a streetwise rapper. But he got so immersed in recreational drugs that he lost his way. He became increasingly unstable and violent and the result was one of the most horrible dismemberment murders in Texan history...

The golden boy

Colton Pitonyak's early life had shown great promise. The former altar boy, born on 5 September 1982, was from a wealthy family and had had every advantage. His father owned a farm machinery company, whilst his mother sold real estate. He grew up with his brother in Little Rock, Arkansas, where his brother liked fishing and shooting with their father, but he stayed home and was closer to his mother. He had musical gifts and was an astute student, outgoing and well liked.

The couple were religious and sent their children to Catholic schools, their secondary education taking place at an all-boys establishment. They also attended the local Catholic church on a regular basis. Colton was also an altar boy, attending the priests during Mass and helping to serve Communion.

At his Catholic high school he opted for a class in moral theology, but he had a wilder side which would especially come to light when he drank and smoked cannabis. He wanted to be popular and thought that he could achieve this by acting tough, though he was badly beaten up by his peers after getting drunk at a party and calling a popular girl a slut and a whore. But, academically, he remained brilliant, never scoring less than 92 per cent in an exam, and in the autumn of 2001 he started to study finance at the University of Texas in Austin.

From the start, he seemed to feel the need to create an image and he wore the same type of clothes as rappers and talked about how often he had bought cocaine when he lived in Little Rock. He continued to drink heavily, but, in his first year, this didn't seem to affect his grades. In his second year, however, his use of cocaine intensified and he began to sell it to his contemporaries. He began to party excessively and sleep late, missing class after class. In winter 2003, he got behind the wheel of his car whilst he was drunk and was spotted by police weaving erratically along the road. He was jailed for driving under the influence but bizarrely saw this as a badge of honour, proof that he was a tough guy, a real man.

He was banned from university and his mother collected him and brought him back to Little Rock, a place he now hated. The following spring, he returned to Austin and enrolled in a community college, studying finance there. Within months he was allowed to return to the University of Texas, but soon dropped out, preferring to spend his days taking drink and drugs. In spring 2004, he went to a party and met Jennifer Cave, a vivacious redhead who had recently split from her boyfriend. She too used drugs recreationally.

But Colton Pitonyak was becoming increasingly aggressive under the influence of cocaine. He lost weight, picked fights and added Xanax, a tranquilliser, to the street drugs that he was already hooked on. He encouraged Jennifer to experiment and she took ecstasy and crack.

There was a fight at his apartment one night and the police came, finding cocaine. He was arrested but bailed himself out, awaiting trial. Meanwhile he returned to class but continued to use drugs and behave aggressively, attending a party and hurling a knife into the wall. Another friend saw him with a revolver and his former friends became increasingly afraid.

Heroin abuse

Pitonyak's attorney persuaded him to enter rehab and he attended prayer sessions there. But when he left he returned to his former lifestyle and was aggrieved when Jennifer refused to live with him. She explained that she loved him as a brother or a friend but didn't want more from the relationship. She moved in with her new boyfriend Scott, a single parent, and promised to help raise his child.

Jennifer continued to be friends with Colton, sometimes spending hours with him or counselling him on the phone. She was using fewer and fewer drugs and had returned to a healthy weight, and she was feeling settled. Colton also professed to want to quit, but he couldn't stop. By now he was injecting heroin and hanging out with a pre-law student, Laura Hall, a goth who idolised him. Friends would later say that he treated her badly, only using her for sex. Under his influence, she began to take more drugs and show up late for her vocational work at a law firm. During an argument, he threatened to shoot her with his gun. On another occasion, he pulled a knife on Jennifer and she fled from his apartment. Laura loved Colton, but Colton still loved Jennifer and always went to her when he was feeling down.

On 10 June 2005, he was sentenced to 60 days in jail for possession of cocaine, but he was released after 20 days. Meanwhile, Jennifer had decided that she wasn't ready to be a wife or mother and she moved out of the house that she shared with Scott and moved in with a female friend. She resumed her drug-taking and remained friends with Colton but only saw him when other people were around as he could be unpredictable. Laura was also realising this, as Colton had fired a gun in his own apartment whilst under the influence. On another occasion he had burnt her on the arm with a cigarette.

By August, his life was spiralling out of control. He owed the local drug dealers several thousand dollars, his car had been impounded for being parked illegally and he got a D grade for one of the few exams he'd bothered to turn up for. He and Jennifer went out dancing but he seemed high and she told another dancer that he was acting strange. Later, at around 1 a.m., she texted a friend to say that they were walking along the street and that Colton was upset and had broken a car window. She said that she was going home soon to get some sleep as she had just started a new job. When she didn't show up the next morning, her new boss was concerned, as were her family when she didn't get in touch.

That day, Colton and Laura went shopping for dusters, air fresheners, gloves, carpet cleaner and a hacksaw. He answered a call from Jennifer's worried mother but said that he hadn't seen her since they'd argued at midnight. He was brusque and uninterested in the fact that she had apparently disappeared. But Jennifer's mother, Sharon, also spoke to Jennifer's friend, who confirmed that Jennifer had still been with Colton at one in the morning.

Dismembered

Sharon phoned the police to report her daughter missing but was informed that they couldn't get involved until 24 hours had elapsed, so she and her boyfriend Jim drove to Pitonyak's apartment, convinced that something had happened to her there. When no one answered, Jim entered via a window and found her decomposing body in the bathtub, with both hands severed at the wrists. Her head was in a binbag in the corner. The hacksaw used to decapitate her was lying on her chest, and, when police arrived, they found a machete in the lounge. Her hands were found in another bag.

An autopsy showed that she had been stabbed in the face and shot in the arm and chest, the latter bullet severing her main artery. She would have bled to death within a moment. The numerous stab wounds on her face and limbs had been made post-mortem, usually the act of someone who is filled with rage. After her head had been cut off, someone had fired another bullet into it via the severed neck.

As the hunt for Pitonyak intensified across Texas, he and his girlfriend played around with a hotel computer in Mexico. He went to the manager's room to watch a cage-fighting show and asked the man to help him sell his car. But he was told that he'd need the paperwork, at which point Pitonyak explained that he couldn't ever return to the States. He refused to elaborate on the reasons and the manager, by now frightened of the increasingly drunk and aggressive young man, didn't ask.

In his absence, Pitonyak had been charged with murder, which carried a potential life sentence. He was caught after Laura phoned a relative, gave out their location and asked for money. The American police contacted the Mexican authorities and they burst into the couple's hotel room at first light and arrested him. Laura Hall had not been charged with any crime so was released. Police later interviewed her and she said that she'd had no idea that there was a body in her boyfriend's bathtub, that she had thought the two of them were just enjoying a romantic getaway.

She logged onto her Facebook page and said that Colton was innocent and she told friends that she loved him. But when she was arrested on her return to Austin, she told police that he had admitted to her that he had shot his best friend and had even showed her Jennifer's corpse. Jailed awaiting trial, she told another prisoner that the six days she had spent with him on the run had been the happiest that she had ever known. Her parents posted bail and she moved in with a friend but continued to talk incessantly about Colton. He, ironically, was faring well in a Mexican jail as he was able to help Hispanic inmates to read and write in English.

Trial

Colton Pitonyak's trial finally began on 22 January 2007 in Austin, Texas. The prosecution said that he had shot and killed Jennifer Cave and had begun to mutilate her body with a view to disposing of it and hiding the crime. The defence alleged that there was no motive and noted that both Colton Pitonyak and Laura Hall's DNA had been found on the gun. (But Laura was with a friend at the time when forensic experts believe Jennifer Cave was killed.)

The defence added that Pitonyak had admitted the murder but had said that it wasn't intentional, that it had been an accidental shooting caused during one of his drugged near-blackouts. They implied that Hall had been responsible for causing Pitonyak to flee the States rather than phone the police. As such, they asked for a not guilty verdict, painting the crime as being a horrible mistake. It was obvious that they hoped for a verdict of manslaughter rather than murder. But, at the end of the first day of testimony, the jury were shown Cave's dismembered body with its numerous post-mortem cuts and some of the jurors wept.

On the second day, they heard about Pitonyak and Hall's flight to Mexico and were shown photos of an unshaven, drug-addicted Pitonyak, who looked very different to the clean-cut young man sitting in court in his expensive grey suit. The manager from the Mexican hotel where they had stayed gave evidence of how he had had to take a knife away from the increasingly aggressive American who changed noticeably under the influence of alcohol, and of how he had noted his crude tattoo, suspecting that it had been acquired in jail (it had). He added that he had become afraid.

Pitonyak took the stand and admitted that he'd been a straight-A student whose life went downhill under the influence of alcohol and drugs. He said that Jennifer had been his friend but denied being in love with her. They had gone out for the evening and he had woken up the next day to find her dead in his apartment, specifically in the bathroom. He added that Laura Hall had cut up the body as he was too squeamish, that it had been her idea to buy the hacksaw though he had accompanied her on the shopping trip.

The prosecution noted that the young man had been cultivating a gangster image since going to university and showed photos of himself that he'd posted on the web wearing gangster clothing and talking about women as whores and bitches. He also carried a gun and a knife.

Another witness told the court that Laura Hall had said she *helped* cut up a body – and Pitonyak's DNA had been found on the machete handle.

In their summing up, the defence relied on the absence of motive, but the prosecution said that Jennifer had been a good customer who wasn't buying drugs from him anymore and this had fuelled his anger. She was increasingly turning her back on a drug-addled lifestyle and this made the addicted Pitonyak feel worse about himself. They believed that he was responsible for the dismemberment as his DNA was all over the machete and knives and Jennifer's blood was all over his clothing. They were convinced that he had shot her in the kitchen, the only room which had been excessively cleaned.

The jury were only out for an hour before returning with a guilty verdict and he was subsequently sentenced to 55 years in prison, and would have to serve half of his sentence before being considered for parole.

That summer, on 28 August 2007, Laura Hall went on trial. The 24-year-old was charged with concealing a crime and mutilating a corpse and pleaded not guilty. The defence painted her as a lovelorn student who was besotted with Pitonyak, a remorseless psychopath. When Pitonyak was arrested in Mexico she had told the authorities that she would kill anyone who hurt him and she had later told friends that Jennifer Cave was a nobody, that this was essentially a victimless crime.

The jury went out and returned the following day with their verdict, finding her guilty of the misdemeanour hindering charge and of the felony of tampering with the evidence. The next week she was given a year for the misdemeanour and five years for the felony. As a result of the latter charge, she would never fulfil her dream of becoming a lawyer. Ironically, by the time of her trial, Laura was involved with another man. Her sentence was later increased to ten years when additional information of her complicity came to light.

In the summer of 2013, Colton Pitonyak's lawyers went to the appeals court and asked for a new trial. The request was denied.

14

THE BANK CLERK
ALAN HOPKINSON

One of the most genteel images of English life must be that of a former bank clerk, from a middle-class family, living in the retirement seaside resort of Eastbourne. But this particular bank worker was a paedophile who kidnapped little girls, held them hostage for days and repeatedly abused them at his squalid flat.

Early life

Alan Hopkinson was born in Eastbourne in 1953, the only child of a respectable married middle-class couple. When he was four, the family moved to Rhodesia (now Zimbabwe) in southern Africa and he went to a good boys-only school where he was found to have an IQ of 159. (The average IQ is around 100 and even postgraduate students only need an IQ of around 130 to cope with their studies, so he was in the top one per cent of the population.) Yet, despite obtaining six O-Levels and three A-Levels, he settled for a series of menial clerical jobs.

It was compulsory at the time in parts of Africa for young men to do military service, so the quiet teenager served time in the Rhodesian military. By the age of 21 he had completed two spells of national service, hating them both.

At 23 he returned to Britain and lived with relatives in Sidcup, Kent, though he again settled for low-level employment. But, when he was 28, he took a computer course, excelled at it and moved into better-paying software-related work. For two years he was a junior clerk in the Bank of England, though later reports, after his offences came to light, would erroneously describe him as a bank manager.

A bank manager has to be able to interact reasonably well with other adults, something that the increasingly reclusive Hopkinson simply couldn't do. When his parents returned to England in 1987 and acquired a house in Maidstone, Kent, the 34-year-old went back to live with them and rarely went out to socialise. He started a relationship with his cousin Jean and moved her into the parental home too.

For years they lived together, but when he lost his job he felt unable to tell her and continued to get up and pretend to go to work every day. The relationship broke down and he would later allege to police and prison staff that he had had what amounted to a nervous breakdown. (This information cannot be taken at face value, however, as paedophiles are incredibly good at portraying themselves as the victim and making people feel sorry for them.)

Sexual offences

The Hopkinsons' neighbours had quickly realised that the attractive, bespectacled clerk had a dark side, as he would stand naked at his bedroom window and tap on the glass when an unsuspecting woman walked by. They had no idea that his darkness extended way beyond such exhibitionism, that he was keeping a diary called *The Evil Rapist*. In July of 1990, he tried to act out one of his rage-filled fantasies, picking up a teenage hitchhiker in Kent. The girl, who was from France, felt comfortable with the attractive, well-spoken

Englishman until Hopkinson stopped the car and turned to grab her. She hit him with her bag and fled.

The predator doubtless realised that he would find it easier to control a smaller victim – and this dovetailed with his desire for girls of around 11 and 12. In November 1990 he grabbed an 11-year-old girl as she walked home from school, threw her into the boot of his car and drove her to the nearest wood, where he sexually assaulted her. He bound her and drove her to his parents' house where he hid her in a tiny cupboard, seeming to view her as a sex toy rather than a human being. Police questioned her classmates and heard that Hopkinson had been giving them sweets and biscuits and making inappropriate comments. They went to his house and found the traumatised child.

They also found child pornography and women's lingerie and Hopkinson admitted that he enjoyed dressing in women's clothes. He was sent to prison in Kent for seven years for kidnapping (for the attempted kidnap of the 17-year-old French hitchhiker and the actual kidnapping of the 11-year-old) rather than for sexual crime.

The fantasy continues

Unfortunately, like most paedophiles, Hopkinson used his prison time to hone his sexual fantasies. Asked to write about his experiences in a therapeutic context, he produced a book called *Foiling the Beast* which examined why men want to abuse little girls. Whilst in jail, he also secretly drew a map of the primary schools in Eastbourne with listings of children in each school district, information that he'd gleaned from local newspapers. He was already planning his next crime, but, like most sex offenders, he was outwardly a model prisoner. Why wouldn't he be, when he had no access to his prey of choice?

Tellingly, when he was offered early release if he would have psychiatric treatment, Hopkinson refused. Whatever his demons were, he wanted to keep them well hidden from view, perhaps even from himself.

Released on licence after serving only four years, the unemployed computer programmer was under supervision in Kent for a mere six months. Thereafter, he moved to Eastbourne, got a council flat a few minutes' walk away from his parents, and returned to his offending behaviour. He befriended many of the local schoolgirls and they would arrive at his shabby bachelor pad above a shopping centre to make cakes.

By now he had greying hair, a neat moustache and could look highly respectable in a suit. He visited his parents every day and was a Mensa member, the type of man who could easily help a child with her homework. He began to groom the two daughters of a near neighbour, who at first had no idea that the debonair white-collar worker posed a threat.

But one neighbour became concerned when a schoolgirl handed her a note to give to Alan which had hearts drawn on the envelope. And the parents of one of the schoolgirls found out about her 'friendship' with this supposed father figure and reported Hopkinson to the police. They warned him that the relationship was inappropriate but he continued undaunted: they were increasingly aware that he was totally obsessed with grooming young girls. A year later another parent complained and detectives were so worried that they tried to secure a court order against him. As they were in the process of doing so, his offending escalated markedly...

A double kidnapping

In November 1998, Hopkinson's parents went on an extended trip to Australia and he had the opportunity to realise his fantasies. Knowing that Eastbourne police were keeping a close watch on him, he drove to Hastings, 14 miles along the coast, on various occasions and noted which routes various children took to their primary school.

On 19 January 1999, a Tuesday, he drew up beside Charlene Lunnon and her best friend Lisa Hoodless, both age ten, and threw them into the boot of his car. (Child victims of sexual abuse are usually given anonymity but, as adults, the girls wrote a book, *Abducted*, under their own names about their ordeal, and have since given many interviews to the press.) Lisa had seen Hopkinson's turquoise car earlier that morning driving slowly past her house.

He at first drove the girls to a field, left Lisa in the boot and spoke to Charlene in the car, telling her that she and her friend had been kidnapped for ransom. But Charlene, who had already been sexually abused by a family friend, wasn't convinced. He also told her that he had kidnapped a girl before and held her for 3 hours but hadn't got any money so this time he was going to do things properly.

He put her back in the boot and drove to his parents' house, where he took Lisa into the house first, concealing her from the neighbours in a holdall, and sexually assaulted her. Going back to his parents' garage, he sexually assaulted Charlene. He then drove both children to the underground car park of his own flat and carried them, one at a time in a holdall, up four flights of stairs.

Once indoors, he tried to make the children feel sorry for him, saying that he felt safer in prison and that he couldn't cope with life on the outside. He asked Lisa to hit him across the face then seemed surprised when she obliged. He said that he never would have taken them if his parents hadn't gone abroad and left him alone. He then added, cruelly, that neither of the girls' fathers would pay the ransom money and that he hadn't decided what to do with them yet.

For the next two days he repeatedly abused the ten-year-olds to the point where they were painfully swollen and in shock, though he tried to convince them that he was being gentle and said that he had children round to his flat all the time to play computer games.

On their third day in captivity he told both girls to have baths then put them in the car and drove them to a chip shop, saying that he was about to drive them back to Hastings. Leaving them in the darkened vehicle, he soon returned with sausage and chips. The girls had barely eaten since the kidnapping but were still too upset to eat much: their main focus was on going home.

But the paedophile drove them to Beachy Head and stared over the cliff edge, holding Charlene over the precipice. Then, after saying that he had decided to keep both girls for one more day, he put them back in the car boot and drove them to his flat, removing the handle from the main door so that they couldn't escape.

The following morning he met his elderly parents at the airport and drove them to their home. Whilst he was out, the girls explored the flat and found lists of children's names and what he had done to them. There were abbreviations like NF which he would later admit to police meant 'naked fun'.

By now Charlene and Lisa's parents feared that they were dead, something which was supposedly confirmed by various local psychics. It was a calculated guess as most children are killed within hours of being abducted and the ten-year-olds had now been missing for four days. Meanwhile Alan Hopkinson fed them more junk food and the sexual assaults and rapes continued relentlessly.

Hopkinson, the girls discovered, rarely slept and survived on a diet of nicotine and coffee. The flat was filthy and smelt bad and there was fungus growing from the ceiling. It was a life devoid of balance, his only focus that of abusing girls.

But luck was at last on the children's side when the police arrived at Hopkinson's door in response to reports that he had been interfering with neighbourhood children. They knocked loudly, shouted 'Police' and kept knocking. Horrified, the paedophile paced up and down swearing under his breath. When he answered, they asked him to come down to the station and answer some questions. He agreed, fetched his wallet and cigarettes and then told them that he had the two girls from Hastings in the flat. Police rescued the children and they were intimately examined by a female doctor before being reunited with their families.

Trial

At his trial at Lewes Crown Court in May 1999, Alan Hopkinson pleaded guilty to all charges and was sentenced to nine life sentences, with Judge Richard Brown telling him that the court should do everything in its power to ensure that he was never again free to prey upon young children. In 2013 he applied for parole but was turned down. Police officers involved in the case have said that he is one of the most deceptively dangerous men that they have ever met.

15

THE CHILDMINDER
JUDY BUENOANO

In her roles of housewife, mother to a disabled child and crèche owner, Judy Buenoano was a sympathetic figure – but, as she tired of each role, those around her began to die...

Orphaned

Judy Buenoano was christened Judias Welty and born into an impoverished family in Quanah, Texas on 4 April 1943, one of four children. Her mother died of tuberculosis when she was only two and she was raised by her grandparents as her father was rarely around. But, when her grandfather died, Judy's grandmother couldn't cope and sent her as a 13-year-old to a children's home. They found her to be out of control and she was moved to a reform school. After her release she went to live with her father and new stepmother in New Mexico, but was so badly treated that she attacked them, resulting in a two-month jail sentence.

By the age of 17, she was back on the streets and determined to have some fun and secure herself a reasonable style of living. She looked and sounded sweet and men were attracted to her. She soon set up home with a handsome Air Force Sergeant called Art Schultz and they had a child together who they named Michael.

Judy and Art split up within a year and she went on to marry Air Force Sergeant Jim Goodyear and had two children with him. Whilst he pursued his military career, she set up a day-care centre for preschool children and had various acquaintances come and work for her. Intelligent and persuasive, she was good at making money and the centre thrived. She told her clients that she was a nurse but friends would later say that she had lied about her qualifications and experience and had only previously worked as a nurse's aid. Ironically, she had less and less time for her own son Michael, who was a slow learner. She seemed to be ashamed of him, so although she lived and worked in Orlando, she enrolled him in a special school in Miami and rarely visited.

The first murder

By the time that she had been married to Jim for over a decade, Judy was bored and disillusioned. She was glad when he was sent to Vietnam for a year and promptly began an affair with Bobby Joe Morris, a local businessman. When Jim returned to their Orlando home, she told a friend that she was thinking about putting arsenic in his meals: the friend joked that she should insure him heavily first. Judy did just that, taking out a policy for $28,000. Shortly afterwards Jim became sick with crippling stomach pains and vomiting and, as the months passed, his health deteriorated alarmingly. Judy told anyone who would listen that he had contracted a mysterious debilitating ailment during his Asian tour.

The unfortunate man was admitted to hospital with kidney failure and liver damage and died there on 16 September 1971, aged 37. His death was attributed to natural causes and Judy collected the insurance payout and treated herself to a sports car and an expensive new wardrobe. (She would also receive a widow's pension for the next 14 years until the crime was discovered.) After her husband's death she changed her surname to Buenoano, which is ungrammatical Spanish for Goodyear. She doubtless figured that a change of name would make it harder for people from her past to track her down.

The second and third murders

Judy and her common-law husband Bobby Joe moved to Pensacola and went into business together, but the venture failed and the couple moved to Colorado. She insured him and he suddenly died in 1978 of what appeared to be a heart attack. Wealthy again, she returned to Pensacola, set up a beauty salon and spent lots of money on jewellery and wild nights out.

But her teenage son, Michael, was cramping her style and she found it costly to keep paying carers to spend time with him. She took over his care, insured him for $100,000 by forging his signature on the documents and inventing the name and signature of a witness. Shortly afterwards, the 19-year-old began to suffer the same symptoms as his stepfather, Jim Goodyear, had. His weight dropped by 30 pounds, he felt incredibly ill and he was hospitalised. Fortunately, he made a good recovery.

The day after he was discharged in the summer of 1980, Judy told him that she was taking him for a canoe ride. The young man was understandably nervous as, with the heavy callipers on his legs and his very limited arm movements, he couldn't swim. But his mother said that he could be propped up on a chair and pointed out that the East River was tranquil and that she was familiar with paddling a canoe.

But, shortly after they set off, Judy swam to shore and told shocked fishermen that her son had drowned after he cast his rod upwards and it tangled in an overhead tree branch, dislodging a snake. She said that the reptile had fallen into the canoe and that Michael had flailed around in a panic, overturning the boat, and that she had been unable to reach him. Again the insurers paid out and Judy went on another spending spree.

The one that got away

Judy and her two remaining children continued to live in Pensacola, where she soon teamed up with businessman John Gentry. He came to live with them but, before long, began to feel unwell. Judy suggested that he take out a $500,000 insurance policy so that she would be protected if anything happened to him. She also insisted that he double the number of vitamin capsules that she was giving him to boost his vitamin C, but John began to suspect that he was allergic and put them in his briefcase, where he promptly forgot about them. He was hospitalised in 1983 after eating one of Judy's salads but assumed that this was due to food poisoning.

A month later, after having lunch at a local restaurant, John got behind the wheel of his car and switched on the ignition, only to have part of the vehicle explode, blowing away part of his stomach and intestines. He lived but was baffled to hear that the explosion had been the result of a home-made bomb which had been hidden under the hood.

Police asked if anyone would benefit from his death and he remembered Judy's insistence that he take out life insurance. He also remembered the vitamin C capsules that she had given him, removed some from his briefcase and gave them to detectives who sent them to the laboratory: tests showed that the powdered vitamin C had been doctored with the deadly poison paraformaldehyde. He did not return to the home that he shared with Judy, and the couple were later divorced.

Detectives now investigated Buenoano's background and found that her common-law husband Bobby Joe had died of a supposed heart attack at a surprisingly young age. They exhumed his corpse and found that it contained enough arsenic to kill 11 people. Her husband Jim's body was also exhumed and found to be perfectly preserved, despite having been in the ground for almost 13 years, as arsenic acts as a preservative.

They looked into Michael's death by drowning and realised that he didn't have sufficient movement in his arms to cast a fishing rod or flail around if a snake fell out of a tree. His body had also been found far upstream of where his mother said that the accident had taken place.

Death penalty

Buenoano's murder trial began on 21 October 1985 in Orange County. The defence said that Jim Goodyear could have come into contact with lethal poisons in Vietnam, but several of Judy's friends and acquaintances came forward and said that she had talked to them about how easy it was to kill with arsenic, adding that no one would suspect its presence unless they were actively looking for it. Jim had had a medical on his return from Asia and had been deemed healthy but had become ill within months of returning to live with his wife. The prosecution said that the victim had received a dose of arsenic (freely available at the time in the form of flypapers bought from the local grocery store) which was 90 times stronger than that needed to cause death.

Arsenic, the jury heard, had also been found in the bodies of Bobby Joe Morris and of Buenoano's son, Michael, who had died from drowning. Buenoano's daughter tried to blame Bobby Joe's death on her half-brother, Michael, saying that Michael had poisoned the man, but she wasn't believed. The jury found Buenoano guilty and recommended that she go to the electric chair.

Judy Buenoano, now looking older than her actual age of 42, pleaded with the judge before sentencing, saying that she had found religion and wanted him to spare her life, but he sentenced her to death.

The years passed with Buenoano filing appeal after appeal. She seemed quietly confident that the state would never carry out the sentence and gave interviews to journalists in which she hinted that she would die of natural causes. But, on 30 March 1998, aged 54, she went to the electric chair, the first woman to be executed in Florida for 150 years.

16

THE CHRISTIAN MOTHER
ELLIE NESLER

Though she believed in the ten commandments, Ellie Nesler shot dead the man on trial for sodomising her son.

Early life

Born on 2 August 1952, Ellie Nesler was the first of three daughters born into a coal-mining family near Jamestown, California. It was a hard life where she earned extra cash as a teenager by driving a tractor for a local farmer and helping to dig ditches. An early first marriage ended in an equally swift divorce. She then met and married a gold miner, Bill Nesler, and they had a son, also Bill. The family moved to Liberia in Africa in the hope of finding gold and Ellie gave birth to a daughter, but when civil war broke out she returned to California with her children, leaving her husband behind. He would visit but return afterwards to Africa. Ellie Nesler now survived on welfare cheques and supplemented this by chopping wood for others in the neighbourhood.

A regular churchgoer, she befriended a Christian parishioner called Daniel Mark Driver and the 34-year-old acted as a father figure to Bill, hoisting him up in his arms so that he could better see the minister delivering the sermon and putting him on his lap when they were watching television at the Nesler home.

When Bill was six in the summer of 1988, he begged his mum to let him go away to Christian camp for a fortnight. Ellie agreed as their trusted family friend Daniel was helping out at the camp as a dishwasher. He was also a nature lover who promised to show Bill the squirrels and other wildlife in the woods near the camp.

But when Bill returned he was a different child, veering between being sullen and argumentative. He began to hit his younger sister and avoided Daniel until Daniel allegedly threatened to kill Bill's mother and sister if he didn't continue to spend time with him. Ellie confided in Daniel that she was finding her son hard to deal with and the two prayed together for divine guidance.

Then, on a sleepover at his aunt's house, Bill told her that Daniel had 'done nasty things to him'. The woman confided in Ellie and Ellie told Bill that she too had been abused at a similar age. She had told a relative but he'd said that this happened to little girls all the time and was nothing to worry about. Now Ellie told her son that he must tell police exactly what happened so that Daniel Driver would be jailed for life.

The little boy confided in police that the abuse had been going on for a year and that he had been sodomised by Daniel Driver at the camp.

Police investigated and found that Driver had previously been found guilty of molesting several boys in San Jose but that his church affiliates had all spoken up for him, saying that he was a good Christian young man who had been dating an older woman with children. They alleged that, when the relationship soured, he had molested her offspring to get back at her so he wasn't really a paedophile. (In reality, paedophiles often target single mothers when the real object of their desire is the children and this was doubtless the case here.)

A judge had let Driver off with probation on the proviso that he signed up for psychological counselling, and so he was immediately free to abuse again. Now he was facing even more serious charges over crimes against Bill and other neighbourhood boys that he had groomed, and he knew that it would be much harder this time to avoid a custodial sentence. He immediately left town and was on the loose for a while, to the horror of the little boys who had described their abuse to the police and social workers. He had told these children that, if they told, he would seek revenge by murdering their favourite relatives. Fortunately, he was caught shoplifting, because he'd run out of money, and was taken into custody.

The hearing

As the date for the pre-trial hearing loomed, Bill became increasingly distraught and vomited repeatedly as he was convinced that Daniel Driver would hurt him if he testified. He didn't want to go to court but Ellie Nesler was determined that he would. No one had pressed charges when *she* was molested and she was going to have justice for her son.

But the hearing went badly as the children weren't allowed to testify from behind a screen, and had to sit close to their alleged abuser. Their discomfort increased immeasurably when the defence asked them to point to the parts of their bodies that Driver had touched. Ashamed – and possibly afraid to touch his own penis as his Christian upbringing had told him that this was sinful – one boy pointed to his thigh and another said that he didn't recognise Driver as his molester. The defence asked the boys questions which included 'How many times did he sodomise you?' and 'Did you like it?' The children were sometimes shocked into silence.

Afraid that the paedophile was going to be set free again, Ellie Nesler entered the Tuolumne courtroom in Northern California on 2 April 1993, walked into the back room where Driver was talking to his legal team, and fatally shot him in the head and neck a total of five times.

She was taken into custody and became a heroine to many for protecting her son and potentially many other children. That sympathetic stance wavered, however, when it was discovered that she'd been high on methamphetamine at the time of the shooting and had been taking the drug for some time. It also transpired that, at age 18, she had stolen a car and served a short sentence in a Californian juvenile detention centre.

In 1994, Ellie was diagnosed with breast cancer and told she would probably only live another five years. She pleaded not guilty due to temporary insanity and many expected the judge to be lenient given the circumstances but she was found guilty of voluntary manslaughter and sentenced to ten years in prison.

In 1996 she was released on appeal but six years later was convicted of buying the tablets used to make methamphetamine and was sentenced to six years in prison. She was released after four.

The cancer which had been diagnosed all those years before gained a stronger hold and she lost all of her hair, though her spirit remained indomitable. She died in a California medical centre just after Christmas 2008, aged 56. Her sisters, who attended her funeral alongside around 50 other mourners, said that she was a heroine.

Sadly, during her incarceration, Bill (raised by one of his aunts) went off the rails and ended up in juvenile hall for numerous offences, including robbery and drugs. At age 23, he assaulted a friend, 45-year-old David Davis (no relation to the author), who he believed was stealing from the family property. He was given a two-month sentence for this. Within an hour of being released early for good conduct, he tracked Davis down and kicked him repeatedly and the man died within hours of his injuries.

In 2005, Bill Nesler was sentenced to 25 years to life. He was serving out his sentence in High Desert State Prison near Susanville, California, when his mother died and he wasn't able to attend her funeral.

A very balanced TV movie, *Judgment Day: The Ellie Nesler Story*, was made about his mother's case.

17

THE CRIMINOLOGY STUDENT
STEPHEN GRIFFITHS

Criminologists can have both a professional interest in and personal fascination with crime, and read widely in their attempts to understand the psychology of the lawless. But one Bradford-based student didn't just want to learn about serial killers – he wanted to be one, and succeeded in his quest...

Psychiatric problems

Stephen Griffiths was born on 24 December 1969 to Moira and Stephen Griffiths. His father was a sales rep for a frozen foods firm, his mother a telephonist. Both were only 20 when they married and Moira was five months pregnant at the time. Two and a half years later the couple had another child, a daughter, and, in February 1976 they had a second son.

Stephen was intelligent and bookish but shy and introverted. He was close to his father and spent lots of time with him when his parents' marriage ended in the late 1970s. He took the break-up badly and began to shoot birds in the garden with his airgun, seeming to take equal pleasure in dismembering them. He also started shoplifting, stole from a garage and was told off by the bobby on the beat.

Determined that he would have a good education, his father spent all of his savings to send him to a private grammar school in Wakefield but, despite his high IQ, he preferred *Dungeons & Dragons* magazines to studying. He was also fascinated by martial arts and spent his pocket money on a dagger and on the martial-arts weapons known as throwing stars. In real life, he was a small thin boy but in his fantasies he was a killing machine and all-powerful. He increasingly retreated into a world of make-believe.

At 16 he dropped out of school and, the following year, was caught shoplifting. When the manager tried to restrain him, he slashed the man across the face with a knife. His victim required 19 stitches and Griffiths was sentenced to three years in a juvenile custodial unit. A psychiatrist found that he was suffering from a personality disorder and after his early release at the end of 1988 he continued to have outpatient psychiatric care.

Alone

By now his mother had forged a new life for herself and was going out almost every night; he became increasingly estranged from her and from his father. His mother's half-brother would later comment that, from the age of 18, the family hardly saw Stephen at all.

After leaving youth custody he rented a flat on his own. He appeared to be depressed and this may have had a genetic cause as, by now, his mother was also suffering from depression.

The psychologist

At 19, Stephen Griffiths started a psychology course at Bradford College. It could have been a new start but, during this period, he was caught with an air pistol and sentenced to 100 hours of community service. He continued with his studies whilst carrying out this community work. Unfortunately, he seemed incapable of staying out of trouble and became convinced that other students were talking about him. He pulled a knife on one terrified female, threatened those who came to her aid and was charged with affray: this time he was sentenced to two years, to be served at the category B Leeds Prison. There, he talked openly of which staff members and prisoners he would like to murder, and a prison warder who'd trained as a psychiatric nurse warned the governor that the young man was a loose cannon and should be monitored closely at all times.

After his release, Griffiths resumed his studies, though he was put on probation the following October for possessing an offensive weapon, a knife, in public. He graduated with a degree in psychology in 1993.

An ongoing quest for attention

Possibly because he had felt ignored during parts of his childhood, Stephen Griffiths continued to do everything in his power to get himself noticed. He dressed as a goth, took numerous photos of himself which he put on his webpage and on Facebook and Myspace, and kept exotic pets such as lizards, which he would take to nightclubs on leads. He also kept boa constrictors and portrayed himself as a macho man.

Unfortunately, the girlfriends he befriended at these clubs soon found that he was misogynistic and controlling. One girl finished with him only to find that her pet dogs had disappeared. They were never seen again and she is convinced that Griffiths took them and possibly killed them. Other young women were subjected to repeated phone calls and verbal threats after ending the relationship.

The unemployed young man was bright and invariably won at the chess games which he played in a local pub, but his mental health and criminal history made it impossible for him to find work so he spent his days walking his lizards or drinking at the flats of various unemployed acquaintances. When he was between girlfriends, he would rent a prostitute, paying her £40 a session. Despite being on benefits, he always seemed to have money for cigarettes and beer.

He often went out in the early hours to chat to the street girls as he lived in the red light district of Bradford and several of them saw him as a brotherly figure. He sometimes invited them back to his place to smoke pot. But he was house-proud and would insist that they take their shoes off before entering the spotless premises, and, if a girl dropped ash on the carpet, he would immediately sweep it up.

Killer friend

One of Stephen's friends at this time was a man called Kenneth Valentine, who charged sex workers £5 a time to bring their punters back to his bedroom. Valentine and Griffiths lived in the same block of flats and were so close that some of the street workers thought that they were lovers. Valentine had drilled a hole in the wall so that he could watch couples having sex.

Kenneth Valentine had served time in prison for the manslaughter of a woman and had been released in 1991, but in 1996 he killed again, strangling sex worker Caroline Cleevey in his home and dumping her body in a storm drain. Griffiths strongly suspected him of the killing and beat him up so badly that mutual friends feared the older man, 43 at the time, would die. In March 1998, Valentine was jailed for life for Caroline's murder and given a minimum of 22 years.

Academic

After the loss of his friend, Griffiths continued to hang out with prostitutes. He had a high IQ and was fascinated by true crime, so none of his acquaintances were surprised when he returned to academia, taking up a place on a PhD course in local history at the University of Bradford. His thesis was on Victorian Homicide, and he spent hours at the local library researching it. He told the other students about his BSc in psychology and explained that he wanted to become a psychologist so that he could understand the killer's mind. It made perfect sense that his small flat was crammed with hundreds of books about crime, but a few of his acquaintances queried the two crossbows which he kept on a shelf in his living room. He explained that he liked them and had bought them from a fishing tackle shop.

But Stephen rarely dated his fellow students, instead picking up women at clubs or answering lonely hearts adverts in the local paper. He liked to feel superior to his girlfriends and told one of them that he was training to be a counsellor. She was perturbed by his lack of emotional warmth and his various peculiarities – he couldn't orgasm from intercourse and went mad if anyone touched his hair – and ended the relationship. Another girl finished with him as he was so controlling and had begun to hit her for perceived slights: in the end, she had to take out a restraining order as he pursued her relentlessly.

By his mid thirties, Griffiths was becoming less and less attractive as a potential boyfriend. He'd put on weight, was balding and had started to use cocaine on a regular basis, which increased his underlying paranoia and speeded up his speech so that he often sounded hyper. He spent hours downloading violent pornography and refused to let his few remaining friends touch his computer when they came round for a beer. He tried online dating but the women he met found him strange and egotistical and no one agreed to a second date.

By March 2009, the PhD student's mental health had declined to the extent that he bombarded a former female friend with hate-filled texts and phone calls, causing her to flee from her home. She was the sixth woman to report him to the police for harassment. He also beat up a former male friend because he believed he had been badly treating prostitutes.

The staff at his block of flats had become aware that he was increasingly unstable and the caretaker had been warned by his manager never to be alone with him. Some of the other tenants thought of him as 'Psycho Steve'. They would have been even more troubled if they'd known that he'd set up a Myspace page on the internet in which he claimed that his alter ego was a misanthropic demon called Ven Pariah who might unleash his rage at any time.

Yet, despite his alleged hatred of humanity, Stephen Griffiths wanted to be remembered by the masses – and, if he couldn't be famous, he was more than happy to be infamous. He knew that murdering two or more women at separate times would render him a serial killer and that he would earn a notorious place in the echelons of true crime. If he used one of the fearsome weapons in his house he would be known as the Crossbow Killer and be as feared as a previous local serial killer, Peter Sutcliffe aka the Yorkshire Ripper, a man who he talked about endlessly and seemed, bizarrely, to admire. But, though he was impressed by the sheer number of victims which Sutcliffe had amassed, Griffiths thought that he had left too many clues at his crime scenes. He told his acquaintances that he was clued up on forensics, that he wouldn't have made the same mistakes. It was classic narcissistic thinking in which the narcissist believes that he – or indeed she – is superior to everyone else.

Three victims

On the evening of Monday 22 June 2009, Griffiths intercepted 43-year-old grandmother Susan Rushworth as she walked to a Bradford park to meet a friend. Susan had collected her methadone prescription that day and was in good spirits. She was known to offer full sex for £30 in order to fund her addiction to heroin. Her family became concerned at her disappearance, as did the police, and the case was featured on *Crimewatch*, but it would be the following year before her murder was verified.

If Griffiths' later account of events is to be believed, ten months elapsed before he killed again. This time the victim was 31-year-old Shelley Armitage, a drug addict and alcoholic who made a living from selling sex. On Monday 26 April she had a mid-evening meal with friends in a cafe and was filmed by a CCTV camera in the vicinity of the red light district – near Griffiths' home – circa 10 p.m., then promptly disappeared.

Four weeks later, on Saturday 22 May, Suzanne Blamires (who used the street name Amber) was out looking for business in the early hours of the morning when she encountered Stephen Griffiths. The 36-year-old had been raised by a successful couple, and had had every material advantage. But in her late teens she had rebelled against her protective upbringing and partied incessantly, soon turning to alcohol and drugs. Now she was hooked on crack cocaine and was also drinking up to 14 cans of strong beer every day. The PhD student invited her back to his flat, doubtless promising her drugs and money. Like the other two victims, she would not leave the building alive…

Caught on camera

That Monday morning, Peter Gee, the caretaker of Holmfield Court, arrived at work as usual and, within an hour, was reviewing the footage taken by the CCTV system. He watched the scene monitored by one of the cameras at 2.30 a.m. on Saturday showing tenant Stephen Griffiths walking into his flat with a petite brunette. Moments later she left the flat at a run with him in hot pursuit. He caught up with her and punched her to the ground, dragged her towards his doorstep, left her there and returned with a crossbow, which he used to shoot her from close range before pulling her into his flat and slamming the door.

Had he just witnessed a murder? The caretaker fast-forwarded through the footage and saw that, 20 minutes after the shooting, Griffiths had re-emerged from his flat with the crossbow, raised it and made a one-fingered gesture to the camera. It was unlikely that anyone could survive being shot with such a fearsome weapon: the CCTV cameras had witnessed what was essentially a snuff movie. A deeply shocked Peter Gee hurried off to find his manager, who promptly called the police.

Within hours, West Yorkshire police had assembled an armed response team, comprising 60 officers armed with pistols and even machine guns. They battered down Griffiths' door but he offered no resistance: after all, he wanted to be caught, to become an antihero. The man who had never held down a job, not even for a single day, was now – in his own eyes – extra special, a serial killer who had despatched his victims in an especially unusual way.

Arrested on suspicion of murdering Suzanne Blamires, Stephen Griffiths said, 'This is the end of the line for me.' At the station he began to talk, saying that he had killed 'loads' of women, before blaming the murders on his alter ego Ven Pariah. (Peter Sutcliffe had claimed insanity in the hope of being treated at a mental health facility rather than a normal prison, but he was initially found competent and jailed accordingly, though later removed to a secure hospital when he showed signs of schizophrenia. But Griffiths had suffered from mental health problems from early adulthood, so it's hard to tell if these simply worsened into full-blown episodes of disassociation – a temporary break from reality during which he acted out his murderous fantasies – or if he was faking insanity.)

The student criminologist told police that he had cannibalised parts of Suzanne (he used her street name of Amber) but this, in itself, isn't proof of madness. Unemployment benefits clerk Dennis Nilsen ate part of most of his victims but was found fit to plead and sent to Parkhurst Prison. Such men tend to want to possess their victims totally and ingesting them is an extreme form of ownership.

Griffiths also admitted to eating parts of his other victims – rendering his cooker unusable when he tried to cook part of the first body only for blood and fat to clog up the oven – before cutting the remains into numerous pieces in the bath using power tools.

He had killed his first victim, Susan Rushworth, with a hammer rather than the crossbow and had attempted to burn parts of her body, inadvertently setting his sofa on fire though he had managed to hide the body before the fire brigade arrived. Despite his hours spent cleaning the premises, forensic experts would find traces of her blood on the walls.

Incredibly, he had made journey after journey on public transport with bags containing dismembered body parts, dumping the limbs and slices of flesh in the River Aire.

A horrifying discovery

The following day, police were still listening to Griffiths' confession when a walker saw a rucksack stranded near the bank of the River Aire. He opened the bag and found a human head: it was that of Suzanne Blamires. The next weekend police divers found more of her body parts, as well as the bags which contained the knives, hacksaws and razor blades used to cut her up. Three days later they found a small piece of Shelley Armitage's spine in that same river. Taken with his confession, police felt confident with charging him with all three murders and he appeared at Bradford Magistrates Court on 28 May 2010.

Asked by the clerk to state his name, he replied 'The Crossbow Cannibal'. After the 3-minute hearing he was taken to Bradford Crown Court, denied bail and sent to Wakefield Prison to await trial.

Unsurprisingly, the disturbed and solitary man did not fare well in the mayhem of a noisy Victorian prison. He slept badly, refused to engage with other inmates and spent most of his time alone in his cell. Within weeks he tried to commit suicide, tying a plastic bag around his head and a sock around his neck. He was spotted on a CCTV camera which monitored his room and was intercepted before any harm was done. He was transferred to a cell in the prison's hospital wing, where he was watched around the clock. After he threatened a guard, he was moved to a segregation cell, where he spent most of his time sleeping. When he was moved back to the general prison population he broke his TV screen and cut his own throat with a piece of the glass.

Later that same month – September 2010 – he tried to asphyxiate himself by choking on a plastic bag but a guard managed to retrieve the offending object seconds before Griffiths lapsed into unconsciousness.

By the date of his next hearing at Leeds Crown Court, the killer had lost several stone in weight. Shortly afterwards he went on hunger strike and also swallowed batteries, though these later passed through his digestive system. Psychiatrists suspected that he was trying to feign symptoms of mental illness in the hope that he'd be found unfit to plead, but he did not get his wish and, in late December, pleaded guilty to all three murders.

The judge heard of the CCTV footage taken outside Griffiths' flat, of how the camera had captured him shooting a bolt into Suzanne Blamires' inert body. Afterwards he had approached another street walker and asked her to return with him, saying that he wanted to take a photo of her bum. He bought crack cocaine for them both but she felt uneasy and decided to listen to her sixth sense and made an excuse to avoid going into his flat.

CCTV footage taken the following day showed the killer going out with what looked like heavy bags and returning with lighter ones. He did the same thing on the Sunday. He had admitted that, during these journeys, he was taking body parts to a dumping site, specifically the River Aire in Shipley.

Police, the jury heard, had looked at numerous pieces of CCTV footage from around the city at the time when Shelley Armitage disappeared and had seen Griffiths make trips towards the river with bags and a rucksack. He had done the same with Suzanne Blamires' body parts. He had told officers that he had cooked and eaten parts of the first two victims but had eaten slices of the third one raw.

The gory evidence continued. Suzanne Blamires had been cut into at least 81 pieces and a knife and a bolt had been found embedded in her head. Blood from all three victims had been found under Griffiths' bath.

The killer's digital camera had been found in his flat and it contained images of Shelley Armitage lying in the bath with the words My Sex Slave sprayed in paint on her back. In other photos, she was bound and gagged and stretched out on cushions. In some photos, Griffiths was fondling the bottom of one of the victims: he had admitted to several of his girlfriends that he had a fetish for buttocks and loved to photograph and fondle them, and he had asked various prostitutes to pose with their bottoms in the air so that he could take photographs.

The court heard that, after his various encounters with the law over the years, Griffiths had been assessed by psychiatrists and found to be both violent and unstable. He identified with – and idolised – serial killers such as the Yorkshire Ripper and wanted to be equally notorious. He had a personality disorder but had known what he was doing at the time of the murders and had taken care afterwards to get rid of the bodies and destroy most of the forensic evidence.

The judge handed down three life sentences, stating that the sadistic nature of the crimes – Shelley Armitage might have been bound and gagged whilst she was still alive – and their premeditated nature, plus the fact that Griffiths had cannibalised all three women, meant that the murders were so monstrous that life, in this instance, should indeed mean life. Three days before his forty-first birthday, the killer was returned to prison where he will remain until his death.

Griffiths used to hint to his acquaintances that he would end up in Wakefield Prison, where he is currently incarcerated. He seemed to have no fear of this, yet he is not making the most of his time there, preferring to lie on his bed rather than go to the recreation room and chat to other prisoners. He has made another two suicide attempts and claims that being watched by the guards is affecting his mental health. When he does enter a communal area, he tends to sit alone and, if approached, tells the other party to go away. Perhaps his delusions of grandeur make him feel superior to the other inmates, though many of them have been jailed for equally callous crimes against humanity.

18

THE PRIEST
GERALD ROBINSON

Everyone knew that one of the hospital priests, Father Gerald Robinson, hated the oldest nursing nun, so he was the immediate suspect when she was found half-naked, strangled and stabbed...

A hate-filled crime

Easter Saturday in 1980 at Mercy Hospital started like any other day, with the nuns ministering to the sick in Toledo, Ohio. But the peace was broken by startled screams when one of the nuns unlocked the chapel's sacristy. For their oldest nurse, 71-year-old Sister Margaret Ann Pahl, lay badly beaten on the floor, her navy habit pulled up to expose her breasts, her panties at her ankles. There were numerous stab wounds to her head, neck and torso, and her arms had been positioned at her sides, almost as if she'd been posed.

The nun hurried to alert the other sisters about the shocking murder and, one by one, they filed into the chapel. Father Swiatecki had just finished performing the last rites when another priest employed by the hospital, Father Gerald Robinson, walked in. 'Why did you kill her?' Father Swiatecki roared, but the younger priest just stared and didn't reply. Not that his silence, of itself, implied guilt, as he had always been a quiet, reserved man.

Early years

Though he was born in America, Gerald John Robinson had a Polish mother (and German father) and grew up in Toledo's Polish community. Born on 14 April 1938, he was their second son. He was a shy boy who wanted a quiet life, and in this he seemed to resemble his father. His mother was the dominant force in the family and very involved in the local church.

She soon decreed that her youngest boy was destined for the priesthood and he immediately acceded to her wishes. By the age of 14, he was enrolled in a seminary that was 60 miles away from home and would live on campus, apart from holidays spent with his parents, for the next four years.

Gerald remained a thin, introverted boy who only really came to life when the seminary put on plays for Polish parishes. He seemed happier playing a part, becoming someone different. In his day-to-day life he was pious, aloof and seemed repressed, preferring to read theology books than socialise with his peers. He was denied a normal, exploration-based childhood, but the years of study paid off and, aged 26, he was ordained and spent the next few years preaching to the Polish community and steadily gaining in popularity.

By 1973, he was an associate pastor and was well respected by his parishioners. However, in what was undoubtedly a demotion, the Diocese of Toledo transferred him after a year to become one of two chaplains at Mercy Hospital. The 36-year-old priest was given two small rooms in the school of nursing, his duties to administer the last rites to patients and say Mass in the chapel every day.

Dealing with the dying on a regular basis was daunting but he soon acclimatised, going out with friends at night so that his life contained some jocularity and was balanced. He often came home late and others at the hospital got used to seeing him wandering about after midnight in the hospital grounds. The chapel where he said Mass was run by 66-year-old Sister Margaret Ann Pahl, the nurse who would eventually be murdered in that very place.

Sister Margaret was a perfectionist whose main job was to organise the thorough daily cleaning of the chapel. Father Robinson apparently found her domineering (she doubtless reminded him of his mother) so there was a personality clash between the two from the start. Because of her increasing deafness, she would become frustrated during a conversation and start shouting, something which the mild-mannered priest despised. Some of the younger cleaning staff also found her difficult to deal with and would leave the chapel in tears.

The clash came to a head on Good Friday, 4 April 1980, when Father Robinson inexplicably cut the service short. A stickler for protocol, Sister Margaret berated him in front of others and he stood there glaring at her before walking away. The distressed nun told colleagues that his conduct was indefensible, that she planned to talk to him again soon. But the following day, she was found dead.

The investigation

Detectives were shocked to find that the nun had been so thoroughly brutalised. 'Who would do this?' they asked the doctors, nurses and nuns who worked at the hospital. Again and again they were given the name of Father Gerald Robinson.

An autopsy showed that what had appeared to be severe bruising on the nun's face was actually the damage caused by six stab wounds to her left cheek. There were another 15 stab wounds to her neck, nine on her chest and one on her shoulder. Other vicious wounds to the torso had penetrated her breastbone and her heart, causing fatal injuries. Her lungs and oesophagus were also injured in the frenzied attack. She had been stabbed a total of 31 times and had probably been penetrated by a finger as a small scratch was found inside her vagina but her hymen was intact. Her assailant had apparently pushed her clothing out of the way in order to defile her, suggesting that he was enraged.

So who could the culprit be? One hospital worker had seen a strange man leaving the office beside the chapel at 7.30 a.m. on the morning of the murder. And one of the nuns speculated that another nun (she had no one specific in mind) might be responsible and had staged the vaginal penetration to make detectives think that the strangler and stabber was a man.

At the time, there was an unwritten rule that detectives must not do anything to embarrass the Catholic Diocese, so when a priest was caught having sex with another man in public, or was reported for interfering with a child, they were taken by the arresting police officer to the Vice Squad, who then called the Monsignor. The priest was then dealt with privately by the church, usually by being moved on to another parish, and didn't face a legal trial. But now the Toledo Police Department was dealing with murder, a much more serious crime.

They interviewed Father Gerald Robinson and, to their amazement, he said that the killer was among his parishioners and had confessed to him two days before. The Catholic detectives were amazed, protesting that there was no way that the priest would ever divulge information given in private in the Confessional. Father Robinson then said that he'd made the story up just to get them off his back.

In his room, they found a dagger-type letter opener which resembled the murder weapon. It had been polished, but, when the police laboratory technician took it apart, he found a tiny dark spot behind the ornate medallion which decorated the opener, a spot which might have been blood. A first test could not rule out blood or positively establish it, and there wasn't enough material for a second test.

Father Robinson failed some of the questions during his first lie detector test, and a subsequent lie detector test was inconclusive, though the results would not be admissible in an Ohio court. He would later explain that he was on Valium for shock after the murder, and that this might have skewed the polygraph's results.

The weeks turned into months and Father Robinson was moved out of Mercy Hospital by the bishop and assigned to three Polish churches. He was beloved by his parishioners as he spoke fluent Polish and his sermons had a conservative air. In time, he moved on to offer pastoral care at various nursing homes in the Toledo area and, by the time that 23 years had elapsed since the murder, he was semi-retired.

Alleged abuse

But, in late 2003, the Cold Case Squad decided to examine Sister Pahl's unsolved murder and spoke to a nun who claimed that she had been ritualistically abused by a satanic cult, which included Father Robinson, from the time that she was five years old, but that she had only recently 'remembered' the extent of her suffering. She alleged that she had seen a three-year-old girl being murdered and that she herself had been raped on an altar at the age of six. By the age of 14, she said, she was being used by men for sadomasochistic sex and one of her abusers had been Father Gerald Robinson.

The apparent surfacing of such repressed memories is understandably controversial, as there is such a thing as false memory syndrome where adults 'remember' events which didn't actually happen. One woman, whilst in the throes of a nervous breakdown, reported that her father had raped her multiple times as a child. When she was examined, however, she was still a virgin, her hymen intact.

The nun was undoubtedly telling her story in good faith but her information could not be verified and mental illness could not be ruled out. If the authorities were to catch the killer, they would have to rely on forensics or a belated confession from Father Robinson.

Police laboratory technicians retrieved Robinson's dagger-style letter opener from the archives and did tests which suggested that it was the murder weapon, especially as one of the wounds had a pattern which resembled the opener's decorative medallion. Furthermore, a receptionist claimed that she had heard frenzied footsteps racing towards Father Robinson's quarters shortly after the murder had taken place. As it was Easter weekend, the student nurses had gone home for the holidays and he was the only person staying on the second floor.

It was hardly a watertight case, but detectives were convinced that they had their man and questioned the 66-year-old in his modest abode – he was now living in the home of his deceased parents. He said that he had never had a key for the Mercy Hospital sacristy. They found this to be untrue: they knew that, during his tenure, he had gone there every day. He said little and went quietly when they told him that he was under arrest.

Detectives searched his house and found a booklet about the occult in which passages on the Black Mass (a satanic service) had been highlighted in marker pen. They also found a box filled with photographs of corpses in coffins. He was charged with the 1980 murder, though he pleaded not guilty at a hearing in Lucas County Common Pleas Court.

The prosecutor had the nun's body exhumed and re-examined and it appeared to show a mark on the mandible which was consistent with the markings on the dagger-style letter opener. They also found male DNA on her underwear and under her fingernails.

The trial

In April 2006, the priest's trial began. Prosecutors alleged that the Father's Easter Friday argument with the domineering nun had been the last straw, that Gerald Robinson had lain awake all night plotting revenge. At 7 a.m., they said, he had entered the sacristy, knowing that she would be there alone, looped an altar cloth around her neck and strangled her for 2 minutes, breaking two small bones. He then, they stated, placed an upside-down crucifix across her heart in a satanic ritual and stabbed her already-dead body repeatedly, then pushed her clothes out of the way and penetrated her vagina with a finger or small crucifix.

Prosecutors also said that he had taken the bloody altar cloth with him but had dropped it outside the chapel when he saw another member of the nursing staff. An hour later the nun's desecrated body had been found.

A lab assistant at Mercy Hospital testified that she had seen Father Robinson coming out of the chapel shortly before the nun's body was discovered. She had told her superiors but had been warned to keep quiet or she would lose her job. A doctor at the hospital had also told investigators that he had seen a priest, who had stared at him coldly, near the chapel around the time of the murder, but they had shown no interest in this information at the time.

The detectives who had originally interviewed Gerald Robinson said that their interrogation had been interrupted when their supervisor and the Monsignor from the Catholic Diocese took the priest away. The supervisor took all three copies of the police report on the case, which subsequently disappeared. A detective admitted that such interference from the Church was common at this time, with paedophile priests merely being moved to other parishes.

The defence noted that the lab technicians had only tested the letter opener against the wounds and hadn't compared them with other potential weapons. They also pointed out that DNA found on Sister Margaret Pahl's exhumed underwear did not come from the Father. It was, of course, possible that there had been contamination when paramedics removed her body from the sacristy, but did that explain the DNA from an unknown male found under her fingernails? It was a curious anomaly, as medics had asserted that the nun had been strangled from behind without a chance to fight back.

The rounded mark on the Sister's forehead, which the prosecution alleged was caused by the letter opener's medallion, was also disputed, as it was pointed out by the defence that it could have been left by a doctor's stethoscope when the body was examined shortly after death.

Verdict

After just 6 hours 30 minutes of deliberation, the jury returned with their verdict, finding Gerald Robinson guilty of murder. The judge sentenced him to 15 years to life. Robinson had told his supporters that he expected to be found innocent (hardly surprising as the evidence against him was purely circumstantial) but remained impassive upon hearing the verdict and as he was led out of court and taken to Lucas County Jail.

In 2006, criminal lawyer John Donahue took on the priest's case pro bono as he was convinced that it was a miscarriage of justice, but he failed to get the elderly priest – now suffering from Parkinson's disease – released from prison. The following year, a woman who had alleged that Gerald Robinson and another priest had ritually abused her in the 1960s had her case thrown out of civil court due to the statute of limitations.

In October 2009, the US Supreme Court refused to consider Robinson's appeal and he remained in prison, distraught that he would not become eligible for parole until 2021. But his health failed long before that landmark date and he had a serious heart attack in May 2014. He was later moved to the prison hospice in Columbus, Ohio, and died there on 4 July of that same year, aged 76.

19

THE POLICEWOMAN
ANTOINETTE FRANK

Though the police sensibly turned down her original application, this young woman proved remarkably adept at fulfilling her desire to become an officer. Unfortunately, she was equally adept at organising an armed robbery and helping to kill the terrified witnesses...

Mass slaughter

Officers responding to a 911 call on 4 March 1995 reporting three murders were shocked to find that one of the dead was a policeman, Ronald Williams. The scene was the Kim Anh Vietnamese Restaurant in New Orleans and the other two victims were 17-year-old Cuong Vu and his older sister, 21-year-old Ha Vu. Their family owned the restaurant but Cuong was training to be a monk and Ha planned to enter a nunnery. She had been kneeling, praying, on the floor when she was shot dead.

Quoc, their brother, had escaped from the restaurant after the shootings, raced to a friend's house and called 911. His other sister, Chau, was still hiding in the kitchen. Upon hearing the police officers arrive, she raced into their arms. Another young woman was rushing from one door to the other, and seemed hell-bent on escape, but officers had secured the area. They were shocked when

Chau identified her as one of the killers, because she was Antoinette Frank, a cop, one of their own.

Taken into custody, the 23-year-old policewoman initially blamed the murders on an 18-year-old she described as her nephew, Rogers LaCaze. She said that they'd gone to the restaurant to get takeaway food but that LaCaze had decided to rob the place and had initially shot and killed Ronald Williams, a policeman who was working security there as a second job.

Brought in for questioning, the teenage boy, in turn, blamed the slaughter on Antoinette Frank. Detective work revealed that the policewoman had actually been dating the teenager, who was no relation, and that he sold drugs.

Asked to give an account of the murders, Chau Vu said that Antoinette Frank, who also worked security at the Kim Anh but who wasn't on a shift that night, had come to the restaurant three times that evening with her boyfriend, LaCaze, and that both of them had been nervous and acting oddly. On the third visit, in the early hours, the restaurant was closed, but Frank had unlocked it from the outside with a key, which she must have stolen earlier, and had again entered the premises with Rogers LaCaze. Having a premonition that they were about to be robbed, Chau had hidden the night's takings in the microwave before hiding in a cupboard with her equally terrified brother, Quoc.

Early ambition

Ironically, Antoinette Frank – born on 30 April 1971 to Mary and Adam Frank in Opelousas, Louisiana – had wanted to be a cop from the time that she was a teenager. She was a meek child who had joined a junior branch of the police, called The Explorers, whilst still in high school. By then the family – comprising four children – had relocated to New Orleans. Their father, a Vietnam veteran, had left the army and worked for a telephone company, though he was often absent from home. The family were deeply impoverished.

At the age of 20, she applied to join the police force, describing herself as a courageous young woman. She passed the Civil Service test but failed the interview with a psychologist who found her shallow, superficial and dishonest (she had been sacked from Walmart for being unable to get on with the rest of the staff, but lied when asked if she had ever had a job-related problem). He found that she was on the defensive and unable to take responsibility for past mistakes. He had no idea that, a few weeks earlier, she had left a suicide note for her father saying that she didn't want to live and had been doomed from the day that she was born. But she didn't follow through on her threat to end her life – and also refused to accept that she had failed the screening process put in place by the police.

Showing remarkable resourcefulness for a young woman, she got a letter of commendation from a lawyer who was also a family friend. But she also faked letters of commendation from her physician and from the mayor. She also paid to be independently tested by a psychologist: he was impressed by the fake testimonials which she showed him and wrote that she was suitable to join the police. They decided to give her a second chance and were at first rewarded for their benevolence as she did well at the police academy. Unfortunately, after graduation, she proved too timid to be a useful worker and none of the other officers, male or female, wanted to work with her. She accused all of the male officers of sexual harassment and the female officers found that she didn't pull her weight – she would stand around and let them grapple with an assailant alone.

Criminality

She continued to fail at her job, but also started to make bad choices at home. In autumn 1993, her father disappeared from the house that they shared together and, the following summer, she moved her older brother Adam in, knowing that he was a fugitive from justice. He had been arrested for two counts of attempted manslaughter but had left town. He had also been convicted of burglary and had broken the conditions of his parole.

Unfortunately, her catalogue of errors didn't stop there. One night she responded to reports of a double shooting and later visited one of the victims, Rogers LaCaze, in hospital to take his statement. The 18-year-old youth had fathered two illegitimate children and had been kicked out of the house by his religious mother for dealing drugs. His brother, Michael, had also been in trouble with the law and had been the victim of a previous shooting that resulted from a bad drug deal, leaving him paralysed from the waist down and wheelchair-bound.

At first glance, Rogers LaCaze was an unlikely romantic choice. He was only 5 foot 2 and had several gold teeth, a trademark at that time in New Orleans of the criminal fraternity. He had an IQ of 71 and struggled to write, whereas Antoinette Frank had excelled in academia. But she fell for the younger man and gave him her virginity, telling other cops that he was 'sweet'. She bought him a pager and clothes, rented him a Cadillac and frequently hung around his favourite haunts until he told friends that she was stalking him.

Formative years and motive

Rogers was born on 13 August 1976, the son of Alice Chaney and Michael LaCaze senior. The couple later split up. Rogers did badly at school and dropped out by tenth grade. By the age of 16, he was unemployed but had lots of money by making a living on the street. The following year he was arrested for illegal use of a firearm and, shortly afterwards, his mother found drug paraphernalia in his bedroom and threw him out. He'd later tell police that, by the time he was 18, he was making a living from selling dope.

Now, questioned about the motive for the triple shooting, LaCaze said that Antoinette's brother, Adam, had tried to kiss one of the girls who worked at the Kim Anh restaurant. She had rebuffed him and the staff had asked him not to return. Hearing of this, Antoinette Frank had allegedly become enraged and had told her boyfriend that she was going to sort the Vu family out. She was apparently also angry at her fellow police officer, Ronald Williams, as he worked the lucrative weekend security detail at the restaurant, whereas she herself was restricted to a midweek shift.

Living witnesses

Chau Vu tearfully gave her version of events, explaining that, when Frank and LaCaze entered the restaurant by using a stolen key, police officer Ronald Williams had his back to them. Williams, aged 25, and Frank, who was slightly younger, worked for the same precinct, so the policeman ostensibly had nothing to fear. But Chau and her brother Quoc heard three shots ring out and hid in the dark recesses of a large drinks cooler which had a glass door. The shots, Rogers LaCaze would later admit, came from his gun as he shot the officer in the neck and head from behind.

As the Vus shrank back deeper inside the cooler, Antoinette Frank entered the kitchen, followed by her boyfriend, and asked a terrified Ha and Cuong where Chau had hidden the money. They knelt to pray, protesting that they didn't know, then relented when the policewoman pistol-whipped Cuong around the face. The terrified siblings told the couple that the cash was in the microwave and Frank retrieved it. Peering through the glass, Chau could see Antoinette clutching a pistol and pointing it downwards. From the angle that Chau was at, she couldn't actually see her brother and sister, but seconds later more shots rang out. (Police would later ascertain that the policewoman had shot Ha twice through the head from a distance of 18 inches, then shot Cuong twice in the torso and twice in the head.)

An unlikely plan

Antoinette Frank had planned to kill everyone in the restaurant so that it would appear that a stranger had broken in, slaughtered every living witness and stolen the takings. Now she decided to drop Rogers LaCaze at his house with the money along with Ronald Williams' stolen wallet and credit card. She then went to the police station and reported that two masked men had shot several people at the Kim Anh, disabled the phone lines and escaped. She returned to the scene ahead of the other officers, unaware that Chau had seen her pointing the gun in the direction of Ha and Cuong and firing repeatedly. When she realised that she had left living witnesses she attempted to escape, but by then her police colleagues had arrived and cordoned off the area.

Police became immediately aware that Antoinette Frank's story hadn't made sense. Why hadn't she radioed for help rather than drive to the precinct? Why had she been at the restaurant after hours? They spoke to Chau and Quoc and believed their version of events. Both of the restaurant workers knew Antoinette well – and Quoc was able to identify Rogers LaCaze as her boyfriend. Both were arrested and charged with first-degree murder.

Antoinette Frank had been a police officer for a mere 18 months and now she was directly responsible for two murders and indirectly responsible for a third, as she had let LaCaze into the locked restaurant and given him the gun that he had used to execute policeman Ronald Williams. Detectives had to break the news to his wife, who had given birth to their second son just ten days before.

Two trials

Rogers LaCaze's trial began on 17 July 1995 and lasted for four days. The defence said that Antoinette Frank had set the younger man up, that he was innocent of the murders. But police who had responded to the crime scene told of how oddly Frank had behaved, how she had seemed desperate to escape the restaurant. Chau Vu had left her hiding place and run into the arms of one of the policewomen, telling her that a small black man had come into the Kim Anh with Antoinette and that they were shooting everyone. The jury were taken to the restaurant and shown where Chau and Quoc had hidden and where their siblings' bodies had fallen. Rogers LaCaze was also identified as the man who had used the dead policeman's credit card later that night to buy petrol. The murder weapon has never been found.

Despite his lawyer's objections, Rogers LaCaze insisted on taking the stand in his own defence. He said that Antoinette Frank had been obsessed with him, that she had multiple personalities. He said that police hadn't read him his Miranda rights but the jury had previously heard his taped confession, in which his rights had been clearly read.

The jury were out for 90 minutes then returned with three verdicts, each finding the young man guilty of first-degree murder. After 3 hours of additional deliberation at the penalty phase, they determined that LaCaze be sentenced to death.

Six weeks later, on 5 September 1995, Antoinette Frank's trial began. The prosecution used mainly the same witnesses as they had used when trying LaCaze, and he appeared in court to be identified as the man who had used Officer Ronald William's credit card at a gas station within an hour of the policeman's death.

The jury also heard Antoinette Frank's taped confession. 'He said shoot them, shoot them – and it went off,' she stated vaguely.

'You shot them?' her interrogator queried.

'Yes,' she replied.

Despite her confession, the defence tried to suggest that her boyfriend was the one responsible for all three murders, but the jury were unconvinced and were out for only 20 minutes before returning with three guilty verdicts. It took them a further 40 minutes, at the penalty phase, to determine that she should be executed by the state.

Another murder

Six weeks later, a dog dug up human remains in Antoinette Frank's back garden. Investigators unearthed the skeleton of a male with a bullet-sized hole in the skull. They are believed to be the remains of Antoinette's father, who had disappeared two years before. The former policewoman refused to give a sample of her DNA, and the authorities have declined to take it by force, so the cadaver remains formally unidentified.

In 2000, Frank asked for a new penalty phase, stating that she had been physically, sexually and emotionally abused by her father, that he had impregnated her several times then forced her to have abortions and that this had a bearing on her behaviour at the Kim Anh restaurant. Her attorneys attended a series of hearings in 2002, arguing that the stress of this abuse had led to their client suffering from post-traumatic stress disorder. But the state refuted this, noting that she was the dominant force in the relationship with LaCaze, whereas abused females tend to enter into other abusive relationships. Instead, she showed signs of suffering from narcissistic personality disorder in that she lacked empathy (she told a prison psychiatrist that she had never experienced guilt) and was quick to fly into a rage. The judge declined to offer her a new penalty phase.

The attorneys tried again in 2006, but the Louisiana Supreme Court ruled that her death sentence should be upheld. She was scheduled for execution in December 2008, but this was delayed so that investigators could keep looking into her claims of abuse.

At the time of writing, both Antoinette Frank (who now claims that she's found religion) and Rogers LaCaze remain on death row. If the authorities go ahead with her execution, she will be the first woman who has been put to death in Louisiana since 1942.

20

THE DOCTOR
PHILIPPE NENIERE

Medics are supposed to 'do no harm', but this doctor and his wife were responsible for the death of one policeman and the serious wounding of another.

A life less ordinary

Though he was born and did his medical training in France, Philippe Neniere and his life partner Agnis Jardel (she was wrongly reported in the media as his wife) relocated to South Africa in the 1980s. By 1998 they were living in a farmhouse near Sutherland, 170 miles from Cape Town, and Philippe was working as a hospital superintendent. Agnis told neighbours that she had previously worked in advertising but that they now wanted to drop out of the rat race, to get away from city life. They were initially sociable towards their new community and Agnis was naturally tactile but, by 2008, they were in thrall to an American-based school of enlightenment and believed in the 'third eye'. They began to greet neighbours by kissing or rubbing them on this third eye, allegedly located on the forehead, and were increasingly at odds with the Christian community.

The pair had been taught by the enlightenment school, which many regard as a cult, that the world would end soon and only believers would be saved. They decided that the end would come in 2012 and began to prepare for this.

Though they loved nature and lived an increasingly hippy-like lifestyle, the couple progressively withdrew from their fellow men and opted to have their groceries delivered to their rented farmhouse rather than go into town. They asked their landlord to build them a survival bunker but he understandably laughed off their request, whereupon they became very angry. They started to steal food from neighbouring homes and Agnis would spend hours alone outside staring forlornly into the local dam. They also burned books which challenged their beliefs.

Convinced that others were the enemy (whereas, in reality, their neighbours were increasingly afraid of them) they started to stockpile guns and ammunition and even bought or made a bullet maker. They also kept tins of food in the cellar which were several years past their use-by date.

Many survivalists are comparatively uneducated and often use military-style fantasies to enliven an otherwise dull existence but, as a doctor, Philippe Neniere didn't fall into that category. His girlfriend had also previously held down an interesting, people-centred job.

Initially, the couple were peaceable and so anti-violence that they wouldn't even kill the snakes around their property, but the brand of religion which they were becoming more and more enthralled by prophesied doom, and it seems that they literally danced to its tune, donning cloaks and taking part in strange night-time rituals. The enlightenment school is also against both paper money and the stock market, so they gave up using banks.

They became thin and unkempt, and would collect twigs and burn them in order to keep warm. They also went into town to attempt to sell small household goods from their home in order to bring in some much-needed cash. Yet they continued to see themselves as special, chosen people who would survive because of their faith. Towards the end, their narcissism knew no bounds so that, when a neighbour offered Philippe work, he said, 'I'm an intellectual. I don't need a job.'

Their landlord had allowed them to live in the house for 12 years rent-free as they provided security for the farm, but when his relatives wanted to renovate the building and move in, he nervously asked the couple to leave. They agreed to vacate the premises by December 2010 but didn't. The landlord went to the police and told them about their attitude and about the fact that they kept a great deal of ammunition on the property.

On 21 January 2011, four unarmed police officers went to the house and the by now 60-year-old doctor greeted them politely. They examined his weapons and told him that his licences were out of date and that they would have to confiscate them. Neniere remained calm and walked out to their vehicle with them but suddenly pulled out a handgun, shooting student officer Jacob Boleme, aged 27. He fell to the ground and the doctor shot him again to make sure he was dead. He shot a second officer through the spine and he was seriously injured. Meanwhile, Agnis fired further shots from the house.

The couple shot out the tyres on the police vehicles, ran off into the fields and lived there, using their survivalist training, for the next four days whilst police hunted them on the ground and with helicopters. Police would later say that the pair knew every inch of the region, which is partially desert, and that they feared they could again become their prey.

But the couple sneaked back into the farmhouse and, after two more days, were spotted by infrared sensors. A gunfight ensued, during which police threw stun grenades into the building. Rather than be taken alive, Philippe Neniere shot his partner, then shot himself. When police searched the house they found camping equipment, bottles of gas, candles, firelighters and water containers. They also found books on survivalist techniques.

For a year the couple's bodies remained at the morgue, but no friends or relatives claimed them, so they were eventually buried at the expense of the local authorities.

21

THE COMMUNITY POLICE OFFICER
KENNETH DeKLEINE

Though he was a pillar of the community, this family man snapped when his estranged wife wanted custody of their children.

A fake suicide

On 10 January 2008, 16-year-old schoolboy Christopher DeKleine entered the laundry room of his home in Michigan, USA, and found himself staring at his mother's dead body. Lori DeKleine had a rope around her neck and it at first looked as though she had attempted to hang herself. She had been suffering from depression for some time.

The police were called and an autopsy showed that the 43-year-old had been murdered. As people are most often murdered by a spouse or family friend, they were keen to interview her estranged husband Ken DeKleine, a 13-year veteran of the local police department. Their first enquiries showed that he was good at his job and very well liked.

But they also established that Lori had taken out a restraining order a few months before and had told friends that she was terrified that Ken would kill her. They were due to have a final divorce hearing the following month, where she was likely to get custody of the children, though her 44-year-old husband had also applied for this.

Outwardly, the couple were deeply devout and church-orientated but a few of Lori's inner circle suspected that Ken was controlling and manipulative.

DeKleine was arrested whilst teaching a self-defence class and found to have a bad lip injury which had required six stitches. He told the authorities that a saucepan had fallen on him from a high shelf. He denied having murdered his wife to investigators but admitted it to his brother, saying that he was ready to go to prison. Hours later, he confessed to detectives, explaining that he had wanted to protect his children from their mother's ongoing emotional distress.

He said that he had gone into his wife's garage and from there gained entry to the attic, entering the main part of the house and assaulting Lori after the children had left for school. He strangled her with a nylon strap but she fought back, biting his lip. She had screamed 'Think of the children!' He had replied, 'I am.'

When she was dead, he dragged her to the laundry room and wound a rope around her neck in the hope that it would look like suicide. He hid her blood-spattered shirt, the gloves he had used and the murder weapon in the attic, where they were duly discovered by police. He threw his own bloody sweatshirt away after leaving the house and went to a cafe for a milkshake before returning to work. He would later admit that he felt a strong sense of freedom at this time and was without remorse.

At his trial in July 2008, the jury heard that the couple had been well-liked churchgoers with many friends. Officer DeKleine had trained police officers in Iraq and had had a parade held in his honour on his return. He was also heavily involved with his children's sports and hobbies. Lori, a former Christian school teacher, worked for a religious organisation and was a loving mother but had been diagnosed as bipolar. Her depression deepened and she asked Ken for a separation in December 2006.

He agreed to this, but rerouted her emails to his computer, eventually realising that she was having an affair with her therapist. (The therapist would later be suspended for six months for inappropriate behaviour.) Ken promptly filed for divorce and told his attorney that he felt that the children – aged 16 and 18 – were being manipulated by their mother's mood swings, and that he wanted her permanently out of their lives. He was also enraged that she was due to speak at a conference about stalking, and he was convinced that his previously good name would be undermined by this.

The medical examiner testified that Lori's death had been painful and terrifying – she had broken bones in her face and neck as well as a head injury, and she had fought valiantly for her life. The jury deliberated for little over an hour before finding him guilty of first-degree murder, which carries an automatic life sentence. He is serving this in a Michigan prison.

DeKleine's imprisonment left his two children effectively orphaned and the local police department held a benefit to raise money for them. Casual acquaintances have shown more concern for the youngsters than their father had. He had failed to heed the counselling advice given to warring couples that they have to love their children more than they hate each other.

22

THE YOUTH PASTOR
RICK PULLEY

Though his outward persona was that of an almost-neutered male, Eugene Richard Pulley (known as Rick) concealed a very dark undercurrent and would ultimately go to jail for the murder of his wife.

Childhood

Rick Pulley was a child of divorce, which was unusual in the 1950s. His mother took him to North Carolina, where they initially lived with his aunt and uncle. Later they moved, still within the city of Raleigh, to live with his grandparents and they babysat him whilst his mother was out at her clerical job. He would later say that he had a happy childhood, was given lots of attention and was taught right from wrong. But he would also tell his wife that he had a series of stepfathers and that some of them had been cruel to him.

At school he was an underachiever but he shone at music and was a percussion player in the school orchestra. Later he excelled at playing the drums. He got a place in college to do business studies but still preferred his extracurricular musical activities, singing in the college choir and taking piano lessons. He also worked as a junior manager in a grocery store, where they thought that he was nice but immature.

During this period, he became more religious and devoted himself more and more to his local church, realising that he wanted to create a music ministry. Young people, he hoped, would be attracted by his Christian music and would stay to hear him preach.

He was delighted when an attractive 18-year-old called Patty Jo Riddick joined the same church as their new choir director. She could play more than a dozen instruments and also had a beautiful singing voice. By the following year they were dating, but, as her musical studies became more time-consuming, she told him that it might be a good idea if they saw less of each other. To her shock and embarrassment, he became visibly enraged. In front of their friends, he grabbed her and said that, if she left him, he would kill her. When the friends intervened, he broke down, cried and apologised. The couple continued dating and were married on 2 January 1982. Patty Jo was 21, Rick was 26.

After the honeymoon, he returned to his grocery store job and she returned to her studies. When she graduated, he quit his job and they relocated to Haven Home in Winston-Salem, Virginia, a church-run house for unwed mothers. They had a roof over their head and their food was provided, but they were not paid a salary and were expected to finance any other expenses from their music ministry. They believed that their God would provide for them, but in reality they often travelled miles to a gig and didn't make enough to pay for their travel expenses, far less their accommodation and meals whilst on the road.

A reality check

Over the next 18 months, they borrowed more and more and got into debt before relocating to the River of Life Church in Ringgold, Virginia. There, they led an intensive Christian training course for teenagers, for which Rick was paid a modest salary. But the couple were still broke and Patty Jo had to teach piano in their home to make ends meet. She was beloved by her students as she was both kind and talented and was able to bring out the schoolchildren's own musical gifts. During this period, she was upset to find that Rick was using up some of their hard-earned cash to phone sex lines, but he was addicted and found it hard to quit.

The rest of the eighties and early nineties passed, with the couple's life still completely revolving around the church. They even travelled internationally as missionaries, spreading their beliefs in various Third World countries. But, by 1994, he had become increasingly attracted to another churchgoer and they began to meet in hotel rooms where, he would later maintain, they masturbated each other but didn't have full sex. He also used this woman as a confidante as he often fell out with other parishioners and wanted someone to sound off to, but after a few months he felt guilty and broke off the relationship.

Afterwards, he suggested to Patty Jo that they should give up their music ministry as this would allow him to become the church's full-time pastor, bringing in a much-needed extra thousand dollars a year. She gave him her backing. They also continued to evangelise abroad.

The following year, on Valentine's Day, he confessed to his wife about his brief affair. She was devastated. She was equally shocked a few months later when she heard him telling another churchgoer, a teenage girl, that he had feelings for her.

By now, Rick was regularly shouting at Patty Jo – and at the children who attended Sunday school – and various parishioners saw him have temper tantrums. Patty Jo admitted to a woman she'd been to college with that she was afraid of his increasing rage. In the summer of 1998, she appeared at church with bruises on her face, legs and arms and, when questioned, stammered that she had fallen down the stairs. But she told a friend that, if she disappeared, they should look at Rick.

Patty Jo was visibly unhappy and began to lose weight. Ironically, Rick, who had always been overweight, kept piling on the pounds and looked very unhealthy. This contributed to the erectile dysfunction which had begun to plague him and he increasingly shunned sex with his wife in favour of his beloved X-rated premium telephone lines. Sex in any long-term relationship requires effort and it was simply easier for him to have sex by himself.

Many couples grow apart and agree to a no-fault divorce (and as a child of divorce he was statistically more likely to have a failed marriage than the children of intact unions), but their religion included a vow of 'till death us do part'. His entire friendship group were equally religious. He had no one to confide in, so his darkest thoughts swirled around and around...

On 14 May 1999 – her last day on earth – Patty Jo got Rick to drop her off at her Friday morning cleaning job, menial work which she had undertaken on a weekly basis for the last six years in order to bolster their income. Her determination to keep her household out of debt was truly commendable. She chatted to the house owner as usual and didn't mention feeling unwell. But, at 4 p.m., when a parishioner phoned to ask if the couple were coming to the school play that evening, Rick answered and said that Patty Jo had a cold and wasn't well enough to attend. He told another enquirer that she had allergies and was below par, and told yet a third person that she had gone to do early-evening shopping in town.

Later that evening, he was seen with scratches on his face and said that he had followed their dog into the brambles and fallen over. He later told police that he had then gone home, showered and changed, and turned up to watch the school play alone but left before the end. He further told them that he'd been surprised to find that their red truck, which both of the couple drove, wasn't outside when he got home from the play. He phoned the 24-hour Walmart and asked them to page his wife in case she was still shopping there, but she didn't respond to the page.

He drove to the store, then to friends' houses, then called the emergency services shortly after midnight and explained that she had been missing for 6 hours. They told him to phone back in the morning if she hadn't returned.

The following day, police found the truck but there was no sign of Patty Jo. They questioned Rick about the play and it was obvious that he hadn't seen all of it and hadn't taken in the storyline. He explained the scratches on his face by saying that they were made by briars, but his interrogators were familiar with briar marks and could see that these looked different. Asked to take his shirt off, he revealed further scratches on his chest and four large bruises on his right arm.

Further investigation revealed that Patty Jo had presented a cheque at a shop on the Thursday but that it had been refused due to lack of funds. She'd been embarrassed and was angry at him for not managing their finances better. He admitted to police that they had argued on the Thursday but said that all was well by the Friday when he'd driven her to her cleaning job.

The days passed and Rick Pulley returned to his pastoral duties without the wife who had stood by him for almost 20 years. Within weeks, he was in debt and, after Patty Jo had been missing for three months, he began to sell her musical instruments, her most precious possessions. He relocated to Lebanon Community Fellowship Church in Virginia, working as a Christian counsellor.

Body found

On 18 December 2002, the remains of a woman were found under the Hyoca Bridge, 13 miles from the Pulleys' old home. Many of the bones were missing but the jewellery and scraps of clothing were identified as belonging to Patty Jo Pulley. Three and a half years after his wife had gone missing, Rick Pulley officially became a widower, though by then he had started a new relationship with a woman that he had met on the internet. His wife's family said that he would be welcome at the funeral but he decided not to attend.

Two months later, detectives arrested Rick Pulley for her murder. He wept and denied responsibility and pleaded not guilty when arraigned. He was told that the charge would be reduced to manslaughter if he confessed, but he turned this down and went on trial for murder.

By the time that the trial began on 18 October 2004, he weighed a massive 21 stone and looked at least 20 years older than his chronological age of 48.

The prosecution told of the Pulleys' difficult marriage, of Rick's overheard threats and of Patty Jo's increasing fear of him. The district attorney recounted that he had been scratched and bruised on the day that his wife had disappeared. He had said that she was driving their red truck that day but, when it was found, the seat was pushed much too far back for her small height and frame – it had obviously been driven by a much larger and taller person. She had loved that truck yet he had sold it within weeks of her going missing, almost three years before supposedly finding out that she was dead.

The DA listed the many issues that the couple argued about, from his reliance on internet pornography and sex phone lines to his affair with another woman. They also told of his inability to handle money and how this had led to rows between the couple, particularly after he took to hiding bills and not telling his wife that they had arrived.

The defence stated that the youth pastor had loved his wife, that he was depressed after her disappearance and that his financial situation had worsened. They added that he had spent days looking for her.

Patty Jo's dentist took the stand and said that the teeth found with the remains had been positively identified as hers. A rope found entwined with the skeleton, close to the collarbone, had most likely been used for the purposes of strangulation though they could not rule out the possibility that it had been used to bind her hands or feet. The medical examiner had concluded that strangulation was the most likely cause of death and that afterwards her body had been dropped over the bridge, to land in the bushes 27 feet below.

On the third day of the trial, the jury heard from a witness who had seen someone fitting Rick Pulley's description walking away from the red truck on the day that his wife went missing. This put him near the body dump scene rather than at the school play as he had claimed. A forensic pathologist said that, though Pulley had had minor marks from briar bushes on his skin, the scratches on his face had been consistent with fingernails and the bruises on his arms had been consistent with being grabbed. The defence again asserted that all of the marks had been caused when the accused fell into the briars.

The DA said that Patty Jo hadn't cashed her pay cheque and that her purse and the red truck's keys had all been found in her home, yet she had planned to go shopping. The inference was that she had been murdered before she had the chance to go to Walmart. She had been working three part-time jobs but the couple regularly had to pay $200 phone bills because of his use of X-rated premium lines. She had written in her diary that he rarely spent quality time with her any more and that she had told him that he had to change his ways.

Dozens of his colleagues and parishioners from his church took the stand and testified that the couple had had a close relationship and that he had been devastated when his wife went missing and again when her remains were found.

Rick Pulley insisted on taking the stand. For the next two days, he talked of his love for his wife and their shared dream of running a music ministry. He wept often. He also cried when questioned by the prosecution about the debts he'd run up through his use of telephone sex lines and about his brief affair with another parishioner. He said that his wife had been disappointed by his failings but that she had forgiven him.

The jury heard a taped interview that Pulley had given to the police in which he said he'd seen all of the play. They had asked him questions about the plot (the police had also been to see the performance in question as their own children had taken part) and he had got the answers wrong.

The prosecution said that there were two likely scenarios. In the first, the couple had argued whilst he was driving her home from her job and he had pulled over, hurt or killed her and thrown her body over the bridge. In the second scenario, he had killed her later in the evening then immediately driven on to Walmart as if searching for her. The defence alleged that he would not have had time to carry out either plot.

The jury were out for less than 3 hours before returning with their verdict – guilty of first-degree murder, after which the court sentenced him to life imprisonment without the possibility of parole. He later appealed for a new trial but this was turned down. In 2008, he was transferred to Nash Correctional Centre, Nashville, a medium-security jail housing 512 prisoners.

23

THE HIGHWAY PATROLMAN
CRAIG PEYER

Though he had both looks and charisma and could have been a successful ladies' man, Craig Peyer actually hated women. At first he merely used his position to frighten them, but one night he gravitated to murder...

A blameless victim

Cara Knott had spent the last three days looking after her boyfriend, who was suffering from flu, but now, on the evening of 27 December 1986, he was feeling better so she phoned her parents and said that she was about to drive home. The drive should have taken 45 minutes, but when the brilliant young student hadn't arrived 2 hours later, her concerned family went out looking for her. The San Diego police weren't initially interested as she hadn't been missing for 24 hours, but when the Knott family found her car abandoned in a dead-end road, which had been blocked by a Road Closed sign, they realised that they might be dealing with a kidnapping or worse.

A search party was formed and one of the officers saw Cara Knott lying on the rocks beneath a nearby highway bridge. She had been beaten about the head and strangled. She also had ten broken ribs.

When the news story broke, a young woman called a local TV station and reported that she had been sexually harassed by a

California highway patrolman the previous month on the same stretch of Mercy Road. The TV station informed the police but the tip wasn't followed up for some time.

Fortunately, another near-victim later contacted detectives to tell of her experience at the hands of a CHP officer who had pulled her over on Mercy Road because she had a cracked headlight. He had kept her talking for an hour and a half and she had felt very uneasy. Both women named the same officer, Craig Peyer. Other women would later admit that Peyer had pulled them over and spent time stroking their hair and patting their shoulders. They had felt frightened but had opted not to make an official complaint. All of the women, like Cara Knott, had long blonde straight hair.

The supreme self-publicist

Peyer, aged 36, was already well known to his colleagues as he was handsome, exceptionally well groomed and articulate, traits which ensured that he was the California Highway Patrol's spokesman and regularly liaised with the media. But, though he masqueraded as a happily married man with two young sons, Peyer was actually on his third marriage and was having an affair with a married woman.

He had been sworn in as an officer in 1980 and the power had gone to his head to the extent that he frequently bragged, 'You don't piss off God or cops.'

When he was called in for questioning, it was found that he had scratches all over his face. When questioned about this, he said that he had slipped and fallen against a wire fence, sustaining injuries to his face, shoulder, arm and foot. Unconvinced, they inspected his cruiser and found three ropes hidden in the trunk: this was significant as Cara had probably been strangled with a rope.

Later, they heard from other women who had been pulled over by Peyer, taken to dark side roads, and made to spend time in the back of his vehicle: he would suggestively caress the gear stick of his car and seemed to enjoy their apprehension and growing fear.

On 4 January 1988, the patrolman's trial began. Despite the fact that gold thread from a CHP uniform patch had been found on the victim's sweatshirt, he was still protesting his innocence. But the tyre tracks found at the scene matched a CHP cruiser and a drop of his blood had been found on Cara's boot.

However, the defence found that the blood evidence only showed two matching markers, meaning it could have come from someone other than Peyer. The ropes, incredibly, hadn't been tested for blood and skin, and the gold threads weren't solely used for CHP uniforms. The following month, the jury admitted that it couldn't reach a unanimous verdict though it was seven to five in favour of convicting him, a result that necessitated a retrial.

Retrial

On 17 May 1988, the retrial began. This time a couple came forward who had seen Craig Peyer pulling over a white VW driven by a blonde girl, Cara Knott. They hadn't realised the importance of their testimony and had gone on their honeymoon. Peyer's colleagues testified that he had falsified his records at the time of Cara Knott's murder and that afterwards he kept asking for updates on the case. He had also said that the perpetrator probably just killed her by mistake. (Other colleagues remained convinced of his innocence and blocked investigative reporters' attempts to find out more about the previous official complaints made against him, many of which mysteriously disappeared from police files.)

This time the jury returned with a guilty verdict and he was sentenced to 25 years to life and sent to the California Men's Colony, a medium-security prison, where he trained as an electrician but has shown no interest in understanding his own pathology. When more sophisticated DNA testing became available in 2004, he turned down the opportunity to have his taken and compared to DNA found at the crime scene. He has since been turned down three times for parole. His last denial came in 2012 and he is not eligible to reapply until 2027.

This news was of some comfort to the victim's family, who set up the San Diego Crime Victims Oak Garden as a tribute to their beautiful and talented daughter. Cara Knott's father, Sam, died there of a heart attack in 2000 whilst tending the trees.

24

THE JUNIOR POLICE OFFICER
STEVEN RIOS

Though on the outside he was deeply conventional, this young man allegedly killed rather than reveal his bisexuality.

A family man

In the years immediately following the millennium, 27-year-old Steven Rios was a thin, bespectacled man who worked as a junior police officer, patrolling the university campus district of Columbia, Missouri. He had a pretty young wife and a newborn son and would hurry home from work most nights to give his spouse a much-needed break from childcare. He also volunteered for various police boards and charities. But the prematurely balding officer had a big secret – he was bisexual and had been having an affair with an attractive 23-year-old male university student, Jesse Valencia, for some time.

The affair started after Rios had arrested Valencia at a party for trying to intervene when other police officers attempted to arrest his friends. Afterwards, Rios visited the young student in his apartment and the two became lovers. Valencia was outwardly gay, championed same-sex marriage and even wrote a column for the university newspaper about his sexual preferences. In contrast, Steven Rios gave him a false name, that of another officer, wore his colleague's police badge when he visited and pretended to be a single man.

Rios hoped to keep the relationship secret but Valencia told several of his acquaintances and his mother, Linda, whom he was very close to. He also had a threesome with Rios and another man, and this man would later identify the married police officer in court. Valencia wanted Steven Rios to have the courage of his convictions, to be open about his sexuality, and may have suggested that he was going to go public about their affair. Certainly, the court system would give this as Rios' motive for the carnage which happened next...

Slain on campus

At 2 p.m. on 5 June 2004, Jesse Valencia was found dead in a back garden close to his East Campus apartment. His throat had been cut and he had bled to death. The police were surprised when, later that same day, Steven Rios arrived at the crime scene, despite the fact that he wasn't on duty, and said that he had arrested Jesse Valencia six weeks previously. He obviously kept quiet about the fact that he had visited Valencia's apartment late at night, and during his work shifts, on at least six subsequent occasions for sex. A colleague, who knew Rios well, helped him secure the crime scene and could see that he was upset and distant, not his usual self.

Police began making enquiries and soon found out that Valencia had been having an affair with a young policeman. Steven Rios then contacted his superiors and said that he wasn't the cop in question but that he suspected it might be one of two other officers. In a particularly callous move, he went as far as to give their names. But, when police spoke to Valencia's best friend, they learned about the third man that had joined them in bed, a man called Andy, who was able to confirm that Steven Rios was the gay officer in question.

Valencia's friends also said that he had been planning to confront Rios about the fact that he suspected he was married and to ask him to tell his wife the truth.

Meanwhile, a television channel had become aware of the identity of Valencia's secret lover and they broadcast a photograph of Steven Rios. When he saw it, he threatened suicide and had to be taken into protective custody. Shortly afterwards he escaped and climbed to the top storey of a five-storey building, where he stood, close to the edge, for 2 hours, holding a photograph of his wife and infant son, until trained negotiators talked him down.

On 16 June, the junior officer officially resigned from the force and shortly afterwards DNA discovered under the victim's fingernails was found to match his own. He was charged with first-degree murder but the authorities were so worried about his continuing suicide risk that he was held in a mental hospital rather than in jail.

The trial began on 17 May 2005. The jury heard that the victim had been brought to the ground, probably by a choke hold, which would have rendered him unconscious in as little as three seconds. The bruises on his neck testified to this. Rios had been taught such a choke hold at the police academy as part of his training on the force. The victim's throat had then been cut so deeply with a knife that it left marks in his spine.

Steven Rios took the stand in his own defence and denied that he'd ever owned a knife, but several officers testified that they had seen him with one and that he had it on a clip in his pocket. Both the clip and knife had subsequently disappeared. He admitted the affair but said that it had been an aberration and that, when the media had outed him, he had asked his wife Libby if they could go to counselling together.

He said that Jesse Valencia was promiscuous and could have been killed by a previous lover and that he himself had been at a party many miles away when the homicide took place. He added that the fact that three of his chest hairs were found on the dead man's body meant nothing as Valencia didn't shower often and they were the result of an earlier intimate act. But Valencia's friends disputed this, saying that he was very hygienic and would even have his nails manicured. He had been an exceptionally beautiful and well-groomed man.

Valencia's friend, Joan Sheridan, told of Jesse's desire to make Steven Rios tell the truth about his sexual predilections, even hinting that he might go to Rios's wife and boss to expose him. She said that Jesse was proud of his sexuality and had hated the junior officer's hypocrisy.

Four days later, the jury went out and, after a day of deliberation, returned with a guilty verdict. Steven Rios, still protesting his innocence, was sentenced to life without parole. His wife and his father said afterwards that they believed in his innocence and that he had their unfailing support.

In April 2007, his conviction was overturned as Joan Sheridan's testimony was now deemed to be hearsay and therefore inadmissible. A jubilant Rios was granted a new trial. But in December 2008, the police officer was again convicted unanimously of the murder of Jesse Valencia and again sentenced to life, though this time with the possibility of parole. Looking much older than his 31 years, he wept copiously.

Afterwards, the prosecution said that Rios had a history of arresting women and then making passes at them (just like highway patrolman Craig Peyer) and that three of these women had been prepared to testify against him. He had also been fired when working for a previous police force, as he had rented storage space in another officer's name.

Steven Rios is currently incarcerated in Sioux Falls, a South Dakota prison, but will be eligible for parole after serving 30 years. His wife divorced him and remarried but still maintains that he is innocent. His supporters believe that he was guilty of having sex when he should have been at work (and guilty of committing adultery) but that someone else killed Jesse Valencia.

25

THE MONK
MYKHAYLO KOFEL

Subjected to a joyless existence in a foreign land, this young man finally snapped and killed one of his oppressors.

Overkill

Sister Michelle Lewis lay, almost naked, in the centre of her bedroom at Florida's Holy Cross Academy, her legs spread apart and her body almost drained of blood. She had been stabbed a colossal 92 times. Her office had been broken into and ransacked and there were blood smears on the entrance door. Noticing a bloody palm print on her forearm and another on her leg, detectives were confident that they would soon find out who had committed the brutal crime.

The religious teacher had lived as a nun but couldn't actually become one as she was a divorcee. She had become resident at the religious campus ten years before and was working as financial administrator at Holy Cross at the time of her murder. But the 12-hour days in the oppressive heat, clad in heavy monastic garments, had taken their toll and she was sometimes short-tempered and tired. She only remained working in this challenging environment as she believed that she was serving God.

On Sunday 25 March 2001, she didn't show up for the liturgy and one of the monastic brothers investigated and found her corpse spreadeagled on the floor. He raced back to alert the brethren and one of them phoned the emergency services.

Whilst they were doing so, another monk, Mykhaylo Kofel, known as Misha, walked past and asked what had happened. The 18-year-old was still wearing his white altar gown. At this stage, no one suspected the young apprentice monk, an academically gifted student who had arrived from the Ukraine on 1 August 1996, more than four years before.

Paramedics examined the 39-year-old sister, finding that she had been battered about the head with a blunt instrument and stabbed repeatedly with a knife. There were self-defence wounds on her hands and one of her thumbs had almost been severed as she fought for her life.

Miami-Dade detectives began to interview everyone who lived on campus and were told by one of the Fathers that he had taken two of the trainee monks out to shop for groceries on the previous afternoon. He had given his set of master keys to one of the boys, Mykhaylo Kofel, so that the teenager could put the groceries away, and had noticed that a key was missing when he got the bunch back.

An isolated childhood

Born on 2 July 1982, Mykhaylo had been a shy 14-year-old boy living with his parents in an impoverished part of the Ukraine when he was recruited for the priesthood by Father Gregory Wendt. The Father had told the boy's parents that he would take the small, sickly teenager – and another teenage boy – back to Miami in the USA and train them in monastic ways. He refused to take two other religious village boys who were in their twenties, explaining that they were too old.

Mr Kofel, a train driver, was struggling to support his family and his wife's parents on his income, so he welcomed the prospect of one less mouth to feed, and Mrs Kofel was a devout Catholic, so both saw merit in letting their youngest son emigrate to America and train to become a monk.

Mykhaylo's life had always been uncertain, as he'd been beaten by both of his parents and had often seen his father beat his mother, but now he suffered a profound culture shock as he left his modest village and moved to the sprawling Florida campus. He spoke only a few words of English so he and three fellow Ukrainian trainees initially communicated with Father Wendt via an interpreter. They were introduced to Sister Michelle, who would be their surrogate mother from now on.

From the onset, the teenagers were subjected to a demanding regime whereby they rose at 6 a.m. and retired at 10 p.m., the hours in between devoted to prayer, study and athletics. Every moment was accounted for and they could not even take a shower outside the allowed showering time without asking for Father Wendt's permission. If he gave them consent to vacate their quarters for an hour, they had to kiss his hand. They were told to leave their letters to their parents unsealed so that the Father could inspect them before putting them in the post. Mykhaylo hated the regime but had learned English quickly, so he was able to communicate with detectives when they quizzed him about Sister Michelle's violent death.

Interview

Mykhaylo was interviewed by detectives within his room at Holy Cross and they immediately noticed that his hands were shaking and had sticking plasters on them. When these were removed, they revealed cuts which were still oozing blood: he said that he had broken a glass two days previously. He made no attempt to explain an equally fresh-looking scratch on one cheek. Convinced that these were recent injuries, and perturbed by his nervous manner, detectives asked him to accompany them down to the station.

The trainee monk was read his Miranda rights and signed a form consenting to have his fingerprints taken. He said that he was confident they would not be found inside the convent as he had never been there. A thorough examination of his body showed other cuts and bruises and these were duly photographed and documented by the police. One of the detectives told Kofel that he believed that he had committed the murder, and the young monk haltingly began to confess.

He said that he had been sexually abused by his alcoholic father on several occasions, that the older man had touched him inappropriately while very drunk. Because of their impoverished living quarters, he had shared a bed with his parents, sleeping in between them, and when his father was inebriated he often reached for his wife but ended up fondling his son's genitals by mistake. Mykhaylo had come to America hoping to escape this abuse but had, he alleged, been sexually abused at Holy Cross by two of the abbots, namely Father Damien Gibault and Father Gregory Wendt. He said that the former was abusing him approximately twice a month by playing with his sexual organs and that the latter had touched him inappropriately on three occasions through his clothes.

Detectives asked if Sister Michelle had sexually abused him and he said that she hadn't but that she had verbally insulted him, calling him 'Ukrainian trash' and 'freak'. He said that she had also verbally abused the other Ukrainian monks as she didn't want them there.

On the night of the murder, he continued, he had drunk a bottle of wine, stolen from behind the altar, and used the key that he had taken earlier to enter the nun's apartment. He carried a steak knife and a poker with him and his intention was to hurt her as she had humiliated him. She'd woken up, jumped out of bed wearing only a short jumper, screamed at him to get out and scratched his face. He had hit her repeatedly with the poker in an effort to get her to shut up, he said, and had stabbed her again and again with the five-inch-bladed knife. He had no memory of shredding her jumper, but remembered touching her breasts during the struggle whilst he lay on top of her.

Afterwards, he realised that he had lost the key to her room so he broke into her office in the hope of finding a duplicate key that he could put back on the master key ring. At about 5 a.m. he had returned to his room, showered and gone to bed but had been too upset to sleep. He had also been kept awake by the throbbing pain in his hands, caused by the cuts made by the knife.

Kofel was charged with murder and taken to the psychiatric unit of the county jail, where he was put under suicide watch. He elected not to attend the hearing a fortnight after the murder and was held without bail.

Autopsy

Meanwhile, the pathologist's report on Sister Michelle made for sombre reading. The 39-year-old had had her skull broken by repeated blows from a poker-like instrument and her right hand, left wrist and nose had also been broken during the prolonged fight to the death. The knife had pierced her lungs, heart and liver and had done massive damage to her chest and abdomen. She had also been jumped on six times and the bloody pattern matched the soles of Kofel's shoes.

Detectives believed the trainee monk's allegations of abuse as he spoke with sincerity and made good eye contact. They got in touch with the Sexual Crimes Bureau and an investigation was soon under way.

When questioned, the other trainee monks said that they had never been sexually abused by either of the Fathers and most of them said that they hadn't been verbally abused by Sister Michelle. But one female Holy Cross student stated that Sister Michelle did mock and humiliate the Ukrainian boys when they didn't understand certain English phrases. She had seen how hurt and dejected Kofel was by this mockery.

The young man was also enraged because he wanted to live the normal life of a teenager but wasn't allowed to play sports, to go on class outings or even to socialise with his classmates. Father Wendt had made it clear to the other Holy Cross students that they must not speak to the trainee monks, that they were there to serve God rather than to make friends. Father Wendt had also, Kofel said, reneged on a promise that he could go back to the Ukraine to visit his parents, and he couldn't travel as the Father had his passport. The repeated sexual abuse, he explained, had caused him to lose his faith.

Closing ranks

Father Wendt and Father Gibault had said, through their lawyers, that – given that they were being suspected of sexual abuse – they were unwilling to testify at Mykhaylo Kofel's trial unless they were granted immunity. Police were enraged, believing that they were thwarting a full enquiry.

Background research had found that the defendant had self-harmed in the month before Sister Michelle's murder, cutting his chest with a knife in an attempt to distract his mind from his increasing depression. The defence psychiatrist had found that Kofel was insecure, afraid, socially isolated and passive. He had a dependent personality and allowed others to take advantage of him. Kofel had admitted being afraid of Father Wendt and had passed a polygraph test in which he was questioned about the allegations of sexual abuse.

Further investigation revealed that monks in America were usually recruited after they had finished their education and were aged 20 or more, and that recruiting 14-year-old boys was highly unusual. Also unusual was the fact that the Ukrainian teenagers' parents had received money from Holy Cross for allowing them to go and live on the Florida campus. Father Gregory Wendt had legally adopted another teenager, who regularly shared his bedroom, and Father Damien Gibault had attempted to adopt Mykhaylo Kofel but his parents had refused to sign the forms.

After a few months, the Sex Crimes Bureau shut down their investigation into the alleged abuse of Mykhaylo Kofel, explaining that they could not corroborate the young monk's story, that churches invariably closed ranks when allegations of sexual impropriety were raised.

The prosecutor went to the Ukraine to talk to Kofel's parents, who said that their son had visited their home with Father Damien Gibault and that the two had shared a bed. Another monk candidate, who had returned to the Ukraine at age 16, said that Kofel had had a key to Father Gibault's apartment and that he often heard the boy leaving the Father's rooms late at night. Afterwards, Mykhaylo would seem depressed and would talk about the fact that he liked girls but was banned from talking to them by his religious superiors.

Petro Terenta, who had arrived from the Ukraine at the same time as Kofel, admitted during Kofel's trial that he had shared a bedroom – and, on at least one occasion, a bed – with Father Gibault, his adoptive parent, and had travelled with him on holiday to Naples on two occasions. On such holidays, he said, Father Wendt and Mykhaylo Kofel would also share a room. Kofel had also visited Belgium and Holland with Wendt, staying in five-star hotels rather than in nearby monasteries.

On 26 November 2002, Father Wendt was ordered to attend a meeting at the public defender's office, where he met with Kofel's attorney but he refused to answer question after question, based on his constitutional rights. He answered fewer than a fifth of the queries put to him. Five more sessions followed, the last in August 2004. At the end of that month, Holy Cross Academy permanently closed.

It was February 2005, almost four years after the murder, before Mykhaylo Kofel – who had by now westernised his Christian name to Mike – had his day in court, where he pleaded guilty to the second-degree murder of Michelle Lewis. The victim's mother addressed Kofel and said that her daughter was now with the angels in heaven, and asked the court to lock Kofel up with the crime scene photos. The judge respectfully declined.

Kofel apologised for his actions and was sentenced to 30 years, a sentence that he is currently serving in Okeechobee Correctional Institution in Florida. With good behaviour, he could be free by 2026, whereupon he will be immediately deported to the Ukraine.

26

THE TRAINEE VET
STEVEN HARPER

Though he was so bright that he could have forged a brilliant career, this young man attempted to kill his girlfriend after she left him, and he succeeded in killing two of her relatives.

Mass illness

Sunday 10 September 1978 started as a normal day for 24-year-old Duane Johnson, his wife Sandy and their two-year-old daughter Sherrie. The father and daughter ate breakfast but complained that the milk tasted strange so Sandy poured it down the sink. Duane, a truck driver, painted the outside of the family's Omaha three-bedroom house whilst Sandy took little Sherrie to the shops for groceries, but the child vomited so Sandy cut short the trip and brought her home.

Later, Sandy's sister Sallie and her husband Bruce Shelton visited, bringing their 11-month baby, Chad, with them. They drank some home-made lemonade from the fridge and Duane, thirsty from painting outside in the sun, had two glasses. The Sheltons went on to a restaurant but soon felt unwell and went home. Meanwhile Duane had begun to slur his words, developed an appalling headache and took to his bed.

The next few days were horrendous for the Johnsons and the Sheltons, as several members became so unwell that they were admitted to hospital and taken to intensive care.

Little Chad Shelton was the first to die. The baby boy cried constantly and was clearly in great pain before he slipped into an irreversible coma and died on 14 September, three days before his first birthday. An autopsy showed that his liver had almost been eaten away and he had blood on his brain and in his stomach. His parents were sick but survived.

Baffled medics continued to treat his uncle Duane, who was in agony with blood dripping from his eyes and pouring out of his nose and mouth. They could see that he was bleeding to death internally and contacted the authorities, who sent investigators from the health department to the house to try to find a cause. The strong and healthy truck driver put up a remarkable fight but his organs bled out and he died the morning after Chad. His little daughter Sherrie eventually pulled through but was left with permanent liver damage.

Sallie and Bruce Shelton had permanent liver damage and suffered ongoing headaches and nausea. They mourned the loss of their baby son, Chad, and wondered if anything in their home had been the cause of death.

A mysterious toxin

An autopsy on both bodies suggested that a chemical toxin had been involved, and each of the victims had drunk milk or lemonade at the Johnson's house, so detectives looked at potential enemies of the family. Their enquiries soon centred on Sandy's ex-boyfriend, Steven Roy Harper. She had been his first girlfriend and he had been devastated when she refused to wait for him to finish his studies and, instead, married Duane. (She had had an early failed first marriage to her childhood sweetheart, so, despite being only 22, Duane was her second spouse.)

Steven, it transpired, was shortly going to start his degree in veterinary medicine at a prestigious Omaha university. But, in the previous months, he'd been working as a research technologist, conducting experiments on rats.

Detectives went to his home and spoke to his father, who explained that he was out of town. They found five empty rat cages in the garage and laboratory notes detailing how the rats had responded to certain chemicals and how and when they had died, so it was clear that he had been experimenting on the rodents in his own time. His workplace admitted that several cages had gone missing whilst he was working there and that his job had included assisting in biochemical experiments on rats and doing autopsies.

In the kitchen, they found containers of sulphur potassium nitrate and potassium chloride as well as other chemicals which could cause a sizeable explosion. And they found satanic literature and magazines in which Harper had scrawled Sandy's initials over demonic female images.

Further enquiries revealed that his mother had brought a Doberman puppy and the family cat to the vet as they were convulsing and obviously in great pain. Both had died despite the vet's efforts and had apparently been poisoned, though the deeply distressed Mrs Harper had no idea how this could have occurred. They had suffered from unstoppable internal bleeding, one of the main symptoms that had beset Chad and Duane, symptoms that the police now believed had been caused by Steven Harper, who had studied biology at university.

A tragic accident

So why had the academically bright young man become so disturbed? The answer lay in his childhood. At age nine, he and some other boys had been setting fire to snakes when he accidentally set himself alight, badly burning over half of his body. He had spent months in hospital in agony and endured 13 operations, was left badly scarred and didn't have the confidence to approach girls. Instead, he had devoted his life to Christian worship and to academia.

But Sandy, whom he'd known at school, had tracked him down when her first marriage broke up and they'd started dating. He was 20 and had never been out with a girl before. She had taken his virginity and he had fallen hard for her. In fact, he was looking forward to marrying her after he graduated. Unfortunately, Sandy wanted to remarry quickly and start a family, so they had split up and she'd wed Duane.

As detectives dug deeper, they found that Harper had attempted to murder Duane in the past. He had become clinically depressed after finishing his pre-veterinary degree and, on 20 June 1975, had an argument with his father in which he threatened to kill the older man. Still enraged, he drove off with his shotgun after threatening suicide and parked on the hill which overlooked the house which Sandy and Duane shared.

The couple returned shortly after 1 a.m., bringing Sallie and her then-boyfriend Bruce, and Sandy's brother Dan and his girlfriend with them. Harper shot at Duane but missed. The terrified man sped off into the darkness and Harper pointed the gun at Sandy and asked 'Where did he go?' Dan shouted at him to leave his sister alone, and Steven Harper promptly shot him in the shoulder. He collapsed, screaming for help, on the lawn.

Sandy's mother popped her head out of a window to ask what was happening (Sandy lived across the road from her) and was shot in the face. Meanwhile Dan got to his feet and was shot a second time, after which Harper sped off.

He abandoned his truck within the hour (it was found with a rifle and a 12-inch hunting knife under the seat) but evaded capture for the next year, taking a coach to Oklahoma, where he lived with an uncle. He consulted a psychiatrist at this time, admitting that he wasn't over his first girlfriend, and she administered the Minnesota Multiphasic Personality Inventory. The results showed that Harper was schizophrenic but he didn't return to the psychiatrist's office to hear the results as he couldn't afford the fees.

Prison time

Almost a year after the shooting he was stopped for a traffic violation on his motorbike and a computer check revealed that there was an arrest warrant out for him. He pleaded no contest and wrote a letter to the court expressing deep remorse for what he had done. He was sent to a Nebraska jail for one to five years, where he spent most of his time talking to his pastor and reading the Bible.

By July 1977 the model prisoner was on work release, and he was paroled four months later. Detectives found that he had gone to Omaha in September as his brother Michael had crashed his motorcycle and needed someone to pick up an accident claims form from the local police HQ. This put him in town at the time of the mass poisoning, and was the final piece of evidence that detectives needed to issue an arrest warrant for the 25-year-old. He was arrested the following day by the FBI in Texas, where he had taken a construction job.

Awaiting trial, Harper brooded over the recent past. He had stolen a bottle of a little-known carcinogen (a cancer-causing agent) from the lab when he was working with the rats and had tried it out on the family cat, which died in agony. Unfortunately, his brother's Doberman had drunk from the same bowl and had also died a horrible death. He had realised then that it would take very little to kill Sandy and Duane. His plan, or so he told a friend, had been to give them a small dose of the toxin so that they would develop cancer years later and the cause would not be traced back to him. It was a horrible way to treat someone who hadn't meant him any harm and had just wanted to move on with her life.

Harper had handed in his notice at the laboratory and, for several weeks, kept surveillance on the Johnson residence, noticing that they went out almost every Saturday night, leaving the house empty. When they next did so, he had sneaked into their house via a side window and put the killer toxin in a pitcher of home-made lemonade and a milk carton which he found in the fridge. He had left by the same window as he arrived, disappearing into the night.

Suicide attempt

By the following month, as he awaited trial, he decided that he no longer wanted to live and broke a window, managing to cut his wrists and write the name Sandy in blood on his cell wall. He was taken to hospital and patched up, then returned to jail.

Detectives interviewed him but he stalled at first, saying that he couldn't remember his movements at the time of the mass poisoning then stating that his attorney had told him to keep quiet. But eventually he blurted out 'I did it', explaining that he had been experimenting at work with cancer-causing chemicals and had stolen a vial of the toxic liquid and used it to adulterate the Johnsons' drinks.

Ironically, Harper wasn't sure which of several toxins he had stolen from the lab: he thought that it was DMBA but investigators determined that it was most likely DMN, or dimethylnitrosamine, which was used as a solvent in the rubber industry but also given to animals by researchers to induce cancer. It was a sweet-tasting concoction which was metabolised by the body within 48 hours, killing but leaving no chemical trace. DMN had previously been used as a means of murder in Germany, when a science teacher used it to kill his wife. She had told hospital staff that she suspected her husband was trying to poison her, and investigators had found DMN in the marmalade. Her husband confessed that he had planned to kill her – and, within hours of him making this statement to police, she had died of liver damage brought on by the corrosive chemical.

Steven Harper's trial began in mid September 1978 in Omaha, though, days before, he had again attempted suicide by taking a razor to his wrists. He was briefly hospitalised before being returned to jail on antipsychotic drugs.

In court, the prosecution alleged that Steven Harper, by adulterating the Johnsons' drinks, had caused the deaths of Chad Shelton and Duane Johnson and caused severe ongoing health problems for Sherrie Johnson, and Bruce and Sallie Shelton. An ex-fellow prisoner, whom Harper had remained friends with after they were paroled, took the stand and admitted that Harper had told him of his murderous plans.

The defence countered that the adult victim, Duane, had worked as a truck driver and sometimes had loads which included chemicals such as anhydrous ammonia. He had also been painting the house on the day that he became unwell and might have used turpentine. They also cast doubt on the fact that the Sheltons had been subjected to DMA, wondering if, instead, they had suffered acute food poisoning after eating tacos at a restaurant.

The following day, the jury reached their verdict, finding Steven Harper guilty. A month later he was sentenced to die in the electric chair and transferred to death row at the Nebraska State Penitentiary in Lincoln.

Steven's nominal date with death was 15 February 1980, but, as is usually the case with death row prisoners, he embarked on a lengthy appeals process. He was expected to die in time of natural causes as Nebraska hadn't executed a prisoner since 1959.

Harper remained deeply religious, reading zealously from his three Bibles and writing to religious authority figures. His favourite possession was a book of hymns. He remained troubled and depressed and rarely socialised with other prisoners, spending hour after hour in his cell and often talking to imagined demons. More than ten years passed in this way.

But, by the winter of 1990, the troubled double-killer had had enough and began to hide his antipsychotic medication under his tongue and stash it away in his cell. On 6 December 1990, he had amassed enough for an overdose and, after writing a farewell note to his parents, he killed himself.

27

THE LAY MINISTER
JEFFREY LUNDGREN

Though he believed that he was a prophet, this preacher killed an innocent family of five and was prepared to kill more.

A difficult childhood

Jeffrey Don Lundgren was born on 3 May 1950 in Independence, Missouri and raised in the Reorganized Church of Jesus Christ of Latter Day Saints (RLDS), a breakaway sect of the Mormon church. His father Don, a construction worker, had a steely gaze which frightened other adults and he was very strict with Jeffrey and his brother. Jeffrey would later say that he was physically abused. He also had difficulties with his mother, Lois, who he perceived as being distant and cold. As a child, he turned to the scriptures as a means of understanding his place in life and could soon recite large sections of the Book of Mormon. At school, though he craved love and acceptance, he was seen as arrogant and odd. Increasingly ostracised, he took his ire out on wild animals, which he tortured and killed.

When he was studying engineering at university, he met a religious young woman called Alice Keehler, who had also had a difficult childhood after her father developed multiple sclerosis and became depressed and violent. She and Jeffrey began dating and, from the start, he told her what to wear for their dates and insisted on taking her from one class to the next, becoming angry when she talked to other boys. But she had little life experience and perceived his stalking behaviour as devotion and love. When he got her pregnant, he dropped out of university and they married in early 1970. His parents disapproved of the relationship so he didn't tell them about the wedding ceremony.

Over the next ten years, the couple went on to have four children (three sons and a daughter) and remained active in the RLDS faith. Unfortunately, Jeffrey couldn't hold down a job as he was lazy and irresponsible. He also had an eye for other women – he was let go from one of his hospital jobs for fondling the breasts of a female co-worker – and the marriage became increasingly strained. After the birth of their third child, he began to hit Alice and once knocked her down the stairs, rupturing her spleen. She would later say that his favourite sexual kick was to smear his faeces over her and that her distaste at this led to most of their fights. Jeffrey Lundgren would deny that he had this rare sexual fetish but it's on record that he cut the pipes leading from the toilet so that faeces piled up in the basement of his rented house.

In 1980, he was working at a hospital as a maintenance man when two television sets went missing. They were traced to his home and he claimed that he planned to repair them. He was let go from this job and from several other jobs.

He became a mass of contradictions for, though he shunned stimulants like coffee, he developed a taste for cola and vodka. And though his religious library was vast, he also amassed hardcore sadomasochistic pornography. Most religions teach that sex is only for the purposes of procreation yet, when the couple left their rented house, the landlord found a dildo coated in faeces which had clearly been used for anal penetration. However, he remained devout and loved to have religious discussions deep into the night. An advocate of 'spare the rod and spoil the child', he beat his oldest son Damon mercilessly and the little boy was terrified.

Breakaway

Lundgren spent a few months in jail in 1981 for writing bad cheques, after which he got a well-paying job in Independence as a biomedical technician. For the first time in years the couple cleared their debts and enjoyed a more luxurious lifestyle and, after he repaid his creditors, his record was expunged.

The local RLDS church invited him to join the lay priesthood and gave him a small house attached to the church. He began to preach to his peers but wanted additional power so set up a breakaway group and held biblical study groups in his home. In 1984 he told his flock that God had told him to move to Kirtland, Ohio and that they should call him Father. He set up a commune there that August, attracting his religious friends from university. Over time, they were joined by a couple of other lost individuals who believed Lundgren's claims that he was receiving visions and had a direct line to heaven.

One of his belief systems was that there would be a huge earthquake on 3 May 1988 (his thirty-eighth birthday) and that only the faithful would survive. He was also convinced that infidels might try to steal the group's worldly goods so they should arm themselves and prepare for civil war. To this end, he began to stockpile guns and ammunition and warned his flock that they might have to shoot to kill. Lundgren himself was an excellent shot as he had often gone hunting with his father when he was a child.

In April 1987, the Avery family – a married couple with three daughters – joined Lundgren's faith group, which now numbered around a dozen disciples. Despite her gender, Cheryl Avery was opposed to the ordination of women priests and she believed that those who approved of this were being led astray by Satan. She loved Jeffrey Lundgren's fundamentalist religious views and soon began to quote him chapter and verse.

Unfortunately, her devotion wasn't reciprocated as Lundgren thought that the Avery family were frumpy and old-fashioned and found them very dull and mousy. They weren't well liked by other church members so relied increasingly for companionship on the Lundgrens, whom they saw as their closest friends. Cheryl cooked them indigestible pies, which they hated, and her husband Dennis questioned Lundgren's teachings at Bible class, something he hated even more. Lundgren also disliked the couple's three daughters, as he said that he sensed they each had a rebellious streak.

Cheryl and Dennis Avery had always been deeply religious (they had met at a religious retreat when she was 22 and he was 29 and it had been the first time either of them had dated) but now she became fanatical, whereas her husband became virtually passive, telling everyone that the Lord would provide.

The Averys had never had much cash but, when they came into some money, Lundgren hoped that he would be first in line for a donation, so was angered when the couple used the money to pay off their mortgage. He had been talking to his followers a great deal about blood atonement and now told them that the Avery family was wicked and that they would have to die. He began to bring home war movies and preached about taking over the local temple by using force. He often toyed with a gun as he made these sermons and increasingly ruled by turning his followers against each other and by creating fear. But he seems to have lost his nerve when it came to storming the temple, perhaps because he knew that the police had become aware of the rumours and were staking the place out.

He was excommunicated by the church after threatening to kill other members and told his disciples that it was a sign from God and that it was time to head off into the wilderness. He also said that they had to kill the Avery family before they left.

Incredibly, his disciples unquestioningly did his bidding by digging a mass grave in the barn and bringing in bags of lime in readiness to sprinkle over the bodies. Meanwhile, Lundgren booked the Averys into a nearby hotel and persuaded Cheryl to write a letter to her mother saying that they wouldn't be in touch for a while.

Lundgren's understanding of the Old Testament led him to believe that evil men should be beheaded and that wicked women should be stripped naked and disembowelled and children swung against the wall by their feet until their skulls caved in. But these methods of execution sounded too grisly even for him and he opted for buying a stun gun to subdue the victims and using a pistol to send them to the afterlife.

On 10 April 1989, everyone sat down to a last supper with Dennis, Cheryl and their three innocent children, the youngest of whom adored Alice Lundgren. Immediately after dessert, Alice took her three youngest offspring to a garden centre to buy picnic tables. She knew what was about to happen to the Averys and had arranged to phone her husband later to see if it was safe to come back. The Avery family, busy clearing the table and doing the dishes, now had moments left to live.

As he relaxed after the meal, Dennis Avery was asked to help sort out some camping equipment but when he entered the barn to do so he was assaulted with a stun gun wielded by one of Lundgren's lieutenants. The stun gun didn't work properly and he didn't lose consciousness as expected, so several of the men present (there were five of them at the scene) jumped on him and pulled him to the ground. Dennis began to scream and plead for mercy as they forced him into the makeshift grave where Jeffrey Lundgren shot him twice, one bullet piercing his heart. A lookout ran a chainsaw just before and during the murder so that the shots wouldn't alert the rest of the Avery clan.

Damon, Lundgren's 18-year-old schoolboy son, began to cry hysterically and was ill with shock, backing away from the pit which held the bloodstained man. He had known what was supposed to happen but now it wasn't just macho talk about blood atonement from his fundamentalist father – it was a real-life homicide.

Next, one of the men brought Cheryl Avery into the barn on a similar pretext, grabbed and blindfolded her, taped her wrists and feet and put her next to her husband in the pit, where Jeffrey Lundgren shot her through the back of the head. The coroner would later state that she had probably taken 5 minutes to die.

The men then told Trina, aged 15, that her parents wanted to talk to her, so she put down her book and wandered over to the barn where she was shot twice in the head by the lay preacher. Becky, 13, was next to be taken and shot, one bullet entering her chest and another her thigh. Though she lapsed into unconsciousness, she didn't immediately die.

The youngest child, Karen, aged seven, was the last to be taken to the outbuilding, where she was taped and blindfolded before being shot in the head. Her death was relatively swift.

Afterwards the men spread lime on the bodies and filled in the grave with rocks and soil before covering the area with old suitcases and assorted paraphernalia. Alice phoned, was told to come home, and joined her husband and Damon on a trip to the Averys' hotel room, where they took the family's possessions to make it look as if they had left of their own accord. Most of the disciples were in tears when they got back, but Lundgren seemed convinced that he had followed God's orders and he told 18-year-old Damon that he was now a man.

Ironically, police officers and the FBI arrived at the Lundgrens' farmhouse the next day as they had received reports that weapons were being kept there illegally. But Lundgren showed them his legal rifles and, after 2 hours of talking and searching, they reluctantly left.

Convinced that they must have bugged the place, Jeffrey Lundgren demanded that the cult talk in whispers. The following morning, they fled south-east, deliberately replicating the direction of a particular exodus recorded in the Book of Mormon.

A new start

The group now relocated to Davis, West Virginia, and set up camp in the Canaan Valley (so called after the biblical promised land), where Lundgren resumed his teachings. They had brought generators and refrigerators so, although they were living in the wilderness, they didn't have an entirely primitive way of life.

Within a month of the murders, Jeffrey Lundgren decided to take a second wife from the group and was indifferent to the fact that she was already married. She would later say that she acquiesced to sleeping with him in his tent as she didn't want her daughter to come to any harm. Her legal husband echoed this viewpoint and read the scriptures in his tent whilst his wife had sex with the self-styled prophet in an adjoining one.

It's been said that absolute power corrupts absolutely, and Jeffrey Lundgren's behaviour increasingly bore this out. He determined that, on numerous occasions, one of the women (he chose which one each time) would enter his tent and hand him her panties. She would then strip and dance erotically to music for an hour whilst he and Alice watched from their makeshift bed. He would masturbate into the panties whilst watching the dance, explaining to the followers that by shedding his semen he was echoing Christ shedding his blood.

When some of the women protested, Alice Lundgren threatened to beat them. Unsurprisingly, the men were equally unhappy with the situation and several of them now fled the group and went to live with friends. Alice began to hit Jeffrey and scream profanities at him as she was enraged to find him bedding one of the younger women and making romantic gestures towards her, such as sipping from the same cup. Jeffrey was seen to run from Alice's tent with blood dripping from his wounds.

With his orderly world crashing down around him, he told his few remaining followers that the group had to disband for a time whilst he regrouped. They had given up their careers, homes, friends and sometimes even their spouses for him and now watched in amazement as he and Alice drove off into the sunset with their children, with Alice unaware that Jeffrey planned to meet his mistress again as soon as possible.

Realising that the disciples were now solo agents, local police spoke to several of them and realised that the Averys had not remained part of the group. Further enquiries showed that no one had seen them since April of the previous year…

On 4 January 1990, investigators went to the barn, were appalled at the awful stench and dug down to find the decomposing bodies. Word reached the media and photographers were swiftly dispatched to the murder scene. Jeffrey and Alice were lying on the bed in their hotel room when they suddenly saw their former farmhouse on the TV.

Arrest and trial

The Lundgrens were arrested at the hotel and their followers quickly joined them in custody. Alice is reported to have said that she was going to plead 'battered wife syndrome' and that she would get off scot-free. She had not been present at the time of the murders, but she had been sitting next to Jeffrey when the murders were discussed and had suggested they find out if 13-year-old Becky was menstruating yet, as this would determine whether she should be killed as a child (by battering her against the wall) or by being disembowelled, the fate of a supposedly evil woman.

Various cult members took the stand at Alice Lundgren's trial and testified that she had threatened them and that she had coached them how to dance in a carnal fashion for her husband. They said that the couple had enjoyed seafood dinners whilst the rest of the cult ate basic food, and that, as Lundgren's wife, Alice had enjoyed many privileges and had never seemed afraid. She had been the one to suggest to the rest of the cult that he was a prophet who was obeying God's commands.

At his trial, which began in June 1990, Jeffrey Lundgren admitted responsibility for the murders but argued that Dennis Avery was a false prophet so had to be killed, and that his family (women and children being subservient to men in biblical texts) had to die with him. The defence's psychologist said that Lundgren truly believed his religious visions, that he wasn't a con man as such, though he had obviously deceived himself. He had been emotionally abused as a child and had felt inferior, but religion had given him a way to relate to his peers. In time, as those around him became increasingly impressed by his vast knowledge of the scriptures, he had become narcissistic and had retreated into a fantasy world.

Lundgren took the stand in his own defence, spoke for a full day and assured the jury that 'It's not a figment of my imagination that I can talk to God, that I can hear his voice'. They weren't convinced and, after a few hours' deliberation, found him culpable. He was later sentenced to death on five counts. Alice Lundgren received a life sentence, as did several of the other cult members. One of the men and three of the women received lesser sentences and were paroled in December 2010.

Many jurors felt pity for Damon Lundgren, who had been subjected to his parents' religious views all his life and had been beaten whenever he dissented. The teenager had been genuinely distressed at Dennis Avery's death.

Damon wept on the stand and begged the court not to execute him, saying that he had been in thrall to his father for his entire life but that he now believed he could make a contribution to society. Still only 19 years old, he was sentenced to life imprisonment. Incensed, his father wrote to him and said that it didn't matter what the jurors thought, that he should concentrate on getting right with God.

The Lundgrens divorced in 1991 but in 1994 he remarried, this time to Kathryn Johnson, another cult member whom he'd previously had a daughter with. She had served a short sentence for knowing about the murders and not alerting the authorities. The couple married in a short prison ceremony (which didn't include a conjugal visit) and afterwards 41-year-old Kathryn said, 'Jeff and I have a positive, beautiful relationship that is not dependent on where he is.'

In jail, the new bridegroom's weight soared to almost 20 stone and, like many overeaters, he became diabetic. (Alice Lundgren, in contrast, lost a massive ten stone and became almost waiflike.) He remained deeply religious, though he eventually told a prison officer that he might have misinterpreted the scriptures.

The end is nigh

For a man who believed that he had a direct link to God and had always done his bidding, Jeffrey Lundgren became surprisingly nervous as his execution date approached. Indeed, he did all that he could to stop it, claiming that his morbid obesity would make his death by lethal injection a cruel and unusual punishment, that he would feel more pain than a slimmer man. But the US Supreme Court refused a last-minute request to stop his execution and, on the morning of 24 October 2006, after a final breakfast of cereal, pancakes, milk and fruit juice he was led into the death chamber. He had wept beforehand and phoned his wife and one of his adult children to say that he loved them. He also phoned his lawyer several times.

He made a final speech saying, 'I profess my love for God, my family, for my children, for Kathy.' Cheryl Avery's brother (who had lost his sister, brother-in-law and three nieces at Jeffrey Lundgren's hands) watched as the lay preacher was injected with the deadly chemicals.

28

THE CLASSICS STUDENT
JOHN TANNER

To most onlookers, John Tanner was a mild-mannered undergraduate, reading the Classics at Nottingham University and dating an Oxford University student. It was only when his girlfriend's body was found that the authorities realised he had a darker side...

A pointless murder

Everyone was baffled when 19-year-old Rachel McLean disappeared from her lodging house in April 1991. The pretty and popular student simply didn't show up for one of her exams and this was so out of character that her tutor alerted the police. They talked to her boyfriend of nine months, John Tanner, and found numerous love letters that the couple had written to each other. John said that he had spent the weekend with Rachel and that he had been waiting with her at Oxford railway station for his train to arrive to take him back to Nottingham when a male friend of hers arrived and offered to drive her back to her house. She had happily left with him. He gave a description of the stranger and a police artist's sketch was made and duly circulated.

The days passed and no one in the media suspected the attractive, long-haired student had anything to do with his beloved girlfriend's disappearance. He was a sensitive, poetic young man who had been born in New Zealand and had attended college there before coming to England to study the Classics. Rachel's parents had really liked him. But police had found Rachel's diary in which she wrote that Tanner was becoming increasingly possessive and she wasn't sure if she wanted such a full-on relationship. Police checked footage taken at the railway station and found no sign of Rachel or the mysterious stranger, and their enquiries made them aware that the jealous Tanner would not have let his beautiful girlfriend leave the station with another man.

The police had already made a search of Rachel's rooming house, but, after 17 days had elapsed, they began to tear the place apart and found her body in a cavity beneath the floorboards inside a walk-in cupboard. She had been strangled. John Tanner was arrested and later tried at Birmingham Crown Court.

The young man told the authorities that he had asked Rachel to get engaged to him that April but that she had refused and also admitted that she had cheated on him on two occasions. (Her friends would later deny this.) In what he claimed was a fit of rage, he had strangled her on the fourteenth of the month. He said, 'I feel I must have lost control because I only have a vague recollection of what happened after. I have never felt this kind of reaction before and I am bewildered that I could do this to someone I loved so much. It was as if something snapped in my mind.'

But the autopsy showed that, when attempts to strangle Rachel manually from the front had failed, Tanner had looped a tie or similar ligature around her neck from the back and tightened it. As she tried to pull the ligature away, she had hauled out some of her own hair. He had spent the night in the same bedroom as the body before disposing of her beneath the floorboards. The cupboard was subject to a continuous flow of cold air so her body hadn't decomposed.

The trial opened at Birmingham Crown Court on 2 December 1991, the defendant pleading not guilty to murder but guilty to manslaughter. John Tanner took the stand in his own defence and said that he'd flown into a rage when Rachel admitted previous infidelities and that he'd called her a tart. She'd struck him and he had lost control and strangled her.

The day after the murder, he admitted, he had written a letter that was ostensibly to Rachel in which he mentioned the mystery man. He said that he had done so because he didn't want to admit to himself that she was dead. He wrote, 'Fancy seeing that friend of yours at the station… it was nice of him to give you a lift.' He added, 'I worry for you being in that house on your own.' (Rachel's flatmates had gone home for the Easter holiday.)

A follow-up letter two days later said, 'I have been trying to reach you all week but I guess the Bodleian Library has had you in its grasp… Being without you is a terrible burden to bear but I live in the knowledge that I will be in your arms next weekend.'

The court also heard extracts from Rachel's diary which illustrated her doubts. She had written: 'Will I marry him? Will I get engaged to him? Will I let it roll over me without intercession or simply because I cannot be bothered to make any effort to stop it?'

She had sent him a Valentine's Day card weeks before her death, in which she called him her 'one and only' and said that he was 'the fulfilment of the heart and mind's desire', but in her diary she wrote that he was 'a sick, childish bastard… generating self-pity'. He was by now making numerous calls to her house and to her friends to check up on her whereabouts and she was feeling stifled by this.

The defence painted Tanner as a man who was blindly in love and whose morality had briefly broken down at the thought of losing his beloved, whilst the prosecution talked of his callous deliberation in hiding the body, inventing the stranger at the railway station and writing the two follow-up letters to Rachel to deceive the police. The trial lasted for four days.

After 4 hours 30 minutes of deliberation, the jury found him guilty of murder rather than the lesser charge of manslaughter and he was sentenced to life imprisonment. A detective involved in the case later described him as a fantasist.

John Tanner served his sentence quietly in HMP Gartree in Leicestershire, during which time he began a relationship with a female student who wrote to him and who had visited various prisoners as part of her criminology course. He was released in 2003, after serving almost 12 years, and deported to his native New Zealand. He settled there with his father in Wanganui and was reunited with his criminologist girlfriend, who had by then found a teaching job in the area.

29

THE RELIGIOUS TEACHERS
COLIN HOWELL & HAZEL BUCHANAN/STEWART

There can be few more respectable images than that of a former lay preacher and a Sunday school teacher but, when these two fell in love, their respective spouses were doomed to die...

A diabolical plot

There was shock and sadness in the small Northern Ireland seaside town of Castlerock, County Derry, when PC Trevor Buchanan (aged 32) and mother-of-four Lesley Howell (31) were found in a fume-filled garage in 1991. It looked as if the pair, who were platonic friends, had committed suicide. Their respective spouses, Hazel Buchanan and Colin Howell, received the sympathy of the community for being widowed at such an early age.

No one suspected them of foul play. After all, Hazel Buchanan was a devout Baptist who taught Sunday school and Colin Howell was a former lay preacher now working as a dentist, who was also a regular at the local Baptist church. Indeed, the two couples had met there and Hazel Buchanan had soon started looking after the Howells' four children, three of whom were pre-school age, while Lesley Howell was at work.

But, whilst they were in a swimming pool in 1990, Colin Howell stroked Hazel Buchanan's stomach. She felt desire for him and they soon began a torrid affair. Both were unhappy in their marriages and enjoyed having illicit meetings. He said that he would teach her to play the guitar and this gave him a reason to come round to her house whilst her police constable husband was doing shift work, without the neighbours suspecting anything. When she became pregnant by him, she travelled to London for an abortion. She would later allege that she felt guilty about having sex outside marriage and told a later boyfriend that she let Howell give her drugs before intercourse so that she would be less repressed.

A double murder

But, when Lesley Howell found out about her husband's affair, she was so distressed that she attempted to commit suicide. She survived, but it gave Colin Howell the idea of killing her. If he and his lover could annihilate both their spouses, they could resume their tempestuous affair. The sensible alternative would have been for them to each file for divorce, but that would have meant risking the disappointment of their religious friends.

Lesley's father died on 7 May and her depression increased, so her husband decided to kill her later that month as it would look as if a second suicide attempt had succeeded. He gassed her using a hosepipe, connected to his car exhaust, as she slept on the settee in her nightdress, his hope being that she would slide painlessly from sleep into death. But she awoke and struggled, crying out for their eldest son – Matthew, aged six – whereupon Colin Howell pressed a duvet firmly over her face. When she stopped breathing, he took off her nightie and dressed her corpse in everyday clothing, phoned his lover to confirm what he'd done, put Lesley's body in the car and drove, as prearranged, to Hazel Buchanan's house.

She, in turn, had given her husband – and the father of her two young children – sleeping tablets in his food so he was out for the count. Colin Howell then began to gas her husband as he slept in bed but he, too, awoke, and fought for his life, so Howell also had to suffocate him with his duvet. Trevor Buchanan – Howell would later admit – stared straight at his killer before he died.

Whilst Hazel Buchanan tidied up the murder scene to hide signs of a struggle and disposed of the hosepipe, her lover drove both bodies to his recently deceased father-in-law's house in Castlerock, drove into the garage and scattered several of his wife's treasured possessions around her. He switched on the ignition and left the garage, closing the door. Later, sounding distraught, he reported his wife missing and there was immediate concern because of her previous suicide attempt. Some of his fellow worshippers mounted a search and were deeply shocked to find both bodies in the garage.

An inquest determined that the friends had committed suicide due to depression, dying of carbon monoxide poisoning. Howell benefited to the tune of several hundred thousand pounds from his wife's will and from insurance policies, allowing him to shore up his flagging dental practice and pay off his debts.

The lovers split up five years later and by 2004 Hazel Buchanan was engaged to a retired police superintendent, David Stewart. When they married she changed her surname to his.

A belated confession

Colin Howell also remarried and his dental practice thrived, but he felt increasingly unhappy. He told his second wife about what he'd done and it was clear that the double murder was preying on his mind. Then, in 2007, his son Matthew died in an accident in Russia, and Howell himself lost £350,000 in an investment scam. The 51-year-old became convinced that he was cursed and confessed his and Hazel's crimes to church elders, who duly informed the police. Once arrested, he told detectives about how his former mistress had agreed to the murder plan, drugged her husband and helped dispose of the evidence.

After a trial, the dentist was jailed for a minimum of 21 years, though the judge said that it would have been 28 years if he had not admitted his culpability. The father of ten children seemed relieved to have eventually confessed. However, he was back in court in 2011, when he pleaded guilty to sexually assaulting nine of his female dental patients after drugging them, the assaults having taken place over several years.

In January 2009, Hazel Stewart – now living in Coleraine – was arrested and pleaded not guilty at Coleraine Court. The court heard that she had known that Colin Howell had murdered his wife and that he was coming round to murder her husband and she had done nothing to prevent this. Indeed, she had encouraged her spouse to take a potent sleeping pill as she wanted him to be sedated before her lover came round. She had left the garage open so that Howell could enter the house and had given him her husband's clothing after the murder so that he could dress his corpse. She had disposed of the gas tubing and had played the part of the grieving widow for many years. Colin Howell testified against her at her trial, and the 48-year-old was jailed for 18 years.

In January 2013 she dropped her appeal against the conviction for her husband's murder and will serve out the rest of her sentence in a Belfast women's jail.

30

THE TEENAGE VOLUNTEER
BERNADETTE PROTTI

Though she was from a devout Catholic family and spent her spare time doing voluntary work in the community, this Californian teenager stabbed a more popular pupil to death when her overtures of friendship were rebuffed.

A religious upbringing

Named after a saint, Bernadette Protti was one of six children born to Elaine and Ray Protti. She was the youngest child and her parents were middle-aged when they had her in 1969. She was embarrassed by their house, which had limited money spent on the decor and paintwork, and her relationship with her parents was increasingly strained. She originally attended a Catholic school but, for reasons unknown, transferred to the larger and more sophisticated Miramonte High School in Contra Costa County, where she tried desperately to fit in and be liked.

She was in awe of one of the most popular students, Kirsten Costas, who was from an affluent family and was a cheerleader, a member of the swimming team and a Lark. Larks did community work, including co-counselling for other pupils who had lost their way. As a Lark herself, Bernadette helped shy, younger pupils to fit in, but she herself felt increasingly adrift. By now her father had retired from his engineering job and she complained that neither parent listened to her.

She was turned down for the cheerleading squad as she lacked the necessary co-ordination and was also turned down when she tried to join the yearbook staff and one of the school's sorority groups, the Atlanthus. But she did find acceptance in another volunteering community group and tried to befriend Kirsten during their frequent meetings. The girls went on a skiing school trip and Bernadette would later tell others that the more popular girl had laughed at her inexpensive skis and boots. She would later say that Kirsten didn't like her but that she thought Kirsten was 'okay'.

The murder

By the summer of 1984, she had figured out a way to get Kirsten alone, though we will never know if the motive was to try to get into her good books or if the murder which followed was premeditated. She phoned when she knew Kirsten was out and spoke to her mother, pretending that Kirsten had a secret invitation to a sorority dinner. She said that it was to be a surprise for Kirsten, that she'd pick her up in a car on 23 June. In reality, she had a vague plan to take Kirsten to a party and become her friend. To this end she borrowed her father's car, telling him that she was babysitting and would feel safer driving home afterwards. (In the TV film made about the case, *The Cheerleader Murder*, the car belongs to her mother, and all names and various details were changed.)

She picked Kirsten up as planned and they parked in a churchyard, where Protti would later allege that Kirsten smoked a joint, but the more popular girl was annoyed when she heard that there was no special dinner. Exiting the car, she made her way to a nearby house, explaining to the couple who lived there that her friend was 'acting weird' and that she wanted to phone her parents and get a lift back home. The phone went unanswered as her parents were still out at a charity dinner, but the man of the house agreed to drive her back so that she could wait for them at her next-door neighbours' house. Protti tailed them in her father's car.

The Good Samaritan who was driving her back commented to Kirsten that they were being tailed by a mustard-coloured Pinto, but she said that it was just her weird friend and that it was no big deal. He parked and watched Kirsten exit the car and go into the grounds of her neighbours' house, where a girl of around age 15 jumped out at her and appeared to make stabbing motions with her right arm. Kirsten fell down, then got up and began to flee towards her neighbours' porch. She had been stabbed a total of five times. The long knife blade had slashed her twice in the back, twice in the front and once in the hand as she tried to protect herself. One of the stab wounds to her body had penetrated her left lung, another had penetrated her right lung, and the third had lacerated her liver.

The Good Samaritan tailed the Pinto for a few minutes but it raced away. However, he was able to give an excellent description of the youthful killer to the police.

Meanwhile, blood spurting everywhere, Kirsten battered on the door and her next-door neighbours phoned an ambulance and asked her who had done this, but she was already having breathing difficulties and couldn't answer. She died shortly afterwards in hospital without naming her equally young killer.

An investigation

Detectives knew from their witness's statement that they were looking for a chubby teenage girl with long fair hair dressed in a yellow shirt and scruffy red jogging trousers. She had been driving a light-coloured Pinto so they interviewed 750 Pinto owners in the area. They also interviewed numerous students at the school which Kirsten had attended, but even though Bernadette Protti's lie detector test was inconclusive the police didn't check the veracity of her alibi.

As the months passed, suspicion centred on another student, who had the courage to dress differently, favouring a goth look over the more conventional preppie one. The girl was victimised repeatedly by other pupils and eventually changed schools.

The community rallied round in a desperate attempt to catch the killer, raising a substantial reward. Kirsten's parents also worked hard to ensure that their daughter's senseless murder wasn't forgotten. Determined to be proactive, they used some of the reward money to hire a private investigator who went over the lie detector results and found that Bernadette Protti's had been misread and that she had actually failed some portions of the test whilst others had been inconclusive. He checked and found that Protti hadn't been babysitting as claimed that night, that in fact she hadn't babysat for the family in question for an entire year.

The police now involved the FBI who reread the lie detector results and called the teenager in for questioning. They pointed out that she fitted the description of the killer and had also been driving a car which fitted the description of the murderer's vehicle. She had lied about where she was at the time of the murder so didn't have an alibi. Convinced of her guilt but aware that all of the evidence was circumstantial, the FBI officer suggested she go home for the weekend and think about what she wanted to do next.

A distraught Bernadette Protti now confided to her priest that she'd committed the murder. She contemplated suicide but believed that, if she took her own life, she wouldn't go to heaven. She asked her mother if she could talk to her, but Elaine Protti said that she was too tired, that it could wait till the following day. The next morning Protti handed her mother a letter, asked her not to read it for half an hour and left the house.

Elaine spent the time in Bible study as she always did, then read the letter, which admitted the murder and said that Bernadette wanted to hand herself in, saying that she couldn't explain why she'd killed Kirsten but that she hated herself. Elaine fetched her husband and they drove to the school, collected their youngest daughter and took her to the sheriff's office, where she made a rambling 90-minute confession, often breaking down in tears.

Trial

At the three-day trial, held in front of a judge, she said she'd found the knife in the car as her sister used it to cut tomatoes to snack on. (In the film, the knife is used by her sister in the car to cut chunks from a cucumber which she then eats, leaving the knife in the front of the vehicle.) But the prosecution argued that no one would keep an 18-inch blade for such purposes.

It was also noted that Protti had been casually dressed considering that she was going to a party, so in court it was suggested that she hadn't planned to go socialising and intended to commit the murder all along. But the girl had a limited budget and rarely wore fashionable clothes.

On 14 March 1985, she was sentenced to a maximum of nine years in the California Youth Authority's Venture School, where she earned her high school diploma. She also found herself a boyfriend, though the authorities were alarmed at how angry she became when they fought.

Under California law, Bernadette Protti had to be released by age 25, but she was actually paroled two years earlier in 1992. She left the area, changed her name, married, got a degree and now enjoys a successful career. She has never again come to the attention of law enforcement agencies.

31

THE IVY LEAGUE LAWYER
JASON BOHN

High-flying attorney Jason Bohn broke the law with repeated acts of domestic violence, culminating in a particularly savage murder.

A difficult childhood

Jason Bohn was the first of two sons born into an increasingly unhappy family, and when his parents divorced he and his brother went to live with their father in a Florida trailer park. Both boys would later allege that their father had a drug problem and that he put beer into their bottles of juice to keep them quiet. Jason would also allege that his father was physically abusive and once stabbed him in the knee. He also said that his father eventually introduced him to cocaine.

By the end of primary school he hated both parents and wrote an essay called '101 Ways to Kill Your Father'. His stepmother found it and was so frightened that she demanded he leave the house. He then lived with his mother for a while but her career in publishing demanded that she travel and he felt abandoned and increasingly lost. By the age of 13 he had been put into foster care, where he regularly got into fights and was suicidal. Aged 14, whilst in a residential children's home, he punched a pregnant 18-year-old girl in the stomach and she promptly miscarried. His rages were becoming legendary, but he rallied when the Jewish Child Care Association took an interest in him and encouraged him to pursue his studies: for years he was their poster child.

Men who hate their mothers sometimes transfer that hatred onto all women and become deeply misogynistic, and Bohn seems to have fallen into that category. Though he graduated from both Columbia University and Florida University and became a successful lawyer, he put most of his energy into controlling his girlfriends. One of them would later tell police that he'd give her lists of tasks to achieve and threaten to kill her if she didn't achieve them. He would go red with anger, his eyes would bulge and he would shout so loudly that spittle would fly from his mouth.

The final straw came when they were at their apartment one night and he called out to her. She took too long to respond to his call and, when she did, he started to choke her and waved a kitchen knife threateningly in her face, shouting that he would kill her and no one would know. Terrified, she left the relationship but was too afraid of the repercussions to report the abuse. Like most misogynists, Bohn soon transferred his rage to another girlfriend.

The violence escalates

Whilst at a football match in Florida, he met Danielle Thomas, originally from Kentucky, a graduate who was working as a financial analyst for Weight Watchers. She loved everything from playing the saxophone to skydiving and the two immediately hit it off. Soon they graduated from dating to set up home together in Queens, New York. She was perhaps too much in love to realise that violent or otherwise inadequate people will often pitch for an early period of cohabitation or even marriage, and are usually unwilling to let a relationship mature slowly for fear that their inadequacies will be found out.

Soon Bohn became increasingly abusive, with horrified neighbours repeatedly reporting to the police that they could hear Danielle screaming. In the spring of 2012 he beat her so badly that she had two black eyes and could only walk with the aid of crutches: her relatives were shocked at the change in her and begged her to leave. That May she went to the police to report the abuse and, whilst she was at the station, Bohn called her. She put him on speaker phone and police were shocked to hear him say that he was going to smash her skull in and that he would hunt her down like a dog in the street. He was arrested for harassment but quickly released on bail. Danielle spent the next two months living in a women's refuge but refused a friend's offer to take her to a hotel.

The lion's den

In June 2012 she made a fatal error, returning alone to their apartment to collect her West Highland terrier. (A woman is most at risk after she leaves a violent man and, if she must return to the property, should only do so with a police escort.) She and Bohn immediately began to argue and he grabbed her by the neck. During the altercation which followed, either his or her phone made a call by mistake and a friend's machine recorded what happened next.

The lawyer was heard to ask who she had previously phoned (he had been going through her phone log) and she whimpered that she didn't know and added that she loved him. Seconds later she gasped out, 'I can't breathe.' He told her she was stupid and said, 'You think I'm going to stop. I won't stop.'

He proceeded to beat and strangle her to death, then filled the bathtub with ice before dumping her body in it, doubtless hoping to slow down the rate of decomposition. But neighbours had phoned the police during the assault and they arrived to find her corpse and two notes from her ex-lover, who had by now fled. One said that it had been a drunken accident and the other said that he loved her. No one who saw her battered body was convinced.

After the murder, Bohn used Danielle's phone to call her family and tell them she was fine, explaining that she'd gone to watch a rally. He also called an ex-girlfriend and said he'd slammed Danielle into the wall during a drunken argument and that, when he woke up the next day, she wasn't breathing and his knuckles were badly bruised. Five days after the killing he was arrested at a restaurant and taken to jail, where he posted a message on his Facebook page (having previously dictated it to a relative, who did the posting for him). The message said that he suspected she had been cheating and that she was a compulsive liar, that this had made him insecure and led to the abuse. He added that on the night he murdered her he was heavily intoxicated and had essentially blacked out.

At his trial in 2014, the 34-year-old admitted murdering Danielle, 27, but said that he had been suffering from intermittent explosive disorder as a result of his dysfunctional upbringing. (Ironically, his mother, a publishing executive by now earning over a million dollars a year, was helping to fund his legal costs.) He hoped to get a manslaughter conviction on the grounds of diminished responsibility, but after less than a day the jury rejected his plea and returned with a conviction of murder and a life sentence without the possibility of parole. Jason Bohn then wept so hard that his nose bled, but there was very little sympathy for his plight and Danielle's grandmother commented that 'only a bully and a coward would do this to such a beautiful woman'. Bohn is expected to die in jail.

32

THE TOWN MARSHAL
DAVID YOUNG

Though the role of town marshal is to uphold the law, this increasingly unstable man was willing to kill a classroom of children so that they would be reincarnated as his followers in a Brave New World...

Early years

David Young was born on the 12 June 1944 in Albany, California but failed to bond with his siblings and soon went to live in Iowa with a relative. At school he was a loner with a high IQ and a desire to see the world. After graduating from high school he joined the navy in San Diego but left with an honourable discharge after only two months: it was apparent by now that he hated taking orders and was becoming more and more anti-authority. Yet a year later he moved to Nebraska, where he majored in Criminal Justice, perhaps hoping that he could rise quickly through the ranks to become a leader rather than a follower. He married for the first time in 1965 and the couple had two daughters who came to live with him after the marriage ended in divorce.

Young's wife would later state that he ruled the roost with an iron fist and that he was increasingly interested in firearms, an interest which frightened her. On the upside, he read widely and was especially interested in sociology.

Left alone with his pre-teen daughters, Young took naked photographs of them and sold these snapshots to the highest bidders to make extra pocket money. Several of his relatives, and some of the locals in his area, knew about this and everyone would later claim to be concerned, but no one reported him to the authorities. He continued intermittently with his law studies, finally graduating in 1975 near the top of his class.

Despite his high IQ, Young was getting lost and even became an admirer of Adolf Hitler. He also developed a great respect for white supremacy organisations and saw himself as a superior being. In June 1975 his pride was further bolstered when he was made Town Marshal of Mountain Home, Idaho. But he couldn't get on with his fellow officers and was arrested when he arrived at the department with a concealed weapon. Within ten months he was let go.

In 1977, he applied to become the Town Marshal of Cokeville, Wyoming, went through their police training course and succeeded in becoming the town's law enforcer. Unfortunately, the power again went to his head and he gave people tickets on trumped-up charges and swaggered around town wearing a huge cowboy hat and toting his guns. He was by now stockpiling weapons and was often seen cleaning and fondling them. Again he caused consternation in the community and was duly fired, this time at the end of his six-month probationary period.

Second marriage

In the same year he married Doris Walters, a twice-divorced country music singer who had lost her teenage son in a car accident and now lived with her teenage daughter. Doris was six years older than him but the pair had a lot in common as they were both atheists who believed in reincarnation and had no fear of death.

The pair set up home in a trailer in Tucson, Arizona with the older of his daughters from his first marriage, the younger one having left home to escape his frightening mood swings. He became diabetic during these years (angry people are more likely to develop type 2 diabetes as their rage causes regular insulin surges) and had to have two injections a day. He decided that he should spend all of his time writing his manifesto, so Doris supported them both with her singing gigs and with working in the local cafe and doing housecleaning work.

In 1978, he put together a manifesto which made absolutely no sense, containing rambling sentences such as: 'Now people come and people go, but always as people, no longer as individuals from which people had risen (or succumb).' It ended with the line: 'We are all ONE and "we" came apart to do "this" for something "to do" in Nothing and Infinity.' He mailed it to Ronald Reagan, then president of the United States, and to various media outlets where it doubtless ended up in numerous wastepaper bins.

In the years that followed, David Young spent most of his time writing journal after journal and had little contact with the outside world. He let his beard and hair grow long and looked unkempt.

Increasingly impoverished, by 1985 he started talking about a scheme that would make his family rich. He thought that, if he could murder a classroom of especially bright children and take his own life, they would all be reincarnated together and the children would see him as their leader. He would have full control of their minds and they would bring him untold wealth.

In mid May 1986, he assembled a complicated bomb which was set to detonate when two pieces of metal were allowed to make contact. The pieces were held apart merely by a clothes peg. On 16 May 1986, a Friday, he was ready to put his plan into action and set off towards Cokeville with his wife, older daughter and two male friends in the van. Earlier that week Doris had visited her daughter from a previous marriage and said she would soon go shopping with her, yet she had written in her journal: 'I wonder what we'll be called in the Brave New World?' She apparently knew that David Young meant to annihilate them all.

When the friends in the van heard him outlining his plan into a tape recorder, they were horrified and said that they couldn't be part of his madness. He promptly held them at gunpoint and handcuffed them to the inside of the van so that they couldn't go to the police. He parked in the playground of Cokeville Elementary School and entered the building with his wife and daughter, carrying guns and pushing the bomb in a shopping cart.

He told the school receptionist that this was a revolution and that the school was being taken hostage. He showed her the shoelace trigger for the explosives which was attached to his wrist.

At this stage it all got too much for Young's teenage daughter and she turned to walk away. Apparently in agreement with her actions, he threw her the van keys and said, 'Get the hell out of here.' She fled to the town hall to report the hostage situation and she was so distraught that they immediately took her seriously. After she left, her father had ushered a total of 135 children and 18 adults into one of the classrooms and told a teacher to phone the sheriff and ask him to get in touch with Congress demanding two million dollars for each child. Now the FBI became involved, as hostage-taking is a federal offence.

It was hard for the adults in the room to ascertain what Young wanted as his messages were confusing. He said that children were precious and that he didn't want to hurt them, then added, 'I'll only shoot the kids with a .22.' He soon lapsed into a sullen silence and his wife became the vocal one, reassuring the crying children that they were safe and praising their many drawings.

But, as the afternoon wore on, everyone began to feel unwell and realised that the bomb's gasoline container was leaking. A teacher persuaded him to let her open the windows and doors. Doris suddenly looked nervous and warned them to keep away from both, hinting that they might be killed by snipers who were stationed outside. She found an EMT (Emergency Medical Technician) radio in an adjacent classroom and was able to find the police channel and listen in. A teacher, sent by Young to the staff room to make another phone call to the authorities, was able to warn the police to stop broadcasting on this. The same enterprising teacher was also able to disable the school bell, knowing that the children would automatically race for the door if they heard it ring.

A teacher put masking tape in a wide square around David Young and told the kids not to cross it to give the jumpy hostage-taker some breathing space. By now he hadn't had anything to eat for several hours and complications from his diabetes were setting in. He felt overheated but had great difficulty removing his jacket as he was understandably terrified of setting off the shoelace trigger. Despite his boast that everyone could be held hostage for the next ten days, he hadn't brought food, a change of clothing or basic toiletries and, now that he'd taken over the class, seemed at a loss as to what to do with them.

Two deaths

Eventually he needed to go to the bathroom so he carefully transferred the bomb trigger to Doris's wrist and left the room. A teacher raised her hand to her head and said, 'I've got a headache.' Doris said that she did too and immediately emulated the gesture.

This triggered the explosive and she went up in a ball of flame. Teachers screamed at the children to run for the doors and windows as thick black smoke enveloped the classroom. Some of the children's clothes were on fire and they were trying to beat out the flames with their bare hands. Fortunately, the leaking gasoline had turned some of the explosive material into paste, preventing it from becoming airborne, and two of the caps did not detonate. Furthermore, most of the force had gone upwards into the ceiling where the soft tiles absorbed much of the heat.

At this point David Young opened the bathroom door and saw his wife screaming and engulfed in flames. He shot at her, but the first bullet missed, so he shot again, killing her, before turning the gun upon himself. The couple were the only two to lose their lives.

An emergency medical team entered the burning building to find that the top of Doris Young's head had been blown off and that she had died of the bullet wound rather than the effects of the fire. David Young had then put his Colt .45 under his own chin and killed himself.

Seventy-nine of the hostages were hospitalised for burns, smoke inhalation and other injuries. One little girl was still having operations for facial burns eight years later, whilst a teacher who was shot during the chaos still has a bullet lodged close to his heart. A burn pattern on the wall resembled angelic wings and several of the children, brought up in a deeply religious community, subsequently said that they had been saved by angels. Some thought that the angels resembled their dead relatives.

An investigative report concluded that David Young had all the hallmarks of a psychopath as he had no consideration for other people. He had been willing to kill dozens of children and was indifferent to the anguish that this would cause to their families and friends.

A book on the subject by Hartt and Judene Wixom was originally called *Trial by Terror* but the title was later bought by a Latter Day Saints publisher, given additional content and renamed *When Angels Intervene to Save the Children*. It was also made into a movie, *To Save the Children* (1994), with the talented Richard Thomas as David Young.

Though he only killed two people, including himself, Young's plan had been to take out all of the school's children, thus becoming a mass murderer. In August 2014, I interviewed Katherine Ramsland, author of *Inside the Minds of Mass Murderers*, looking for further insight. Katherine, a professor at De Sales University, has also authored books on everything from medical killers to forensic medicine. Her most recent offerings, both eBooks, are part of the *Notorious USA* series and are called *Under the Light of the Moon* and *The Murder Game*.

I asked her if David Young was typical of the mass murderers that she had studied. She agreed that, in many ways, he was: 'David Young had the rigid personality that I've written about. An examination of the backgrounds of many mass murderers makes it clear that they had behaved in ways that suggested they might one day explode: an inability to deal with stress, veiled threats, angry outbursts, or retaliations against others. The build-up of anger appears to derive from the way they learned (or did not learn) to manage stress and disappointment.'

She continued, 'Their individual cognitive processing is key. Those who experience higher exposure to violence in their environment appear to have a greater tendency to duplicate it, especially if it is turned against them and/or they have military experience later in life. But if they're angry, or experience a great need to control their environment (and that of others), their frustration level can reach the point of exploding. To their minds, someone must pay for their discomfort. Or, if they feel like nobodies, they might decide that a grandiose gesture of violence will at least turn them into somebodies. Young was narcissistic and would have been frustrated by his lack of recognition. With his other traits and his approval of violence as a means to an end, he was primed for becoming a violent individual.'

I had noted that very little was known about Young's childhood but that it was obvious that he hadn't bonded with his family. I asked Katherine whether this was typical for mass murderers or whether the alienation usually occurred in adulthood.

She explained: 'Without more being known, it's not possible to say when and how it all started (with David Young). The alienation grows throughout life, typically, because a percentage of our temperament is biological. Other kids would have noticed how rigid he was. Also, if he had delusions or an inability to make his thoughts understood, they would have avoided him. This would only anger him and make him want to control them.'

She clarified: 'There is no clear causal relationship between the child and the adult when it comes to predicting violence, but since behavioural patterns in adapting to stress can point toward the potential for more serious problems down the line, it is still helpful to identify those individuals in need of anger management and other forms of counselling. Behaviours to be concerned about in children and adolescents include a marked increase in deception, blaming others, avoiding responsibility, avoiding efforts to achieve goals, using intimidation to control others, showing lack of empathy for others, exploiting others' weaknesses, developing a pattern of overreaction or anger, being depressed or withdrawn, carrying weapons, complaining about loneliness, and having excessive television or videogame habits – three or more hours a day. Any kind of obsession with violence is a significant red flag.'

I asked which personality disorders, if any, did she think he was suffering from.

'It's not possible to say from the available description. You mention an investigative report that concluded that he was a psychopath, but my impression from the description you have is that he possibly had a functional psychosis or a serious schizotypal disorder. He had strong delusions about reality and had managed to convince his wife, apparently. But a diagnosis cannot be made on such sparse information. There could be a lot of factors and behaviours that we aren't aware of.'

I asked whether David Young was unusual in bringing his wife (and initially his daughter) with him.

'Most mass murderers act alone, but Young had more of a cult mentality, in that he supposedly wanted followers. Apparently, he'd found this in his wife. He also needed a helper given the complexity of his plan. We do see a few mass killers who operate in teams, because they want the affirmation of the other person, who is usually a follower. The fact that Young seemed to think that his daughter and the two men in the van would go along with the plan indicates a person with a distorted sense of reality. He didn't see them as anything other than pawns in his game.'

I asked Katherine to say more about her findings regarding mass murderers.

'Society needs to grasp the fact that children can form the intent to kill, whether or not they understand what they're doing. They can develop those fantasies that may eventually manifest as mass murder. Any sign of a lack of empathy or of devaluing another person's life must be noticed and treated.

'Among the specific traits or behaviours that, when a number of them are present together, provide a constellation of red flags for the potential for explosive violence are: a preoccupation with themes of violence or death, especially in the form of attention to other such incidents; warnings about impending violence; complaints about auditory hallucinations; complaints of being bullied; having a violent or criminal parent; chronic substance abuse; previous aggression or arson; dramatic mood swings; viewing other mass murderers as heroes or "competition"; low frustration tolerance/no resilience; sudden significant stressors; expressions that indicate the collection of injuries or injustices and a tendency to blame others for life's unfairness.

'Other warning behaviours include expressions of dehumanisation of others; withdrawal from social activities; expressions of superiority or entitlement; an excessive need for attention; an intolerant and rigid temperament; reactive paranoia, especially if it's delusional; a collection of weapons, including bombs, or approval of war or assault; requests for assistance buying weapons; and anger at specific parties that fails to be absorbed or resolved. There's often a list of grudges.' She concludes that 'we see quite a few of these in Young'.

33

THE AIRLINE PILOT
RICHARD CRAFTS

As a pilot for a large respected airline and a part-time police officer, Richard Crafts was a pillar of the community who allegedly took drastic measures when his wife asked for a divorce.

A focused childhood

Richard Crafts was born on 20 December 1937 in New York to Lucretia Crafts, who owned a clothing store, and John Crafts, who owned an accountancy firm. John had been married before, a fact he kept secret from most of his family, and was 13 years older than Lucretia. He was a cold, secretive man, given to temper tantrums, and a strict disciplinarian.

The couple went on to have two daughters and it was a privileged upbringing for all three children, involving private schooling. But Richard did badly at school, rarely rising above a C grade for anything. He failed to bond with the other children and often threw books at them. He was suspended for antisocial behaviour and later dropped out of university, opting for a stint in the military instead and flying helicopters. In this, he was following in his father's footsteps as the older man had been a pilot in the First World War.

Whilst in the Marines he became interested in police work and would later pursue this on a part-time basis, but after leaving the service he first became a pilot, flying various types of aircraft. He had his father's cold, secretive manner, but this endeared him to women who liked a challenge and he often persuaded them to sleep with him again on future occasions as he was considered to be good in bed.

In 1969 he added Helle Nielsen from Copenhagen to his growing list of girlfriends. She was 22 at the time, whilst he was 33 (a similar age difference to the one between his parents). They met in Florida, where she was training to be a flight stewardess and he was on a stopover with other cockpit crew.

Commitment phobia

The next few years were confusing for Helle as Richard Crafts got close to her with his stories of military service in Asia. After telling them he sometimes woke up screaming. She wanted to comfort her attractive lover but, every time she got emotionally close, he moved away. Sometimes he did so physically, relocating to Miami whilst she was stationed in New York. In 1973 he briefly moved in with her then had second thoughts and rented a bachelor pad. Their fights were legion and friends begged her to end the relationship, but she remained in love with him.

He had promised that they would marry if she ever became pregnant but, when she did, he beat her up and she had an abortion. They reconciled and she became pregnant again. He again had second thoughts and she scheduled a second termination but, in the autumn of 1975, he agreed to marry her and the termination was cancelled. His airline colleagues would later regard this as a marriage of convenience as they thought him to be incapable of love (and his erstwhile military colleagues had seen his cruel side in Asia when he strapped monkeys to small parachutes and launched them from his plane, knowing that they would claw or bite at the material and fall to their deaths).

On 29 November 1975, he wed his four-months-pregnant bride and they bought a house in Newtown, Connecticut. Helle had undoubtedly hoped that he was truly hers at last but, even when commitment-phobic men marry, they remain emotionally unavailable and will set up barriers to intimacy. They will often choose to work away from home, as Crafts did, and many will also avoid romantic meals and even shy away from hugs. Some will also ruin red-letter days such as birthdays and anniversaries. Crafts fit strongly into this category and didn't even show up for the birth of their third child, so Helle had to drive herself, in labour, to the hospital.

The couple occasionally got into physical fights and, at a friend's house in 1977, he knocked her to the floor. Three years later he hit her so hard that she had two black eyes and feared that her nose was broken. She admitted to her colleagues that she was considering getting a divorce.

The trainee policeman

Ironically, in 1982 Crafts became a special constable, helping to keep crowd control at public functions. His colleagues found him to be overly macho and he was less popular with them than he was with his fellow pilots, many of whom admired him. By 1986 he had gravitated to nearby Southbury as an auxiliary constable.

Meanwhile, he maintained his relationships with previous girlfriends and would stay with one of them for days at a time without letting Helle know where he was. But her sadness turned to fear when he was diagnosed with colonic cancer in August 1984 and his prospects for recovery were poor. They became closer as she nursed him, but that closeness ebbed away when, after major surgery to remove part of his intestine, he recovered and returned to his piloting work and to his adulterous ways.

By 1986, Helle had had enough and hired a private eye who took photos of Richard Crafts kissing another woman. Helle went to see a divorce lawyer and admitted to her husband that she'd done so and that the lawyer had told her she'd get alimony and child support. The plan was to serve him with the papers on 12 November but he kept evading the sheriff. With nothing resolved, Helle's work took her out of town for a few days.

The freezer

On 17 November Richard Crafts bought a huge new freezer and insisted on paying cash for it and collecting it in a truck at a later date rather than having it delivered. The manager remembered him as it was such an unusual transaction, one he had never seen before in his entire retail career. Crafts had previously arranged to hire and collect a large woodchipping machine on 18 November, the following day.

On 18 November, Helle finished her latest shift as a flight attendant and told colleagues she was going home to her nanny and three children. She hoped that her husband would be there but she wasn't certain as he often disappeared for days at a time. She also said to several people that if something happened to her it would not be an accident, a comment she had made on several previous occasions. She got home safely, showered and changed into her favourite pyjamas but shortly afterwards stopped answering her phone. Friends then called her husband and were surprised when Richard said that she was in Denmark visiting her sick mother. Helle hadn't mentioned that her mother was ill, only that she'd given her money to enjoy a December skiing trip.

On 19 November, the nanny was woken by Richard Crafts at 6 a.m. He said that Helle was out and that everyone else in the household had to accompany him to a relative's house as the power had gone out and the house would soon be freezing. His hair was wet and he looked exhausted. Even more strangely, he took them out the front door rather than their usual route through the garage, a route which would have taken them past the freezer. He was so tired that he fell asleep at the wheel and the nanny had to wake him up. That same day, he bought new bedding for the marital bed, including a duvet and two pillows, unusual for a man who normally resented spending any money on the house and who had let it fall into serious disrepair.

On the evening of 20 November, a man drove past a large woodchipping machine that was in use in the area and noted that the person operating it was wearing a police-style hat and cowering against a nearby truck as if he didn't want to be noticed. He could see plastic bags inside the truck. A fellow constable was equally surprised to see Crafts with a woodchipper and asked what he was using it for. The pilot replied that the snow had brought down three tree limbs but the machine seemed much too big for that particular task. On 21 November, Crafts again did a stint as a policeman and was back working as a pilot the following day.

On 22 November, the nanny discovered a large dark stain on the rug in the master bedroom; when she next checked, Crafts had disposed of it. He said that he had dropped kerosene on the rug and that it had left a stain.

The days passed and Richard Crafts didn't inform his wife's airline that she wouldn't be at work. He also fobbed off her friends with suggestions that she'd gone on her travels. But they went to the police, who duly questioned him on 2 December. He was questioned by a neighbouring police force, not the one he served with, and said that he had not seen or heard from Helle since the nineteenth of the previous month.

Increasingly suspicious, they began to investigate and found that Helle had been fearful that her husband would hurt her. They found blood on the marital mattress and on recently laundered towels and on a washcloth. The spatter on the mattress suggested that someone had been making the bed when they were hit over the head with a heavy implement.

They discovered Crafts' surprise purchase of a new freezer and his hiring of the woodchipper and went to the area where he'd been spotted using the machine. Hidden in the woodchips on the ground they found shreds of blue material which matched the pyjamas Helle had been wearing when she was last seen. They also found pieces of a charity appeal with Helle's name on, from a document which they surmised had been in her pyjama pocket. Ironically, it was from a cancer charity as she had been donating to them since her husband's illness. They also found a label from a vitamin packet, though at the time they didn't realise the significance of this: Helle Crafts sold vitamins to her friends and relatives. They recognised a piece of a painted fingernail, with flesh attached, and also recognised what looked like bone fragments. They took bags of biological samples from the woodchipper and surrounding area and sent them to the laboratory for further tests.

Investigators were convinced that the pilot, unwilling to pay alimony, had put his wife's corpse in the freezer as it would be much easier to put a frozen body through a woodchipper machine than a pliant one. They only hoped that she had been dead rather than just unconscious when she was placed in the large freezer chest.

On 13 January they arrested Richard Crafts for the murder of his younger spouse. He arranged for a relative to take care of his three children (whom he had become closer to since becoming a single parent) and went calmly to the police station.

Trial

It's rare to get a conviction without a body but, in this case, it was evident that Helle Crafts was dead. The prosecution's case was that Crafts had chipped his wife into tiny pieces and disposed of them in the nearby river. They had recovered two dental crowns, strands of dyed hair which looked identical to Helle's, a piece of skull and a tiny part of a finger and two fingernails. Though modern forensics were in their infancy in 1986, an orthodontist testified that the dental crowns were identical to those that Helle had worn. The smattering of blood found on the marital mattress, and the removal of the rug, suggested that the bedroom had been the murder scene. The prosecution speculated that she had been changing the bed when her husband approached her from behind and battered her, possibly with his heavy police flashlight, causing her to fall to the floor.

They showed a video of a pig, which has similar flesh to that of a human, being put through a woodchipper to show just how efficiently it could process an adult-sized corpse.

Unusually, the defendant took the stand. Crafts testified for a day and a half in his own defence, saying that he hadn't taken the divorce threat seriously. He said that Helle was unhappy about his other women so was always asking him, 'Don't you want to be married to me?' He said he'd rented the woodchipper to clear brush from the area around his property and that he'd disposed of the rug in the marital bedroom after staining it with kerosene.

His defence team said that they believed Helle was still alive but the prosecution countered that she would never leave her children. The defence said that the jury surely couldn't convict a man for murder when all that had been found was two-thirds of an ounce of bone.

All bar one of the jurists believed that he was guilty. The one who did not had served, like Crafts, in south-east Asia and seemed to see him as a fellow spirit and maintained that he was innocent. This juror became increasingly difficult for the others to talk to and finally the court had to declare a mistrial.

The second trial commenced on 7 September 1989 with much the same evidence and witnesses as last time but a different jury. The jurors were out for four days before finding Richard Crafts guilty of murder in the first degree.

When it came to sentencing, the judge bore in mind Crafts' exemplary military record and his service as a pilot, but he said that he had also to take into account the premeditation of the murder and the fact that Crafts had robbed three children of their mother and indeed of their childhood. To almost everyone's surprise, he sentenced the shaken man to 50 years.

In 1993, Richard Crafts lost his appeal for a new trial. At the time of writing he remains incarcerated but is a model inmate who may well be paroled at any time.

34

THE CHURCH ORGANISER
MARY JANE FONDER

Mental illness, perhaps exacerbated by intense loneliness, seems to have turned this eccentric Lutheran into a killer.

An odd childhood

Mary Jane Fonder was born on 5 July 1942 to Edward and Alice Fonder in Philadelphia. When she came into the world she already had a three-year-old brother, little Ed. Her father was a factory machinist whilst her mother was a proofreader for a publishing company. The couple argued constantly and also picked on the children for trivial things. On the upside, however, they were comparatively wealthy and Mary Jane enjoyed regular stays at their summer house in Bucks County and took part in longer road trips in the family car.

A nervous child, Mary Jane had what she would later describe as a breakdown at the tender age of eight and became so withdrawn that her parents bought her a puppy. This seemed to lift her spirits and distract attention from the fact that she struggled to make friends or connect with youngsters her own age. She regarded her brother, who also struggled to socialise, as her best friend and she looked up to him.

But when Ed went away to university, Mary Jane felt totally alone. She became increasingly agoraphobic and would hyperventilate in social situations. Though she was a bright child and advanced for her age, she was unduly anxious about passing her exams. At 16 she attempted to commit suicide by taking all of her anti-anxiety medication and spent the following month in a mental-health facility.

Shortly after being released from the mental hospital, she dropped out of school. She spent more and more time with her dog and often went to the family's holiday home to paint or crochet garments. On her return to Philadelphia she took up ceramics, living the life of a much older woman. Though she was attractive and had the occasional boyfriend, she would never marry.

She also struggled to find fulfilment in her work. She was a shop assistant then a factory hand, swiftly moving from one employer to another. Her longest term of employment was for a company which manufactured Bibles: she stayed there for over eight years. She lived with her parents until she was 26 then got her own flat but soon moved on to another apartment and then another. She seemed to be searching for something – or someone – and confided in friends that she wished she could find a good man.

Her father disappears

The years passed and by 1987 both of her parents were in failing health and she moved back to Springfield, 40 miles from Philadelphia, to care for them. Her mother went into hospital in the spring of 1992 to have a leg amputated but there were complications and she lapsed into a coma, dying that September when her feeding tube came loose. Mary Jane would later tell acquaintances that her father was mean to her mother whilst she was ill and that she, Mary Jane, was angry with him because of that.

For most of the next two years she cared for her father, whilst working in a fast food restaurant to pay the bills, but the widower became increasingly cantankerous and they alternated between rowing and not speaking. He sometimes went to the woods which bordered their property though he couldn't go far and had to lean heavily on his stick. She became increasingly depressed by her circumstances, as many carers do, and was put on medication for both depression and insomnia. Soon she was contemplating suicide.

But on 26 August 1993, her burden lifted when her 80-year-old father mysteriously disappeared one sunny morning. She told police that she'd got up very early then gone for a lie down at 7 a.m. and had heard the outside door bang, so she assumed her father had gone to the front path to pick up the newspaper. After dozing for 4 hours she had got up to find the house still empty and the paper lying untouched outside.

She told police that he had wandered off but, when they searched her car, they found that she'd taken everything out of the boot and cleaned it. Later, her father's dog was found dead in her freezer and she said it had somehow eaten her father's diabetic medication and died.

During another interview at her house she said, 'I don't think I did anything to my pop,' and added, 'maybe the drugs did something.' When the lone officer pressed her further she clammed up.

By the following interview she had hired herself a lawyer and refused to take a lie detector test. Detectives were convinced that she had murdered her father and perhaps dumped the body in an old well or in heavy woodland or water but, without a body and with the evidence purely circumstantial, they couldn't proceed.

The following year she hired a tree cutter to trim the forested areas around her property but she refused to let him cut timber in one particular area. Later she accused him of stealing her father's tools and made death threats to him, his wife and even his children, saying that she knew how to murder them and get away with it. She subjected the entirely innocent family to so many harassing phone calls that they took her to court. The civil case was settled and the phone calls thankfully stopped, but the community understandably became increasingly wary of the unstable woman in their midst.

A vengeful nature

She continued to be employed as a waitress but her behaviour was becoming more and more erratic. One day she would be sweet and easy-going, the next she would stop making sense. On her off days, she rambled and had a wild look in her eyes.

By now her brother had moved in with her, but he went to another church and had dissimilar interests, so they lived separate lives.

In December 1994 she had an argument with her manageress, claiming that the younger woman had stolen one of her recipes. She repeatedly said that she was going to kill her and repeated the threat over the next few days. Two managers (they had doubled up for protection as she was so angry) fired her and escorted her from the premises whilst she screamed abuse in front of alarmed customers.

She remained apoplectic and took the case to an employment tribunal. On the morning of the hearing she bought a gun but fortunately left it in her car. When the ruling went against her, she accused the board of all sleeping with the manageress and made other equally bizarre statements. More and more people concluded that she was a Jekyll and Hyde character.

A church-based life

As the years passed and she became a pensioner, Mary Jane Fonder felt increasingly invisible. She would talk at people rather than spend half of the conversation listening and would phone up new acquaintances and ramble for hours. As a result, she never became part of the town's ladies-who-lunch crowd, a fact she resented bitterly. With her lopsided wigs (which she sometimes wore back to front), prematurely wrinkled face and large body she was equally unattractive to men. She spent more and more time in church, the one place where she couldn't be turned away.

One day was pretty much the same as the next until 2005 when a handsome new pastor took over at Trinity Evangelical Lutheran Church. Only 56, Gregory Shreaves was a former golfing professional, a slim grey-haired man who was over 6 foot tall. He was kind to the older woman because that was his job and it never occurred to him for a moment that she would view him in a romantic light.

He got to know her better after a funeral in 2006 when she described her artistic skills and he asked her to decorate the church. When it transpired that she'd oversold her painting ability and the decor wasn't up to standard, he found other work for her, putting the church newsletters into envelopes and doing basic administrative tasks. She would also do voluntary work before the Sunday service, went to adult Sunday school classes, sang in the choir, attended evening choir practice and was a regular at the church's senior citizens club.

She developed a huge crush on the pastor and went to his office with photos of herself as a young girl, taken when she had been slender and attractive. During the hour-and-a-half conversation which followed, she talked about her life now and the ballet lessons she'd enjoyed in her youth. The pastor, who was already aware of her loneliness and the fact that she didn't really fit in with the other congregants, nodded encouragingly and let her talk. But he was deeply shocked when she alluded to the attraction between them. Though embarrassed, he made it abundantly clear that he didn't think of her in those terms. Expressionless, she got up and quickly left the room. The pastor phoned a Lutheran bishop and reported what had transpired as he wanted an official to be aware of the pensioner's inappropriate remarks.

As part of his duties, Pastor Shreaves counselled another congregant, Rhonda Smith, who was bipolar and had once been in an abusive relationship. Another of her unsuitable suitors had been a married man. The pastor had helped her through these difficult times and, in turn, she had begun to do voluntary work at the church. Rhonda was dark-haired and had a beautiful smile, but she had no idea that Mary Jane Fonder saw her as a rival for the religious leader's affections.

Deciding that the way to a man's heart is through his stomach, Mary Jane began to leave bags of groceries in Pastor Shreaves' porch and once, when he had left the door unlocked, went into his kitchen and gleefully restocked his refrigerator. Afraid that he was being stalked, but equally afraid of angering her, he politely asked her to stop. She began hanging around the church and engaging him in long, rambling conversations and, when he went out of his way to avoid her, began to leave equally lengthy messages on his home answerphone. When it cut her off after 4 minutes, she'd redial and leave another message and another. He put a block on her number but she managed to ring him from her mobile phone instead.

Unable to persuade her to stop buying him groceries, he left them outside his house until they rotted. She was incensed and snarled down the phone that he was ungrateful, that he was snubbing her. When she called back late one night he suggested she should find another place to worship, but she ignored his request.

Meanwhile, Rhonda was struggling to pay her bills and Pastor Shreaves got her financial help from the church, enough to pay her rent arrears. At the start of January 2008, she made a short speech at the end of the Sunday service, thanking everyone for their financial and emotional support. Detectives would later surmise that this further angered the increasingly unstable Mary Jane Fonder, who had never received such friendship or largesse. Leastways, everyone else was smiling and some of the congregants were moved to tears, but the 65-year-old remained stony-faced.

She told other congregants that she had decided not to return to church, choir practice or the senior citizens club for a while, that she was too upset.

The murder

On 23 January 2008, a church helper found that the door to Trinity Evangelical Lutheran Church was unlocked. She was equally surprised to see a light on in the church office as no one was scheduled to be there that Wednesday afternoon. Entering, she found church volunteer Rhonda Smith lying on the floor, a huge pool of blood around her head. It was apparent to paramedics that she had been shot behind the ear and she was rushed to hospital and pronounced dead.

The church's choir director, Steve, now had to phone the other members of the choir and tell them that a fellow choir member had been shot and that that night's choir practice was cancelled. Everyone was deeply shocked to hear what had happened to the vibrant 42-year-old – everyone except Mary Jane Fonder. To the man's surprise, she virtually ignored the news and started talking about her trip to the hairdresser's.

Thinking that she had misunderstood the seriousness of the situation, Steve reiterated that Rhonda had been shot, but Mary Jane began talking about the shopping that she'd done that day.

The murder enquiry

Several congregants immediately had their suspicions that Mary Jane Fonder was responsible for the younger woman's murder as she hadn't liked her and had, bizarrely, seen her as a rival for the pastor's affections. She had access to the church and had known when Rhonda would be working alone in the office, where she acted as temporary church secretary, a job which the older woman probably coveted. She had been shot twice in the head with a .38 revolver and state records showed that Mary Jane Fonder had owned such a weapon since 1994. The autopsy showed that Rhonda Smith's killer had stood three to four feet away, so the killing was up close and personal.

Mary Jane didn't attend the funeral but sent a long letter to the victim's parents which included the words 'we all loved our pastor' and 'that should have been me in the ground'.

When detectives went to choir practice to interview everyone, she immediately volunteered that she had phoned the church on the Monday of that week and had been surprised when Rhonda answered. The younger woman had explained that she was there for a three-day period whilst Pastor Shreaves was attending a residential religious course elsewhere. On the Tuesday, she told detectives, she had gone to look at an apartment in the same building as Rhonda's because she was tired of living with her brother and was considering getting a new place for herself. She said that afterwards she had eaten alone at a burger bar.

Detectives asked her how she'd spent her Wednesday – the day that Rhonda Smith was killed – and she said she'd had a hairdresser's appointment at 11.30 after which she'd gone shopping for fabric and hadn't returned home until three.

This meant that she didn't have an alibi for the time that Rhonda Smith was killed, shortly before 11, so detectives asked her about the gun she owned and she said she had tossed it out of the car window onto the roadside on a winter's day in 1994. She said that she had fired it first in her garden in order to try it out.

Later, two officers went to the home that she shared with her brother but were shocked to find newspapers piled to the ceiling, animal faeces on the floor and ancient cobwebs over piles of junk. Ed, the brother, let them in but asked them not to tell his sister as she didn't like inviting people into the house. The policemen asked if he could confirm her whereabouts on the morning of the murder and he produced a journal in which he had written that he spent the day at his church and hadn't returned home until late. Detectives established that he had an alibi but his sister didn't.

Detectives fetched her spare wig from the hairdresser's, where it was scheduled to be cleaned, and found traces of the elements used in gunpowder but not enough for the test to be considered conclusive.

Interviewed again, Fonder constantly changed the subject, talking about everything from her knee surgery to her father's disappearance. She complained that she was tired of living in her filthy house and said she'd looked at an apartment in the murder victim's block but realised she couldn't afford it. One of the men asked, 'How do you think Rhonda managed to afford it?' and she told them that the younger woman had had financial help from the church, something that she herself had never enjoyed.

She added that she'd never been part of the in-crowd at the church like Rhonda, had never been invited to one of the Tupperware parties held at various churchgoers' homes. She insisted that the pastor had taken to her though, that he was 'a man, a real man' and was attractive and kind. As the interview progressed she admitted that she'd had sexual feelings for him but that this wouldn't have been a valid reason for her to hurt Rhonda. One of the detectives asked if the killer could be saved and she said they would be if they believed in Jesus Christ.

She continued to talk, saying that she'd wondered if Rhonda was romantically involved with the pastor. After 4 hours of chat she said that she wouldn't talk further without an attorney.

The police took her car away to search it and she confided in another congregant that what had happened with her father ten years ago was coming back to haunt her, but she refused to elaborate.

Shortly afterwards a local fisherman and his son found her missing gun in shallow water and handed it in to police, who could see that it had been fired and that the bullets matched those which had shot Rhonda Smith. Mary Jane Fonder was arrested at her home on 1 April but remained stoical. Confronted with the evidence that they had found her gun and that it was the murder weapon, she said that someone else must have found it and used it to kill the younger woman. She added, bizarrely, 'I got the Devil crawling on me.'

As she was being driven in a police car to the nearest correctional facility she added that she was feasting her eyes on the grass as she might never see it again.

Trial

At her trial in October 2009, the prosecution said that Mary Jane Fonder's gun had not been in the lake for the past 14 years, that it was in excellent condition with very little rust on it. To find her not guilty, the jury would have to believe that she'd thrown away the gun in 1994 and that someone had immediately found it, kept it for 14 years, used it to shoot Rhonda Smith then discarded it in the lake. The prosecution also pointed out that gunpowder residue had been found inside her car.

The defence countered that the gun could have been cleaned by the finder, though the fisherman had robustly denied this. They also said that her car could have been cleaned by a hunter and that this would give an innocent explanation for the gunpowder traces.

As for the motive, Mary Jane Fonder had been jealous of Rhonda Smith's friendship with other congregants and angry that the younger woman had been chosen as the substitute church secretary. She had also been upset that Rhonda had been given financial assistance by the church.

She had written 'Rhonda murdered' on the relevant day of her calendar, though investigators believed she had done so after the killing in order to keep track of events. They also found that Fonder was still receiving her father's pension, despite the fact that he had been declared dead many years before. As a result, she was ordered to pay back almost $33,000 to the pension benefits fund.

After deliberating for 6 hours the jury found her guilty of first-degree murder. Later she was sentenced to life imprisonment and responded with the words, 'I'll go wherever the Lord sends me.' But at the sentencing hearing she told the judge that she was being murdered by the system, that she was innocent.

A change of heart

After a few weeks in prison, Mary Jane Fonder claimed that she was having dreams about Rhonda Smith and added that, though she still couldn't remember killing her, she realised that she must have. She said that she had vague memories of going to the lake (where the gun was found) afterwards. She explained that she had had blackouts for many years and must have had one at the time of the homicide. She continued to deny playing any part in her father's disappearance.

She originally appealed against her sentence but dropped the appeal in February 2010 and seemed to become more at peace with life in prison. She has apparently become a mother figure to some of the younger female inmates at Muncy State Correctional Institution in Pennsylvania, has taken up painting and become much healthier, losing almost 4 stone in weight. Ironically, she has gained an acceptance in prison that she never had in the outside world.

35

THE CRIMINAL JUSTICE STUDENT
DONNY TISON

Despite his difficult childhood, Donny Tison was the family's success story and had plans to join the state police. Then he agreed to help his brothers break their father out of prison and six innocent people died.

Early years

Donny Tison was the first of three sons born to Dorothy and Gary Tison in Casa Grande, Arizona on 1 January 1958. Gary Tison was attractive, charismatic and intelligent and the couple had met when she visited him in prison at the urging of a friend. Dorothy was a quiet, bespectacled woman from a strict Pentecostal family who worked as a secretary and idolised her attractive husband despite his inability to live within the law. Donny became a friendly, helpful and sociable little boy, and the couple went on to have two more children, Ricky and Raymond, and all three were well behaved and well liked, asking their Sunday school teacher to pray for their dad so that he would remain out of prison.

Gary Tison worked for an irrigation company but was in and out of jail for robbery and passing bad cheques. The day after Donny's fourth birthday, his father was sent to prison for 20 to 25 years for armed robbery. The prison report labelled him a sociopath with violent tendencies who took no responsibility for his bad behaviour and was incapable of feeling remorse.

But Dorothy refused to believe that her husband could do any wrong and she told all three sons that he had been wrongly taken away by the authorities, that it was a miscarriage of justice. She took the boys to visit him every Sunday afternoon and during these visits Tison would act the involved father, asking the children about their homework, studying their report cards and telling them when they needed to study harder at school or required a haircut. He never once hit them, unusual for a man who had been brutalised by his own convict father.

Dorothy wrote endless letters to the authorities on her husband's behalf and persuaded others in the community to write as well, saying that they would offer him employment and emotional support if he were released early. They acceded to her pleas and he was set free in 1966, having served only five years of a 25-year sentence. The next ten months would be the only ones that his sons would spend with him outside of the prison walls. They went hunting and fishing and swimming and Donny, now aged nine, saw his father as a heroic figure. He was desperate for a male role model and loved going horseback riding into the desert with his dad.

That Christmas their father bought them a model rail track and they played with it for hours, listening intently to his fabricated tales of being a war hero. Their mother agreed with him about everything so they were given the impression that their father was always right.

But by February 1967 Gary Tison had returned to his old ways, passing a bad cheque: he was caught but let off with a warning. The judge had no way of knowing that he was already involved in a smuggling racket, but he was later caught bribing Mexican officials and was returned to jail to serve the rest of his remaining 20 years.

As he was being driven from the courthouse to jail, he produced a pistol and kidnapped the driver, a prison guard. They stopped in a field for a cigarette and Gary Tison shot the man three times at close range in the chest. He then stole a station wagon from a young mother, holding her and her baby at gunpoint, and shot at police before they arrested him. He led them to the prison guard's body but was unable to explain why he'd shot him dead rather than just leave him handcuffed to a tree.

This time he was sentenced to life imprisonment with no possibility of parole. Dorothy, despite the urging of her friends and family, stood by her man and told her three sons that there had been another miscarriage of justice, that their father had shot another in self-defence. With no one to talk to them honestly about what had happened, the younger boys believed their mother and saw their father as a wronged man, a veritable hero, but Donny – the brightest of the three boys and the most outgoing – began to secretly have his doubts.

Like most sociopaths, Gary Tison soon found out how to win friends and influence people. He took college-level courses in jail and became something of a jailhouse lawyer, helping other prisoners with their appeals. He also became editor of the prison newspaper and wrote positive features about prison life which endeared him to the prison governor. He was so charismatic and intelligent that he was allowed to talk to journalists and local politicians about life behind bars, becoming a regular spokesperson for the prison.

Conjugal visits weren't allowed in the jail but Tison persuaded the guards to look the other way when he had sexual relations with his wife at the picnic table in the prison garden. Shockingly, he would tell his three sons to turn away and hold up newspapers as a shield, then Dorothy would fellate him, sometimes several times in the same afternoon. Various prison visitors complained but the guards were in Tison's corner as he regularly grassed up other prisoners. The guards also looked the other way when he dealt marijuana to boost his income, though he wasn't a user himself.

The model student

Despite this bizarre upbringing, Donny Tison was a model student. He did well at school and during his stint in the Marines, often visiting his father whilst wearing his uniform. He joined the service to put some distance between himself and his family and it seems that it gave him some serious thinking time. He told friends that he never wanted to be like his father and, though he still loved the man, he wanted to get a good education and perhaps join the police. When he left the Marines, he became a criminology student and briefly had a girlfriend, though her family made her end the relationship when they found that he was killer Gary Tison's son. But, at this stage, he in no way resembled his father – he had no criminal record, had never resorted to bullying and he and his siblings had a deference for authority that his father lacked.

Meanwhile, Ricky and Raymond Tison had dropped out of school and spent most of their days watching television, but they were not troublemakers and the family was well regarded in Casa Grande. People felt sorry for the fatherless boys and for Dorothy, who suffered from appalling migraines and struggled to cope with day-to-day life.

Everything changed, however, when Gary Tison asked his two younger sons to help him break out of jail, claiming that he would be killed by a tougher inmate if he remained behind bars. This was a lie as he was a strong man who was feared by the other prisoners. But he was bored with prison and wanted to start a new life in Mexico.

Gary Tison didn't involve Donny in the original plan as the 20-year-old was the sensible one who might try to talk his younger brothers out of it. Instead, various friends and relatives were approached but everyone thought that the scheme – which involved taking a helicopter across the border – was madness. Finally, the brothers persuaded Donny that their beloved father would be murdered if he didn't help them to secure his freedom. Depressed, he quit his evening job, telling his employer that he was having family problems and needed some thinking time. He also confided in a cousin about how low he felt. He said that he'd been looking forward to completing his criminology course and joining the state police but that his life might be about to change. He also started telling people how much he loved his father, yet he hadn't previously verbalised this love on a regular basis. It was as if he was psyching himself up to help carry out the great escape, an escape which would cost several innocent lives…

On the run

On 31 July 1978, Raymond Tison, aged 18, visited his father as usual, bringing what looked like an ice box filled with cans of cola and sandwiches. The guard, who had known him since he was a baby, didn't search under the picnic foods. If he had, he would have found several guns.

Also in on the plan was prisoner Randy Greenawalt, a 28-year-old sociopath with a high IQ who had killed at least two truck drivers. Greenawalt, a former Baptist ministry student, was joined in the foyer by Ricky Tison (19) and Donny Tison (20).

Raymond Tison trained a gun on the other visitors whilst Donny Tison reassured them that no one would get hurt. They took the guard's keys, locked the frightened captives into a room and unlocked the doors to freedom. Twenty minutes later the two adult killers and three boys were in their getaway car, though they soon swapped it for another vehicle, a Lincoln, left for them by friends.

Originally, the authorities issued a statement saying that the five weren't considered dangerous. 'I'll second that,' Donny Tison said, listening to the radio.

The first four murders

But the escapees' vehicle began to play up on the rough desert roads and Gary Tison decided they should steal a new car. He sent Raymond, the smallest of his boys, to stand by their car at midnight and flag down a passer-by.

The first vehicle to stop belonged to John Lyons, a sergeant in the Marines, who was accompanied by his wife Donna and their 23-month-old son, Christopher. Their 15-year-old niece Terri Jo was also in the car with her little dog. She had been visiting the family and together they were now en route to Omaha to show off the baby to some other relatives.

John Lyons got out of his car to examine Raymond's vehicle, only to find himself being held at gunpoint by Gary Tison. He pleaded with the killer, saying that they didn't want any trouble and told them where to find his money and his guns. Keeping their cards close to their chests, the prisoners drove both cars off the road so that they were hidden by the brush from prying eyes.

Suddenly (it appears to have been an impulsive act) Gary Tison shot out the lights and radiator from his old car as the trembling family stood by the side of the vehicle. John Lyons again begged them not to hurt anyone and promised that, if they were given water, they would stay out of sight until mid afternoon.

But Gary Tison herded the family into the back seat of the car they planned to abandon and he and Randy Greenawalt leaned into the open doors and shot them, then reloaded and shot again. When Tison stopped to examine the carnage he found that baby Christopher was unhurt so shot him twice at close range.

Donny Tison and his brothers heard the gunfire and realised what was happening. They felt numb as they resumed their journey, especially as the original plan had been for them all to separate on the day of the escape as soon as they'd driven a fair distance from the prison walls. Within the hour, John Lyons regained consciousness next to his dead wife and fell from the car, where he too died. Fifteen-year-old Terri Jo had only been hit once in the hip and managed to drag herself a thousand yards before she was too weak to go on. Her little dog had followed her and she took off its collar and fastened it around her ankle, her way of letting her finders know her identity. She died of blood loss whilst her Chihuahua died in the blistering heat. In one of those inexplicable moments, her mother woke in the early hours believing that one of her children was calling her name.

The next two murders

The boys now had various opportunities to escape but they stayed with their father and Randy Greenawalt. Donny was sent to sell their vehicle and buy another and the salesperson found him to be edgy and taciturn. A family friend, who had been enlisted to go with him, said he seemed afraid of displeasing his dad. For the first time, he had seen his father's violence and unpredictability rather than the affable mask that the man had worn for their Sunday visits to the prison.

As the hours passed, Donny Tison loosened up a little, telling the friend that 'it was all a horrible mess' and that it wasn't supposed to turn out that way. He added that metaphorically their father now had a knife at their throats all the time and mumbled, 'I'm very, very tired. I'd just like to rest.' But his father, fearful of capture, kept them all on the move.

On 6 August, the broken Lincoln with the partially decomposed bodies of John, Donna and Christopher Lyons was found and a $10,000 reward was offered for information leading to the arrest and conviction of the killers. Later, Terri Jo's body was also found.

The days passed with the men and boys taking turns at the wheel and driving for hours along back roads until they reached an airstrip in New Mexico. They hoped that a relative would have left a piloted Cessna there for them but they arrived many hours before the designated time and staked out the airstrip only to see that the police and press had arrived before them. Changing their plans, they drove to Colorado, where their vehicle began to fail and they started to scout around for another one. It was now Wednesday 9 August.

Near a campsite at Chimney Point, they espied newlyweds Margene and James Judge's van. The two convicts forced the young couple to drive to a more remote area where they made them get out, shot them both through the head, and took their vehicle. Shortly afterwards, either Ricky or Raymond Tison bought cigarettes at a small store, using the crisp $100 note that Margene had been given by her father as additional spending money for her honeymoon.

Donny now left their old vehicle at a garage, telling the owner that he would return for it in a fortnight. He'd come up with this idea so that the vehicle wouldn't look abandoned, as this would alert the authorities. He seemed tired and nervous at the garage, as well he might given that six innocent people had now died at his father and Randy Greenawalt's hands, murders that he had done nothing to prevent.

The clan now decided to backtrack to Arizona and head for the Mexican border, hoping that the authorities were still looking for them in New Mexico. It was Donny's turn to drive the vehicle and he was stunned to see a roadblock ahead of them. He begged his father to let him stop but Gary Tison swore that he would never be taken alive.

He screamed again and again for Donny to race past and, on the third order, Donny did so, squeezing between the parked vehicles as his father and Randy Greenawalt shot out of the side windows, aiming at the startled officers. Moments later they ran into a second roadblock and officers shot at them, getting Donny Tison in the right side of the head. He collapsed onto the steering wheel, suffering massive blood loss, and the car ran into a ditch.

Shouting 'Every man for himself', Gary Tison fled into the desert. The remaining three fugitives – Ricky Tison, Raymond Tison and Randy Greenawalt – clambered out and got obediently down on their stomachs and were taken into custody. Donny Tison, half of his head shot off, died at the scene.

For the next 11 days, the authorities searched for Gary Tison and, on 22 August, his bloated corpse was found lying in the brush within sight of a chemical plant. He had been sucking cactus plants in a bid to find some moisture in the relentless summer heat. He and his oldest son were buried in an unmarked grave.

On trial

Various trials followed and originally all three survivors were sentenced to death. But various people in the community who had known the boys said that they deserved to be sentenced for helping their father to escape but not for the murders, noting that it was the two men (already remorseless murderers at the time of the breakout) who had committed all six killings. That said, the boys had been culpable after the first four homicides in not leaving to alert the authorities.

Dorothy Tison was sentenced to 30 months in prison for being aware of the plot, and, after being paroled, returned to making weekly prison visits, though now she was visiting her two remaining sons rather than their father. The teenagers' sentences were later reduced to life and Ricky Tison is now a teacher's aide in prison whilst Raymond Tison is a prison clerk. Randy Greenawalt was executed by lethal injection in 1997.

Immortalised

The story was made into a TV movie in 1983 called *A Killer in the Family*, with James Spader giving a sensitive portrayal of Donny Tison whilst his sociopathic father was ably played by a brooding Robert Mitchum. The film, which was well received by the public, has subsequently become available on DVD.

36

THE HEADMISTRESS
JEAN HARRIS

Though she was a highly intelligent career woman, Jean Harris became suicidal when her lover lost interest in her. She went to his house with a loaded gun, a decision which would have fatal results...

A prosperous childhood

Jean Harris was born on 27 April 1923 to Mildred and Albert Struven in Cleveland, Ohio. Her mother was a housewife and her father was a civil engineer who designed oil refineries all around the world. Though the Harris family had a summer house and expensive vacations, it wasn't an idyllic childhood as her father suffered from depression and mood swings which blighted his life and led to him having electro-convulsive therapy. Similarly afflicted, one of Jean's uncles committed suicide. She would later note that her father was a tortured and bitter man whom she feared greatly, and that feelings were never discussed in her family.

Though her mother loved her children (Jean was the second of four children), she would wash their mouths out with soap if they uttered any kind of profanity. The family were originally Episcopalian but Jean's mother became a Christian Scientist, a group which believes that ideally we should treat sick and diseased people with prayer rather than with medicine. Mildred would spend her life tiptoeing around her increasingly unstable spouse.

Education and marriage

Jean was a bright child who excelled at school and ultimately went to university, where she gained an economics degree. The following year, she married an older man, Jim Harris, because she knew it would upset her father and the latter cried bitterly throughout the wedding ceremony. Jim was a kind man and a good provider who, outside of work, was at his happiest pottering around the house and garden, whereas Jean Harris was an intellectual who yearned for spirited debate. The couple had two sons who loved their father, but Jean didn't. After 19 years of marriage, she told her husband that she wanted a divorce.

She had already been teaching but now moved to Philadelphia with her teenage boys and accepted a much more highly paid post as a school administrator. It was at a dinner party here in 1966, when she was newly divorced at the age of 42, that she met Hy Tarnower, the doctor that she would ultimately kill. (His former Christian name was Herman but he was always known as Hy, sometimes spelt as Hi, to his friends.)

Hy was 56 and had never been married though he had had numerous relationships. A beak-nosed and balding man with large ears, he seemed at first sight an unlikely playboy but was exceptionally bright, funny and well travelled. His medical practice had been so successful that he had a chauffeur and also domestic staff. They got on well at the party and, a few weeks later, he sent her a book. It should have been an early warning sign, as a man who is truly interested in a relationship doesn't wait for weeks to make contact, but she was pleased and was also appreciative when she went into hospital afterwards for a minor operation and he sent flowers.

This began what initially seemed to be a whirlwind romance. Hy had just been dumped by a previous lover who had tired of waiting for a marriage proposal and now, on the rebound and worried that some of his patients regarded him as being homosexual, he took Jean Harris to the best restaurants and sent her roses. He also wrote love letters which said 'I love you very, very much' and 'my love for you grows deeper all the time'. It was probably too much too soon, a trait common in commitment-phobic men who offer too much then panic and backtrack, unable to cope with growing intimacy. Within months he had proposed and given her a diamond-and-emerald engagement ring which cost $10,000, the same as her annual salary.

But within weeks he broke off the engagement, admitting that he was too afraid to go through with it. His father had died young and Hy would spend over 40 years entirely supporting his mother, so he possibly feared an additional financial burden, but it's more likely that the day-to-day familiarity of a marriage is what terrified him most. It was surely better to tell her this rather than go through with the ceremony, feel caged and soon be filing for divorce.

Hy ended their relationship and she sent back the ring but, within three weeks, had driven to his palatial home for a visit. Afterwards she wrote and said that she loved him and was willing to continue their affair. Hy was delighted and the couple continued to socialise and holiday together for the next 13 years. Jean Harris didn't see anyone else as she remained very much in love, but Hy slept with various new women and a former girlfriend also came back into his life. Even when they were abroad together he would send postcards to his other girlfriends and buy gifts to take back to them.

It's telling that he never spent a single one of her birthdays with her – including her landmark fiftieth – yet she organised numerous birthday parties for him.

When, early in their relationship, she had complained of back pain, Hy gave her painkillers. Later, when she complained of fatigue (a well-known menopausal symptom which would have cleared up naturally given time), he prescribed Desoxyn, better known today as methamphetamine. He would continue to send her packages of this (despite its addictive nature and its ability to induce psychosis if taken at higher levels) throughout their relationship. The drug would have kept her weight down but also led to a permanent jittery feeling and she earned a reputation for being increasingly highly strung. The staff at her school noticed that she had mood swings, barely ate and complained of chronic insomnia. All were side effects of the methamphetamines she was taking, but Hy's solution was to send her three different types of sleeping tablets, all of which were depressants. For a woman who already felt out of touch with society (though she hid it well) it was a disaster waiting to happen.

Jean Harris moved to Connecticut in 1971 and lived close to Hy's cardiology practice and for several years they spent almost every weekend together, but at some stage he also began to date his younger secretary, Lynne Tryforos, a 37-year-old divorcee who nicknamed him Super Doc. Both women seem to have gone all out to please the ageing playboy, with Lynne painting his garden furniture whilst Jean arranged to have his antique chairs restored. His friends wryly referred to Lynne as his weekday girl and to Jean as his weekend girl.

Hy was very rich but Jean Harris struggled to fund her share of their foreign holidays and cruises so she sought more lucrative employment and succeeded in becoming headmistress of the esteemed Madeira girls' boarding school in 1977. This entailed a move to Virginia, so she was now a 5-hour drive away from her increasingly emotionally distant lover.

By now Herman Tarnower was telling her more and more often that he wanted and needed nobody, but Jean Harris wasn't ready to hear this. She looked for ways to make herself more attractive to him (though she was in truth a beautiful woman) and considered having a facelift, going as far as to consult a plastic surgeon. Fortunately, she felt unable to go through with it.

Around this time Lynne Tryforos began receiving anonymous hang-up calls, as did Jean Harris. Both women suspected the other and complained to Hy, who responded by telling Harris that he didn't want to see her for a while. Hurt, she wrote to him and outlined her hectic schedule, adding that she wouldn't interrupt her day to phone up 'a little receptionist'.

She later wrote to him again, complaining, 'Your casual call cancelling a weekend with you that I have spent a summer of work looking forward to – like light at the end of a dark tunnel – is the kind of punishment I have not earned.'

Aware of her terrible loneliness, her sons gave her a dog (and on another occasion her pupils gave her a puppy) but what she really wanted was a strong male that adored her and would make some of life's many decisions for her. She had been unable to win her father's love and now she tried desperately to win Hy's…

In 1978 a Sunday newspaper mentioned the diet sheet which Hy Tarnower gave to his cardiology patients. It basically said 'no fatty meats, no bread, no butter, no alcohol, no rich desserts'. A publisher phoned and suggested he base a book around these guidelines and he hired a freelance writer, but Jean Harris hated the first draft so much that she gave up her entire two-week vacation to rewrite it.

Cruelly, whilst she was burning the midnight oil at his house to polish the manuscript, Hy gave her a burger to eat and took Lynne Tryforos out to dinner.

Harris was again deeply hurt later that year when he sent her a cheque for her work on the book, as she had very much viewed it as a labour of love. She wrote to him remonstrating, 'You ask every woman to be as incapable of love as you are.' She longed for him to take on a husbandly role so that she had some emotional support, but Hy Tarnower simply didn't have this to give. In the acknowledgements section of his book, *The Complete Scarsdale Medical Diet*, he would thank both of his lovers, Jean Harris and Lynne Tryforos, for their splendid help.

Jean Harris became increasingly distraught. She was on campus seven days and seven nights a week dealing with the endless problems of her teenage pupils and their parents, but she didn't feel that she was well liked or supported by the school board and had nowhere to turn. In November 1978 she bought a gun, a light .32 calibre. Like many people, she found the thought of suicide a comfort, a way out if it all got too much.

Six months later, in March 1979, she helped her lover celebrate his sixty-ninth birthday with a week in the Bahamas. When they returned to Hy's house she found that someone had cut all of her clothes to shreds.

Her working life continued to go downhill and she confided in a colleague that she had never felt close to another woman, that, in fact, they terrified her. She said that there was no warmth between women yet those members of staff who tried to get close found her cold and aloof. She phoned Hy more and more often but, beginning to feel the effects of his age, he no longer wanted to spend hours commiserating with her on the phone and told her to make a new life for herself. He also instructed his domestic staff to say that he was out. Jean Harris decided that he was probably dining with Lynne Tryforos, her more easy-going arch enemy. Unable to cope with Harris's increasingly emotional outbursts, the doctor increased her prescription of Desoxyn in the hope that she would have renewed energy for her work.

By now his diet book had topped the bestsellers chart for many months and he was enjoying appearing on television chat shows. His life was getting better and better whilst Jean felt that hers was almost unbearable, as she felt both lonely and overwhelmed by her responsibilities. She had to deal with girls who were anorexic, pregnant, lovelorn and suicidal as well as coping with their parents and with the school board.

She phoned her pastor for help but didn't feel that he was particularly interested in counselling her. She then talked to Hy and he mentioned that he planned to take Lynne Tryforos as his guest to a very special lifetime achievement charity dinner being given the following year in his honour for his seventieth birthday. All of the friends that Jean and Hy had socialised with over the past 13 years would be there so it would be the most public of humiliations for a woman who had always tried to put a brave face on things.

In February 1980, one of Jean Harris's sons married and Hy toasted the bride and gave the bridegroom $1,000. He told Jean, 'It was better that we didn't get married. I don't ever want to worry about what retirement home your mother is in, and I didn't want you to worry about where mine was. I don't want to watch you die of cancer and I don't want you to play nursemaid to me.' It was an honest answer, just not the one she wanted to hear.

That aside, they had an enjoyable weekend which culminated in their making love and he promised she could attend his lifetime achievement dinner. She drove home ecstatic (even phoning a colleague to say that she and her lover were happy again), with the opening chapters of Hy's new book, ironically called *How to Live Longer and Enjoy Life More*, in her briefcase for editing. He had just weeks left to live…

Soon the fun weekend was a distant memory as someone sent her a copy of Hy's will, which left money to Lynne Tryforos and her sons and, apparently, nothing to herself. (He had, in fact, left Jean Harris almost a quarter of a million dollars but this had been scored out by the unknown sender.) To make matters worse, she had run out of methamphetamines so was having withdrawal symptoms of agitation, melancholy and an inability to cope. She phoned Hy numerous times to remind him to send her the prescription medication, but he was spending the weekend with Lynne Tryforos and had asked his domestic staff to fend off Jean Harris's calls.

Distraught, she wrote him a letter which said: 'Your phone call to tell me that you preferred the company of a vicious adulterous psychotic was topped by a call from the Dean of Students ten minutes later.' The call had been about marijuana which had been found on campus, a find which would lead to Jean Harris expelling four well-liked pupils. Upset by this and by the belief that Lynne Tryforos was the main beneficiary of his will, she went on, 'Give her all the money she wants, but give me time with you.'

Throughout the Saturday she added more and more pages to the increasingly rambling letter and eventually posted it. She rewrote her will, had it witnessed by her staff and gathered her insurance and personal papers together so that her sons would find them easily. She would later say that ten years of a growing depression had culminated in this latest plan to take her own life.

On Monday morning she finally got hold of the doctor at his medical practice and asked him not to read the letter when it arrived and added that she would like to see him for a few minutes that evening, but he said that he had a young relative coming to dinner. She knew instinctively that Lynne Tryforos would also be there. Hy said he'd rather see her tomorrow but she pleaded for it to be today and he said, 'Please yourself' and put down the phone.

At teatime that day, 10 March 1980, she loaded her gun, which she had bought previously whilst feeling suicidal, got in her car and drove for 5 hours to Hy's palatial New York home, getting there late that night when the house was in darkness. Herman Tarnower was in bed but she let herself in through the garage carrying a bunch of flowers and a handbag which contained the gun. She would later say that her plan was to say goodbye to him and then kill herself at the lake adjoining his property, but it's much more likely that she planned a murder–suicide.

Hy told her that it was the middle of the night and that he didn't want to talk. He settled down under the covers and, enraged, she went into the adjacent bathroom and began to throw things around the room, including a box of curlers which belonged to her rival. They flew through to the dressing room and smashed a small window there. Enraged beyond measure for the first time in his life (he was known as a man who rarely got angry or ruffled), Hy got out of bed and, as she walked back into the bedroom, he hit her in the face.

Jean Harris's response to this was to return to the bathroom where she threw a jewellery box and a hand mirror, both of which crashed to the floor. Hurrying back into the bedroom, she grabbed her bag and pulled out the loaded gun.

Her take on things, as told later to police and again at her trial, was that she put the gun to her head but Hy grabbed it to stop her committing suicide and, in the struggle which followed, he was shot in the hand. It transpired that the same bullet had then gone into his chest but she said that neither of them was aware of that at this point.

Cursing, Hy Tarnower had stumbled into the bathroom, wrapped a wet towel around his hand and returned to the bedroom, where he pressed the buzzer to summon his live-in butler and cook. When they didn't appear he attempted desperately to phone for help but the line was dead. Meanwhile, Jean Harris had located the gun which had fallen half under the bed and, according to her testimony, she again tried to kill herself with it, but Hy again wrestled with her, she said. She thought that she had the muzzle of the gun facing her stomach so pulled the trigger, but the muzzle had actually been facing her lover and she shot him in the arm.

She left the house and drove to the nearby community centre which had a phone, planning to call for help, then heard police sirens (Hy Tarnower's staff had heard the shots and called the emergency services) and returned to the house. When she saw the doctor, pale and lifeless-looking on a stretcher, she fainted. He died of blood loss shortly after being admitted to hospital. Jean Harris told a detective shortly afterwards that she had hoped the doctor would kill her and added, 'I've been through so much hell with him. I loved him very much. He slept with every woman he could and I've had it.'

As she was awaiting trial, she spoke at length to a psychologist who found that she had a lifelong sense of inferiority and emptiness, that she had sought approval from her lover because he was a father figure. She felt ambivalent about suicide and had gone to Tarnower's house hoping that he would talk her out of it.

Trial

Awaiting trial, Jean Harris received almost 400 letters from former pupils, staff, neighbours and old friends offering to be her character witnesses in court. In replying to them, she never faltered from her story (which she did seem to believe) that she had planned to take her own life that night and had merely gone to say goodbye first to her lover of 14 years. Yet he was dead as the result of bullets fired from her gun and she was still alive.

The autopsy showed that he had been shot in the palm, the shoulder and arm, causing massive internal bleeding. She had told detectives that she recalled shooting him in the palm as they wrestled for the gun but was hazy about what had happened next. The prosecution alleged that the first bullet, which had gone through his palm and into his chest, had been fired whilst he was in bed, that it was a defensive injury, whilst the defence said that the blood-flow spatter showed that both parties had been standing when the bullet went into the doctor's palm. The bullet had severed an artery, making the doctor bleed internally, and another bullet had entered his shoulder from the back. The last bullet – fired when she claimed she intended to shoot herself in the abdomen – had entered his right arm and broken it.

She cried daily throughout the trial but, the rest of the time, looked impatient and haughty, a demeanour which did not endear her to the jury. When she took the stand in her own defence for the first time on the eighth day she frequently wept. She said that she had taken on the roles of headmistress and Dr Tarnower's girlfriend but that, deep down, she didn't know who she was. She added that, from the time she was a young woman, her only prayer had been: 'Just give me the strength to get through this day.' If this was true, it spoke of a deeply insecure individual who had known very little happiness.

But the letter that she had sent to Hy was damning with its references to Lynne Tryforos as a slut and whore. Harris had returned to a theme that had occurred countless times in her letters to Tarnower, that Lynne Tryforos was of a lower class than him and that the relationship demeaned him. Now the jury had to decide if that rage had made her want to kill, if she'd taken an if-I-can't-have-him-nobody-can approach. They were out for 13 days before returning with their verdict, guilty on all counts, and she was sentenced to a minimum of 15 years.

Asked if she wanted to make a statement, she said, 'I want to say that I did not murder Dr Herman Tarnower, that I loved him very much, and I never wished him ill, and I am innocent as I stand here.' She concluded a moment later by saying that this was a travesty of justice.

Righting the wrong

Though Jean Harris could never bring Herman Tarnower back and his friends continued to miss him, she had returned to her previous dutiful self after the murder, spending lots of time with the newborn babies in the prison nursery at Bedford Hills Correctional Facility, a maximum-security women's prison. She also tried to help their mothers to appreciate nature rather than material goods, noting wryly that they knew the name of every designer perfume yet couldn't identify the birds or plants in the prison grounds. She made them aware that, if they spoke to their children kindly and answered their questions, the youngsters would go to school with good language skills and would be better equipped to benefit from the educational system. She also spoke out, saying that society needed more Head Start programmes, that too many children were already permanently damaged by poor parenting when they went to school at age five.

Harris became friends with her biographer, the late Shana Alexander, who visited her often in prison and noted that Jean Harris had survived for years by self-deception, that she suppressed painful truths and denied her anger. Though she had many good qualities, she didn't know herself or her true motivation at all.

Early parole

Jean Harris had two heart attacks in prison and there were ongoing fears for her health, so her sons campaigned vigorously for her to be paroled. By now her own book, *Stranger in Two Worlds*, and that written by Shana Alexander, *Very Much a Lady*, had been published and she was increasingly seen as a sympathetic figure. The governor granted her clemency and she was released three years early in 1993. She continued her charitable work with female prisoners and died on 23 December 2012 in an assisted-living facility at the age of 89.

37

THE CHURCH YOUTH CAMP LEADER
DONALD MILLER

Though his entire life revolved around religion, this young man murdered at least four women and badly hurt another girl and her little brother.

Early years

Donald Miller was born on 28 December 1954 to Elaine and Gene Miller. His father had served in the navy during World War Two and was now a successful businessman who taught Sunday school, and his mother was a housewife. The couple also had several daughters and lived in East Lansing, Michigan.

Donald was a deeply religious boy whose social life consisted of church and Bible study group and in the mid 1970s he met an equally religious teenager, Martha Young, and they began dating. They were both teetotal. They went to Bible study together, worshipped at the same church and wrote long letters to each other littered with biblical quotes and prayers.

Don, as he soon preferred to be known, became a criminal justice major at Michigan State University and had a slightly apologetic expression. His favourite phrase was 'Praise the Lord'.

But Martha became uneasy around him as he only wanted to champion religious activities and was unhappy when she went to athletics or wanted to spend time with her friends. She also thought that his father spoke disrespectfully to his mother and said that his parents' house was so untidy that they couldn't entertain guests. She put distance between herself and Don when she went away to university in Texas but became homesick and returned to her divorced mother's house in Michigan, planning to start a different course at the local college the following year.

She resumed her romance with Don and got engaged but again had doubts, writing down her prayers which included the lines 'Oh Lord, how hard it is to know what to do. I'll take him at his word… and leave the rest to you… Is that okay, Lord?'

Continuing to feel stifled, she broke off the engagement towards the end of December 1976 but he asked if they could remain friends and she agreed. Outwardly easy-going, he even insisted that she keep the engagement ring.

On the last day of the year, Martha went out to babysit for friends, telling her mother, Sue, that Don would be keeping her company and that she wouldn't be late back. But when Sue woke up on 1 January her 19-year-old daughter still hadn't returned home. She phoned Don and he said that he'd dropped Martha at her front door and that she'd sat on the steps, gazing at the stars, whilst he drove down the road to his own parents' place.

Sue Young was immediately suspicious as the temperature the previous night had been minus 17 and Martha had been lightly dressed as she just planned to be indoors, babysitting. And there were no tyre tracks in the snow to indicate she'd ever made it home. She was a dependable girl who had been looking forward to resuming her studies and starting a part-time job at the bank so had no reason to run away. The couple she had babysat for confirmed that she had left their house in good health with Don after they returned home.

That Sunday, Don Miller stood up in church and asked the congregation to pray for his missing friend. His Bible study group told investigators that he was a pillar of the community and could do no wrong. But police discovered deep scratches on his car, indicating that he had driven through coarse bushes, marks that he struggled to explain. He failed two polygraph tests but remained emotionless and stuck by his story even though it contained several anomalies. He had said that Martha's house was in darkness when he delivered her home but Sue had left on several lights. She was also a light sleeper who usually heard when a car drew up and parked outside her property. Detectives warned the Millers that their son might be a killer but they insisted that he was the perfect son. (It would transpire much later that he was sexually abusing a young female relative at the time.)

The months passed and, that April, Don Miller sent a flower to Sue Young on Martha's birthday. It said 'Martha was a rose', and it did not escape anyone's notice that he used the past tense.

That summer he became a Bible teacher at a Christian youth camp for the summer and his church newsletter described him as 'a fine youth'. He began dating another churchgoer who was convinced that the rumours about his involvement in his former girlfriend's disappearance were untrue.

In the autumn, nine months after she disappeared, Martha Young's bag containing her driving licence was found by two hunters in Bath Township, Michigan. All of her clothing was found nearby and everyone now accepted that she was dead.

Three more murders

The following summer, on 15 June 1978, Don Miller struck again, abducting a 28-year-old television executive, Marita Choquette, either from her workplace at a TV station or from her apartment in Grand Ledge, Michigan. A well-liked graduate from Michigan State University, she had last been seen putting her rubbish into the outside dustbin the previous evening. Her car was found at work the next day but was at the back of the parking lot, a lengthy distance from her designated parking space.

The young woman's body was found two weeks later by a farmer, south-east of Lansing, 30 miles from her home. She had been displayed in a praying position in a small wooded area, her corpse surrounded by concrete blocks, and had been stabbed multiple times. Bizarrely, her hands had been cut off and placed by her sides. Apart from being of a slightly heavier build, she bore a striking resemblance to Martha Young.

On 28 June, Miller abducted a 21-year-old student called Wendy Bush, who was last seen alive walking with a man at the James Madison College campus at Michigan University at around 10 p.m. She disappeared without taking her bag or cash and didn't reappear to collect her student loan so police again feared the worst.

On 14 August, Miller claimed his fourth victim, a 30-year-old teacher, Kristine Rose Stuart, who lived a few blocks from his parents' home, where he still lived. At 9.30 a.m. she had dropped her car off to be repaired and was seen walking the short distance to the house that she shared with her husband. She, too, resembled Martha Young. A female driver who drove past Miller's car saw a woman resembling Kristine being held down on the seat. She contacted police and underwent hypnosis after which she recalled him plunging a knife into his terrified victim. Kristine's husband was desolate.

The net closes in

By now, Don Miller seemed to be in a lust-filled frenzy. The following day he entered an unlocked house in East Lansing and asked the 14-year-old girl that he encountered, Lisa Gilbert, if her father was home. When she said no he grabbed her in a chokehold, put a knife to her throat and dragged her into her parents' bedroom where he bound, blindfolded and raped her. He then tied her feet together and began to strangle her with a plastic belt which promptly snapped. He continued the assault by choking her with his bare hands.

Lisa was close to losing consciousness when her younger brother, Randy, walked into the house. Miller dragged him up the stairs and slashed him repeatedly with a knife before attempting to strangle him. Hearing his screams, Lisa managed to untie herself and fled outside where she flagged down a passer-by, screaming that she had been raped and that her brother was being hurt.

It was Don Miller's turn to flee but the passer-by got a good look at him, and, after entrusting Lisa to the care of two women, he jumped in his vehicle and tailed him. Miller escaped but the man had memorised his number plate. Police arrested the serial killer later that afternoon when he arrived at the home of his new girlfriend.

That same month he was charged with attempted murder, sexual assault, breaking and entering and weapons charges. He did not attempt to post bail, perhaps aware that there were vigilantes in the community who wanted their revenge.

At his trial his attorney posited a mental-health defence, saying that Miller contained both an angel and a demon, that he was essentially suffering from multiple personality disorder. A psychiatrist said that Miller had looked at the teenage schoolgirl Lisa and seen a demon. But the prosecution said that he had seemed remarkably composed, telling the girl to lie down on the floor, drawing the curtains and shutting the door. He had also stopped strangling Lisa as soon as her brother Randy entered the house and had tried his best to murder him. Indeed, Randy had lost so much blood in the attack that paramedics feared he would die en route to hospital.

Another defence witness said that Miller had a distant relationship with his father and feelings of ambivalence towards his mother and other females. He was psychotic and a religious fanatic. The prosecution countered that he was sane and knew exactly what he was doing at the time of the attacks.

After being found guilty, he was sentenced to 30 to 50 years for each charge, to be served concurrently. Under Michigan law, this meant that he would be eligible for parole in a mere 13 years, when he would still be a young, healthy man.

A plea bargain

Miller went to jail knowing that he would soon be back in court charged with the murder of Martha Young. Whilst in custody, he spoke to his lawyer and said that he would plead guilty to manslaughter in the deaths of Martha and Kristine and lead police to the bodies if they promised not to charge him with the murders of Marita and Wendy. As Michigan doesn't allow for consecutive sentencing, the families had nothing to lose and much to gain. They would be spared the trauma of another trial and would get to bury their loved ones at last.

This suited Miller as he didn't want to be charged with first-degree murder in the future if the women's bodies were discovered. If the charges were reduced to manslaughter he would still be eligible for early parole.

Don now admitted all four murders and, in July 1979, showed police where to find the undiscovered skeleton of Martha Young, who had been buried for over two years, and the more recent remains of Wendy Bush and Kristine Stuart. His second victim, Marita Choquette, had been discovered earlier in a wooded area as previously mentioned. The killer pointed out the dump sites and remained in the car as detectives uncovered the makeshift graves and verified the information. He remained emotionless.

The years passed and Miller was a model prisoner who taught other convicts how to read and write. In 1989, after serving just over ten years of his sentence in a cell shared with two other prisoners, he became eligible for parole. The victims' relatives were horrified, as was the local community, and sent hundreds of letters annually urging the authorities to keep him behind bars. The years passed without parole being granted and, in 1995, he received an additional two-year sentence because a weapon had been found in his cell at Kinross Correctional Facility, a Michigan prison which ironically offers a wide range of religious activities. But in February 1999 he would automatically be released as, with a reduction due to good behaviour, his sentence would have been served.

A group of locals now got together and formed a committee aimed at protecting the community from Lansing's only serial killer. They hired a legal team who looked more closely at the report of the weapon which had been found in Miller's cell and realised it was a garrotte which had been fashioned from shoelaces which were 72 inches long and large buttons modified into handles, tied with a large knot at each end. They went to court, where Lisa Gilbert testified that he had strangled her with a belt, showing that choking with the aid of a device was his method of choice.

Miller's defence team (and his parents) stated that the bootlaces could have been used innocently as a makeshift belt but prison officers explained that they had gone into his padlocked locker as part of a routine search and found a box which included a crucifix.

There was a plastic package and when they unrolled it they found the shoelaces with wooden handles at both ends.

The jury, who had not been told of his murderous history, deliberated for less than 3 hours before finding him guilty of making a weapon. His lawyers asked for leniency and Miller himself said that, as a criminal major, he would not commit the offence of making a weapon and keeping it in his cell. Unconvinced, the judge said that he did not appear to be reformed and sentenced him to an additional 20 to 40 years. He appealed and his appeal was denied so he appealed again to the Supreme Court. That, too, was denied.

But Michigan residents cannot sleep soundly yet as, in 2018, Don Miller – by then aged 63 – will again become eligible for parole.

SELECT BIBLIOGRAPHY

Alexander, Shana *Very Much a Lady* (1983, Pocket Books)

Clarke, James W. *Last Rampage* (1988, Berkley Books)

Cox, Bill G. *No Safe Place* (2000, Pinnacle)

Davidson, Peter *Murder at Holy Cross* (2007, Berkley)

Dittrich, Stacy *Murder Behind the Badge* (2010, Prometheus Books)

Dixon, Cyril *The Crossbow Cannibal* (2011, John Blake)

Earley, Pete *Prophet of Death* (1991, Avon Books)

Flowers, R. Barri *Masters of True Crime* (2012, Prometheus Books)

Gilbert, Alloma *Deliver Me from Evil* (2008, Pan Books)

Glatt, John *Forgive Me, Father* (2008, St Martin's)

Glatt, John *For I Have Sinned* (1998, St Martin's)

Guillen, Tomas *Toxic Love* (1995, Dell Publishing)

Herzog, Arthur *The Woodchipper Murder* (1989, Zebra Books)

Holmes, D. A. *Abnormal, Clinical & Forensic Psychology* (2010, Pearson Education Ltd)

Hudson, Dale *Kiss and Kill* (2008, Pinnacle)

Hustmyre, Chuck *Killer with a Badge* (2004, Penguin)

Jones, Aphrodite *The FBI Killer* (1992, Pinnacle)

Jones, Tobias *Blood on the Altar* (2012, Faber & Faber)

Lane, Brian *The Murder Yearbook* (1992, Headline)

LaRosa, Paul *Tacoma Confidential* (2006, Signet)

Lunnon, Charlene and Hoodless, Lisa *Abducted* (2009, Penguin Books)

Markman, Ronald and Bosco, Dominick *Alone with the Devil* (1991, Futura)

McEvoy, Colin and Olanoff, Lynn *Love Me or Else* (2012, St Martin's)

Rosen, Fred *Deacon of Death* (2000, Pinnacle)

Sasse, Cynthia Stalter and Widder, Peggy Murphy *The Kirtland Massacre* (1991, Zebra Books)

Scott, Robert *Married to Murder* (2004, Pinnacle)

Sharkey, Joe *Above Suspicion* (1993, Simon & Schuster)

Spangler, Sharon *On Foot in the Grand Canyon* (1989, Pruett Publishing)

Spry, Christopher *Child C* (2008, Simon & Schuster)

Wixom, Hartt and Judene *When Angels Intervene to Save the Children* (1994, Cedar Fort Incorporated)

Young, Sue *Lethal Friendship* (2005, iUniverse)

Filmography

A Killer in the Family (1983, Warner Home Video)

Death of a Cheerleader (1994, Odyssey)

Empty Cradle (1993, Odyssey)

Judgment Day: The Ellie Nesler Story (1999, USA Network)

To Save the Children (1994, Odyssey)

ACKNOWLEDGEMENTS

I'm grateful to Dr David Holmes, senior lecturer in psychology at Manchester Metropolitan University and author of *Abnormal, Clinical and Forensic Psychology* for his insight into borderline personality disorder and psychopathy. I interviewed Dr Holmes for a previous book and appreciate him giving up more of his valuable time.

The same is true of Dr Katherine Ramsland, a professor at DeSales University, author of around 50 non-fiction books and one of my co-contributors at *Serial Killer Quarterly*. Katherine regularly adds insight to the true crime television series *Born to Kill?*

I'd also like to thank Robert Drew, Senior Assistant Editor at Summersdale, and copy-editor Ray Hamilton for their valuable comments and suggestions. Thanks also to Hamish Braid for designing the cover.

Last, but not least, I appreciate the input of criminologist R. Barri Flowers, recipient of the prestigious Wall of Fame award from Michigan University, whose books include *Murder Chronicles*, *College Crime* and *Prostitution in the Digital Age*.

Have you enjoyed this book?
If so, why not write a review on your favourite website?

If you're interested in finding out more about our books,
find us on Facebook at **Summersdale Publishers** and
follow us on Twitter at **@Summersdale**.

Thanks very much for buying this Summersdale book.

www.summersdale.com